50% OFF
Online PHR Prep Course!

By Mometrix

Dear Customer,

We consider it an honor and a privilege that you chose our PHR Study Guide. As a way of showing our appreciation and to help us better serve you, we are offering **50% off our online PHR Prep Course.** Many PHR courses cost hundreds of dollars and don't deliver enough value. With our course, you get access to the best PHR prep material, and **you only pay half price**.

We have structured our online course to perfectly complement your printed study guide. The PHR Prep Course contains **in-depth lessons** that cover all the most important topics, **video reviews** that explain difficult concepts, over **750 practice questions** to ensure you feel prepared, and over **300 digital flashcards**, so you can study while you're on the go.

Online PHR Prep Course

Topics Include:

- Business Management
    - *Mission and Vision Statements*
    - *Ethical and Professional Standards*
- Talent Planning and Acquisition
    - *Interviewing and Selection Techniques*
    - *New Employee Orientation Processes*
- Learning and Development
    - *Coaching and Mentoring*
    - *Employee Retention*
- Total Rewards
    - *Job Analysis and Evaluation*
    - *Benefits Programs*
- Employee and Labor Relations
    - *Diversity and Inclusion*
    - *Performance Management*

Course Features:

- PHR Study Guide
    - Get content that complements our best-selling study guide.
- 5 Full-Length Practice Tests
    - With over 750 practice questions, you can test yourself again and again.
- Mobile Friendly
    - If you need to study on the go, the course is easily accessible from your mobile device.
- PHR Flashcards
    - Our course includes a flashcard mode consisting of over 300 content cards to help you study.

To receive this discount, visit our website at <u>mometrix.com/university/phr</u> or simply scan this QR code with your smartphone. At the checkout page, enter the discount code: **phr50off**

If you have any questions or concerns, please contact us at <u>support@mometrix.com</u>.

SCAN HERE

FREE Study Skills Videos/DVD Offer

Dear Customer,

Thank you for your purchase from Mometrix! We consider it an honor and a privilege that you have purchased our product and we want to ensure your satisfaction.

As part of our ongoing effort to meet the needs of test takers, we have developed a set of Study Skills Videos that we would like to give you for <u>FREE</u>. These videos cover our *best practices* for getting ready for your exam, from how to use our study materials to how to best prepare for the day of the test.

All that we ask is that you email us with feedback that would describe your experience so far with our product. Good, bad, or indifferent, we want to know what you think!

To get your FREE Study Skills Videos, you can use the **QR code** below, or send us an **email** at studyvideos@mometrix.com with *FREE VIDEOS* in the subject line and the following information in the body of the email:

- The name of the product you purchased.
- Your product rating on a scale of 1-5, with 5 being the highest rating.
- Your feedback. It can be long, short, or anything in between. We just want to know your impressions and experience so far with our product. (Good feedback might include how our study material met your needs and ways we might be able to make it even better. You could highlight features that you found helpful or features that you think we should add.)

If you have any questions or concerns, please don't hesitate to contact me directly.

Thanks again!

Sincerely,

Jay Willis
Vice President
jay.willis@mometrix.com
1-800-673-8175

Mometrix
TEST PREPARATION

PHR

Study Guide 2023-2024

3 Full-Length Practice Tests

Secrets Prep Book for the HRCI PHR Certification Exam

5th Edition

Written and edited by the Mometrix Test Prep

Printed in the United States of America

This paper meets the requirements of ANSI/NISO Z39.48-1992 (Permanence of Paper).

Mometrix offers volume discount pricing to institutions. For more information or a price quote, please contact our sales department at sales@mometrix.com or 888-248-1219.

Mometrix Media LLC is not affiliated with or endorsed by any official testing organization. All organizational and test names are trademarks of their respective owners.

Paperback
ISBN 13: 978-1-5167-2205-1
ISBN 10: 1-5167-2205-1

DEAR FUTURE EXAM SUCCESS STORY

First of all, **THANK YOU** for purchasing Mometrix study materials!

Second, congratulations! You are one of the few determined test-takers who are committed to doing whatever it takes to excel on your exam. **You have come to the right place.** We developed these study materials with one goal in mind: to deliver you the information you need in a format that's concise and easy to use.

In addition to optimizing your guide for the content of the test, we've outlined our recommended steps for breaking down the preparation process into small, attainable goals so you can make sure you stay on track.

We've also analyzed the entire test-taking process, identifying the most common pitfalls and showing how you can overcome them and be ready for any curveball the test throws you.

Standardized testing is one of the biggest obstacles on your road to success, which only increases the importance of doing well in the high-pressure, high-stakes environment of test day. Your results on this test could have a significant impact on your future, and this guide provides the information and practical advice to help you achieve your full potential on test day.

Your success is our success

We would love to hear from you! If you would like to share the story of your exam success or if you have any questions or comments in regard to our products, please contact us at **800-673-8175** or **support@mometrix.com**.

Thanks again for your business and we wish you continued success!

Sincerely,
The Mometrix Test Preparation Team

Need more help? Check out our flashcards at:
http://mometrixflashcards.com/HRCI

---

ii

TABLE OF CONTENTS

Introduction

Thank you for purchasing this resource! You have made the choice to prepare yourself for a test that could have a huge impact on your future, and this guide is designed to help you be fully ready for test day. Obviously, it's important to have a solid understanding of the test material, but you also need to be prepared for the unique environment and stressors of the test, so that you can perform to the best of your abilities.

For this purpose, the first section that appears in this guide is the **Secret Keys**. We've devoted countless hours to meticulously researching what works and what doesn't, and we've boiled down our findings to the five most impactful steps you can take to improve your performance on the test. We start at the beginning with study planning and move through the preparation process, all the way to the testing strategies that will help you get the most out of what you know when you're finally sitting in front of the test.

We recommend that you start preparing for your test as far in advance as possible. However, if you've bought this guide as a last-minute study resource and only have a few days before your test, we recommend that you skip over the first two Secret Keys since they address a long-term study plan.

If you struggle with **test anxiety**, we strongly encourage you to check out our recommendations for how you can overcome it. Test anxiety is a formidable foe, but it can be beaten, and we want to make sure you have the tools you need to defeat it.

Secret Key #1 – Plan Big, Study Small

There's a lot riding on your performance. If you want to ace this test, you're going to need to keep your skills sharp and the material fresh in your mind. You need a plan that lets you review everything you need to know while still fitting in your schedule. We'll break this strategy down into three categories.

Information Organization

Start with the information you already have: the official test outline. From this, you can make a complete list of all the concepts you need to cover before the test. Organize these concepts into groups that can be studied together, and create a list of any related vocabulary you need to learn so you can brush up on any difficult terms. You'll want to keep this vocabulary list handy once you actually start studying since you may need to add to it along the way.

Time Management

Once you have your set of study concepts, decide how to spread them out over the time you have left before the test. Break your study plan into small, clear goals so you have a manageable task for each day and know exactly what you're doing. Then just focus on one small step at a time. When you manage your time this way, you don't need to spend hours at a time studying. Studying a small block of content for a short period each day helps you retain information better and avoid stressing over how much you have left to do. You can relax knowing that you have a plan to cover everything in time. In order for this strategy to be effective though, you have to start studying early and stick to your schedule. Avoid the exhaustion and futility that comes from last-minute cramming!

Study Environment

The environment you study in has a big impact on your learning. Studying in a coffee shop, while probably more enjoyable, is not likely to be as fruitful as studying in a quiet room. It's important to keep distractions to a minimum. You're only planning to study for a short block of time, so make the most of it. Don't pause to check your phone or get up to find a snack. It's also important to **avoid multitasking**. Research has consistently shown that multitasking will make your studying dramatically less effective. Your study area should also be comfortable and well-lit so you don't have the distraction of straining your eyes or sitting on an uncomfortable chair.

 The time of day you study is also important. You want to be rested and alert. Don't wait until just before bedtime. Study when you'll be most likely to comprehend and remember. Even better, if you know what time of day your test will be, set that time aside for study. That way your brain will be used to working on that subject at that specific time and you'll have a better chance of recalling information.

Finally, it can be helpful to team up with others who are studying for the same test. Your actual studying should be done in as isolated an environment as possible, but the work of organizing the information and setting up the study plan can be divided up. In between study sessions, you can discuss with your teammates the concepts that you're all studying and quiz each other on the details. Just be sure that your teammates are as serious about the test as you are. If you find that your study time is being replaced with social time, you might need to find a new team.

Secret Key #2 – Make Your Studying Count

You're devoting a lot of time and effort to preparing for this test, so you want to be absolutely certain it will pay off. This means doing more than just reading the content and hoping you can remember it on test day. It's important to make every minute of study count. There are two main areas you can focus on to make your studying count.

Retention

It doesn't matter how much time you study if you can't remember the material. You need to make sure you are retaining the concepts. To check your retention of the information you're learning, try recalling it at later times with minimal prompting. Try carrying around flashcards and glance at one or two from time to time or ask a friend who's also studying for the test to quiz you.

To enhance your retention, look for ways to put the information into practice so that you can apply it rather than simply recalling it. If you're using the information in practical ways, it will be much easier to remember. Similarly, it helps to solidify a concept in your mind if you're not only reading it to yourself but also explaining it to someone else. Ask a friend to let you teach them about a concept you're a little shaky on (or speak aloud to an imaginary audience if necessary). As you try to summarize, define, give examples, and answer your friend's questions, you'll understand the concepts better and they will stay with you longer. Finally, step back for a big picture view and ask yourself how each piece of information fits with the whole subject. When you link the different concepts together and see them working together as a whole, it's easier to remember the individual components.

Finally, practice showing your work on any multi-step problems, even if you're just studying. Writing out each step you take to solve a problem will help solidify the process in your mind, and you'll be more likely to remember it during the test.

Modality

Modality simply refers to the means or method by which you study. Choosing a study modality that fits your own individual learning style is crucial. No two people learn best in exactly the same way, so it's important to know your strengths and use them to your advantage.

For example, if you learn best by visualization, focus on visualizing a concept in your mind and draw an image or a diagram. Try color-coding your notes, illustrating them, or creating symbols that will trigger your mind to recall a learned concept. If you learn best by hearing or discussing information, find a study partner who learns the same way or read aloud to yourself. Think about how to put the information in your own words. Imagine that you are giving a lecture on the topic and record yourself so you can listen to it later.

For any learning style, flashcards can be helpful. Organize the information so you can take advantage of spare moments to review. Underline key words or phrases. Use different colors for different categories. Mnemonic devices (such as creating a short list in which every item starts with the same letter) can also help with retention. Find what works best for you and use it to store the information in your mind most effectively and easily.

3

Secret Key #3 – Practice the Right Way

Your success on test day depends not only on how many hours you put into preparing, but also on whether you prepared the right way. It's good to check along the way to see if your studying is paying off. One of the most effective ways to do this is by taking practice tests to evaluate your progress. Practice tests are useful because they show exactly where you need to improve. Every time you take a practice test, pay special attention to these three groups of questions:

- The questions you got wrong
- The questions you had to guess on, even if you guessed right
- The questions you found difficult or slow to work through

This will show you exactly what your weak areas are, and where you need to devote more study time. Ask yourself why each of these questions gave you trouble. Was it because you didn't understand the material? Was it because you didn't remember the vocabulary? Do you need more repetitions on this type of question to build speed and confidence? Dig into those questions and figure out how you can strengthen your weak areas as you go back to review the material.

Additionally, many practice tests have a section explaining the answer choices. It can be tempting to read the explanation and think that you now have a good understanding of the concept. However, an explanation likely only covers part of the question's broader context. Even if the explanation makes perfect sense, **go back and investigate** every concept related to the question until you're positive you have a thorough understanding.

As you go along, keep in mind that the practice test is just that: practice. Memorizing these questions and answers will not be very helpful on the actual test because it is unlikely to have any of the same exact questions. If you only know the right answers to the sample questions, you won't be prepared for the real thing. **Study the concepts** until you understand them fully, and then you'll be able to answer any question that shows up on the test.

It's important to wait on the practice tests until you're ready. If you take a test on your first day of study, you may be overwhelmed by the amount of material covered and how much you need to learn. Work up to it gradually.

On test day, you'll need to be prepared for answering questions, managing your time, and using the test-taking strategies you've learned. It's a lot to balance, like a mental marathon that will have a big impact on your future. Like training for a marathon, you'll need to start slowly and work your way up. When test day arrives, you'll be ready.

Start with the strategies you've read in the first two Secret Keys—plan your course and study in the way that works best for you. If you have time, consider using multiple study resources to get different approaches to the same concepts. It can be helpful to see difficult concepts from more than one angle. Then find a good source for practice tests. Many times, the test website will suggest potential study resources or provide sample tests.

Practice Test Strategy

If you're able to find at least three practice tests, we recommend this strategy:

UNTIMED AND OPEN-BOOK PRACTICE

Take the first test with no time constraints and with your notes and study guide handy. Take your time and focus on applying the strategies you've learned.

TIMED AND OPEN-BOOK PRACTICE

Take the second practice test open-book as well, but set a timer and practice pacing yourself to finish in time.

TIMED AND CLOSED-BOOK PRACTICE

Take any other practice tests as if it were test day. Set a timer and put away your study materials. Sit at a table or desk in a quiet room, imagine yourself at the testing center, and answer questions as quickly and accurately as possible.

Keep repeating timed and closed-book tests on a regular basis until you run out of practice tests or it's time for the actual test. Your mind will be ready for the schedule and stress of test day, and you'll be able to focus on recalling the material you've learned.

Secret Key #4 – Pace Yourself

Once you're fully prepared for the material on the test, your biggest challenge on test day will be managing your time. Just knowing that the clock is ticking can make you panic even if you have plenty of time left. Work on pacing yourself so you can build confidence against the time constraints of the exam. Pacing is a difficult skill to master, especially in a high-pressure environment, so **practice is vital**.

Set time expectations for your pace based on how much time is available. For example, if a section has 60 questions and the time limit is 30 minutes, you know you have to average 30 seconds or less per question in order to answer them all. Although 30 seconds is the hard limit, set 25 seconds per question as your goal, so you reserve extra time to spend on harder questions. When you budget extra time for the harder questions, you no longer have any reason to stress when those questions take longer to answer.

Don't let this time expectation distract you from working through the test at a calm, steady pace, but keep it in mind so you don't spend too much time on any one question. Recognize that taking extra time on one question you don't understand may keep you from answering two that you do understand later in the test. If your time limit for a question is up and you're still not sure of the answer, mark it and move on, and come back to it later if the time and the test format allow. If the testing format doesn't allow you to return to earlier questions, just make an educated guess; then put it out of your mind and move on.

On the easier questions, be careful not to rush. It may seem wise to hurry through them so you have more time for the challenging ones, but it's not worth missing one if you know the concept and just didn't take the time to read the question fully. Work efficiently but make sure you understand the question and have looked at all of the answer choices, since more than one may seem right at first.

Even if you're paying attention to the time, you may find yourself a little behind at some point. You should speed up to get back on track, but do so wisely. Don't panic; just take a few seconds less on each question until you're caught up. Don't guess without thinking, but do look through the answer choices and eliminate any you know are wrong. If you can get down to two choices, it is often worthwhile to guess from those. Once you've chosen an answer, move on and don't dwell on any that you skipped or had to hurry through. If a question was taking too long, chances are it was one of the harder ones, so you weren't as likely to get it right anyway.

On the other hand, if you find yourself getting ahead of schedule, it may be beneficial to slow down a little. The more quickly you work, the more likely you are to make a careless mistake that will affect your score. You've budgeted time for each question, so don't be afraid to spend that time. Practice an efficient but careful pace to get the most out of the time you have.

Secret Key #5 – Have a Plan for Guessing

When you're taking the test, you may find yourself stuck on a question. Some of the answer choices seem better than others, but you don't see the one answer choice that is obviously correct. What do you do?

The scenario described above is very common, yet most test takers have not effectively prepared for it. Developing and practicing a plan for guessing may be one of the single most effective uses of your time as you get ready for the exam.

In developing your plan for guessing, there are three questions to address:

- When should you start the guessing process?
- How should you narrow down the choices?
- Which answer should you choose?

When to Start the Guessing Process

Unless your plan for guessing is to select C every time (which, despite its merits, is not what we recommend), you need to leave yourself enough time to apply your answer elimination strategies. Since you have a limited amount of time for each question, that means that if you're going to give yourself the best shot at guessing correctly, you have to decide quickly whether or not you will guess.

Of course, the best-case scenario is that you don't have to guess at all, so first, see if you can answer the question based on your knowledge of the subject and basic reasoning skills. Focus on the key words in the question and try to jog your memory of related topics. Give yourself a chance to bring the knowledge to mind, but once you realize that you don't have (or you can't access) the knowledge you need to answer the question, it's time to start the guessing process.

It's almost always better to start the guessing process too early than too late. It only takes a few seconds to remember something and answer the question from knowledge. Carefully eliminating wrong answer choices takes longer. Plus, going through the process of eliminating answer choices can actually help jog your memory.

Summary: Start the guessing process as soon as you decide that you can't answer the question based on your knowledge.

7

How to Narrow Down the Choices

The next chapter in this book (**Test-Taking Strategies**) includes a wide range of strategies for how to approach questions and how to look for answer choices to eliminate. You will definitely want to read those carefully, practice them, and figure out which ones work best for you. Here though, we're going to address a mindset rather than a particular strategy.

Your odds of guessing an answer correctly depend on how many options you are choosing from.

Number of options left	5	4	3	2	1
Odds of guessing correctly	20%	25%	33%	50%	100%

You can see from this chart just how valuable it is to be able to eliminate incorrect answers and make an educated guess, but there are two things that many test takers do that cause them to miss out on the benefits of guessing:

- Accidentally eliminating the correct answer
- Selecting an answer based on an impression

We'll look at the first one here, and the second one in the next section.

To avoid accidentally eliminating the correct answer, we recommend a thought exercise called **the $5 challenge**. In this challenge, you only eliminate an answer choice from contention if you are willing to bet $5 on it being wrong. Why $5? Five dollars is a small but not insignificant amount of money. It's an amount you could afford to lose but wouldn't want to throw away. And while losing

$5 once might not hurt too much, doing it twenty times will set you back $100. In the same way, each small decision you make—eliminating a choice here, guessing on a question there—won't by itself impact your score very much, but when you put them all together, they can make a big difference. By holding each answer choice elimination decision to a higher standard, you can reduce the risk of accidentally eliminating the correct answer.

The $5 challenge can also be applied in a positive sense: If you are willing to bet $5 that an answer choice *is* correct, go ahead and mark it as correct.

Summary: Only eliminate an answer choice if you are willing to bet $5 that it is wrong.

Which Answer to Choose

You're taking the test. You've run into a hard question and decided you'll have to guess. You've eliminated all the answer choices you're willing to bet $5 on. Now you have to pick an answer. Why do we even need to talk about this? Why can't you just pick whichever one you feel like when the time comes?

The answer to these questions is that if you don't come into the test with a plan, you'll rely on your impression to select an answer choice, and if you do that, you risk falling into a trap. The test writers know that everyone who takes their test will be guessing on some of the questions, so they intentionally write wrong answer choices to seem plausible. You still have to pick an answer though, and if the wrong answer choices are designed to look right, how can you ever be sure that you're not falling for their trap? The best solution we've found to this dilemma is to take the decision out of your hands entirely. Here is the process we recommend:

Once you've eliminated any choices that you are confident (willing to bet $5) are wrong, select the first remaining choice as your answer.

Whether you choose to select the first remaining choice, the second, or the last, the important thing is that you use some preselected standard. Using this approach guarantees that you will not be enticed into selecting an answer choice that looks right, because you are not basing your decision on how the answer choices look.

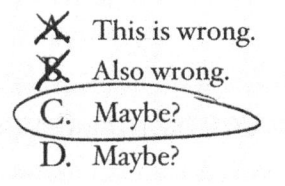

This is not meant to make you question your knowledge. Instead, it is to help you recognize the difference between your knowledge and your impressions. There's a huge difference between thinking an answer is right because of what you know, and thinking an answer is right because it looks or sounds like it should be right.

Summary: To ensure that your selection is appropriately random, make a predetermined selection from among all answer choices you have not eliminated.

Test-Taking Strategies

This section contains a list of test-taking strategies that you may find helpful as you work through the test. By taking what you know and applying logical thought, you can maximize your chances of answering any question correctly!

It is very important to realize that every question is different and every person is different: no single strategy will work on every question, and no single strategy will work for every person. That's why we've included all of them here, so you can try them out and determine which ones work best for different types of questions and which ones work best for you.

Question Strategies

☑ READ CAREFULLY

Read the question and the answer choices carefully. Don't miss the question because you misread the terms. You have plenty of time to read each question thoroughly and make sure you understand what is being asked. Yet a happy medium must be attained, so don't waste too much time. You must read carefully and efficiently.

☑ CONTEXTUAL CLUES

Look for contextual clues. If the question includes a word you are not familiar with, look at the immediate context for some indication of what the word might mean. Contextual clues can often give you all the information you need to decipher the meaning of an unfamiliar word. Even if you can't determine the meaning, you may be able to narrow down the possibilities enough to make a solid guess at the answer to the question.

☑ PREFIXES

If you're having trouble with a word in the question or answer choices, try dissecting it. Take advantage of every clue that the word might include. Prefixes can be a huge help. Usually, they allow you to determine a basic meaning. *Pre-* means before, *post-* means after, *pro-* is positive, *de-* is negative. From prefixes, you can get an idea of the general meaning of the word and try to put it into context.

☑ HEDGE WORDS

Watch out for critical hedge words, such as *likely, may, can, sometimes, often, almost, mostly, usually, generally, rarely,* and *sometimes.* Question writers insert these hedge phrases to cover every possibility. Often an answer choice will be wrong simply because it leaves no room for exception. Be on guard for answer choices that have definitive words such as *exactly* and *always.*

☑ SWITCHBACK WORDS

Stay alert for *switchbacks*. These are the words and phrases frequently used to alert you to shifts in thought. The most common switchback words are *but, although,* and *however.* Others include *nevertheless, on the other hand, even though, while, in spite of, despite,* and *regardless of.* Switchback words are important to catch because they can change the direction of the question or an answer choice.

⊘ FACE VALUE

When in doubt, use common sense. Accept the situation in the problem at face value. Don't read too much into it. These problems will not require you to make wild assumptions. If you have to go beyond creativity and warp time or space in order to have an answer choice fit the question, then you should move on and consider the other answer choices. These are normal problems rooted in reality. The applicable relationship or explanation may not be readily apparent, but it is there for you to figure out. Use your common sense to interpret anything that isn't clear.

Answer Choice Strategies

⊘ ANSWER SELECTION

The most thorough way to pick an answer choice is to identify and eliminate wrong answers until only one is left, then confirm it is the correct answer. Sometimes an answer choice may immediately seem right, but be careful. The test writers will usually put more than one reasonable answer choice on each question, so take a second to read all of them and make sure that the other choices are not equally obvious. As long as you have time left, it is better to read every answer choice than to pick the first one that looks right without checking the others.

⊘ ANSWER CHOICE FAMILIES

An answer choice family consists of two (in rare cases, three) answer choices that are very similar in construction and cannot all be true at the same time. If you see two answer choices that are direct opposites or parallels, one of them is usually the correct answer. For instance, if one answer choice says that quantity x increases and another either says that quantity x decreases (opposite) or says that quantity y increases (parallel), then those answer choices would fall into the same family. An answer choice that doesn't match the construction of the answer choice family is more likely to be incorrect. Most questions will not have answer choice families, but when they do appear, you should be prepared to recognize them.

⊘ ELIMINATE ANSWERS

Eliminate answer choices as soon as you realize they are wrong, but make sure you consider all possibilities. If you are eliminating answer choices and realize that the last one you are left with is also wrong, don't panic. Start over and consider each choice again. There may be something you missed the first time that you will realize on the second pass.

⊘ AVOID FACT TRAPS

Don't be distracted by an answer choice that is factually true but doesn't answer the question. You are looking for the choice that answers the question. Stay focused on what the question is asking for so you don't accidentally pick an answer that is true but incorrect. Always go back to the question and make sure the answer choice you've selected actually answers the question and is not merely a true statement.

⊘ EXTREME STATEMENTS

In general, you should avoid answers that put forth extreme actions as standard practice or proclaim controversial ideas as established fact. An answer choice that states the "process should be used in certain situations, if..." is much more likely to be correct than one that states the "process should be discontinued completely." The first is a calm rational statement and doesn't even make a definitive, uncompromising stance, using a hedge word *if* to provide wiggle room, whereas the second choice is far more extreme.

⌀ BENCHMARK

As you read through the answer choices and you come across one that seems to answer the question well, mentally select that answer choice. This is not your final answer, but it's the one that will help you evaluate the other answer choices. The one that you selected is your benchmark or standard for judging each of the other answer choices. Every other answer choice must be compared to your benchmark. That choice is correct until proven otherwise by another answer choice beating it. If you find a better answer, then that one becomes your new benchmark. Once you've decided that no other choice answers the question as well as your benchmark, you have your final answer.

⌀ PREDICT THE ANSWER

Before you even start looking at the answer choices, it is often best to try to predict the answer. When you come up with the answer on your own, it is easier to avoid distractions and traps because you will know exactly what to look for. The right answer choice is unlikely to be word-for-word what you came up with, but it should be a close match. Even if you are confident that you have the right answer, you should still take the time to read each option before moving on.

General Strategies

⌀ TOUGH QUESTIONS

If you are stumped on a problem or it appears too hard or too difficult, don't waste time. Move on! Remember though, if you can quickly check for obviously incorrect answer choices, your chances of guessing correctly are greatly improved. Before you completely give up, at least try to knock out a couple of possible answers. Eliminate what you can and then guess at the remaining answer choices before moving on.

⌀ CHECK YOUR WORK

Since you will probably not know every term listed and the answer to every question, it is important that you get credit for the ones that you do know. Don't miss any questions through careless mistakes. If at all possible, try to take a second to look back over your answer selection and make sure you've selected the correct answer choice and haven't made a costly careless mistake (such as marking an answer choice that you didn't mean to mark). This quick double check should more than pay for itself in caught mistakes for the time it costs.

⌀ PACE YOURSELF

It's easy to be overwhelmed when you're looking at a page full of questions; your mind is confused and full of random thoughts, and the clock is ticking down faster than you would like. Calm down and maintain the pace that you have set for yourself. Especially as you get down to the last few minutes of the test, don't let the small numbers on the clock make you panic. As long as you are on track by monitoring your pace, you are guaranteed to have time for each question.

⌀ DON'T RUSH

It is very easy to make errors when you are in a hurry. Maintaining a fast pace in answering questions is pointless if it makes you miss questions that you would have gotten right otherwise. Test writers like to include distracting information and wrong answers that seem right. Taking a little extra time to avoid careless mistakes can make all the difference in your test score. Find a pace that allows you to be confident in the answers that you select.

⊘ Keep Moving

Panicking will not help you pass the test, so do your best to stay calm and keep moving. Taking deep breaths and going through the answer elimination steps you practiced can help to break through a stress barrier and keep your pace.

Final Notes

The combination of a solid foundation of content knowledge and the confidence that comes from practicing your plan for applying that knowledge is the key to maximizing your performance on test day. As your foundation of content knowledge is built up and strengthened, you'll find that the strategies included in this chapter become more and more effective in helping you quickly sift through the distractions and traps of the test to isolate the correct answer.

Now that you're preparing to move forward into the test content chapters of this book, be sure to keep your goal in mind. As you read, think about how you will be able to apply this information on the test. If you've already seen sample questions for the test and you have an idea of the question format and style, try to come up with questions of your own that you can answer based on what you're reading. This will give you valuable practice applying your knowledge in the same ways you can expect to on test day.

Good luck and good studying!

Business Management

Vision, Mission, Values, and Structure of the Organization

MISSION AND VISION STATEMENTS

Mission statements and vision statements are similar in that they are both intended to clarify the objectives of the organization. However, a mission statement is only intended to define the broad mission an organization is attempting to carry out on a daily basis. A vision statement is intended to define the specific goals an organization hopes to achieve in the future.

A mission statement is a declaration of the reason an organization exists. This is important in determining standards, values, strategies, and other organizational aspects and serves as a guideline for establishing the processes to achieve goals. For example, the mission statement of a retail chain might be "to provide the best shopping experience possible for our customers." As a result, a decision might be made to implement standards and practices that promote high levels of customer service.

A vision statement is a declaration of the goals the organization wishes to achieve at some future point, which is important in designing and implementing the strategies necessary to meet those goals. For example, the vision statement of a retail chain might be to become the largest retail chain in the United States. As a result, the decision might be made to implement strategies that allow for rapid expansion, like finding and purchasing new locations and training new personnel quickly.

OPERATIONAL STRUCTURES

The two main types of operational structures that an organization may use are organic and mechanistic. A mechanistic structure is any structure in which the operations of an organization are extremely well regulated and defined. Mechanistic structures are usually centralized, have a large number of departments, have a large number of managers with very limited spans of control, have an extensive chain-of-command, are extremely formalized with a large number of policies and procedures, and usually have a large number of extremely specialized tasks. An organic structure, on the other hand, is any structure in which an organization is loosely regulated and possibly less defined. Organic structures are usually decentralized, have a small number of departments, have a small number of managers with each assigned a large span-of-control, have a short chain-of- command, have virtually no formalization so that only basic policies and procedures are established and usually have fewer specialized tasks than mechanistic structures.

Mechanistic and organic operational structures each have their own distinct advantages and disadvantages. As a result, the specific type of structure that is best suited for a particular organization can vary depending on the specific situation. If an organization wants or needs to maintain control of the individual processes and tasks that are performed by the various parts of the organization and the organization is in a business environment that is relatively stable, then it may be wise for the organization to use a structure that is more mechanistic. If the organization is in a business environment in which it needs to implement changes frequently and/or creativity is essential to the its success, then it may want to use a structure that is more organic. However, regardless of whether an organization is primarily mechanistic or primarily organic, it is impossible for an organization to be completely mechanistic or organic, as each organization needs some combination of the two operational structures in order to continue functioning.

Legislative and Regulatory Knowledge

FEDERAL BILL PROCESS

The process of creating a new law begins with a bill being introduced by either the Senate or the House of Representatives. The bill is then referred to a committee that determines if the bill should be considered further by a subcommittee, considered further by the entire floor of the House or Senate, or if the bill should be ignored. If the bill reaches the floor of the House or Senate, the bill is debated and a vote is taken to pass or defeat the bill. If the bill is passed in the Senate, then the bill is passed on to the House to be considered in the same way and vice versa. After both the House and Senate have approved a particular bill, the bill is sent on to the president to be signed into law. However, the president can veto the bill (refuse to sign it into law), or the bill may be returned to congress. It will become law automatically if the president ignores it for 10 days while Congress is in session. It will die automatically if it is ignored until after Congress is out of session.

INFLUENCING LEGISLATION

There is a wide range of methods that an individual, such as an HR professional, might use to influence upcoming legislation, but the three most common methods are by mail, by scheduling meetings with elected officials, or by lobbying. To influence legislation by mail, a formal letter can be sent to an elected official such as a state senator, a congressman or congresswoman, a local mayor, etc. To influence legislation through meetings, a meeting should be scheduled with an elected official or a member of his or her staff to discuss the issue of concern. To influence legislation by lobbying, members of similar organizations, possibly even competitors within the same industry, should be found and the entire group should express their opinions to an appropriate elected official by mail or in person.

Corporate Governance

GOVERNANCE PROCESS

Organizations have certain responsibilities to their employees, consumers, investors, and to society, in general. These responsibilities include abiding laws and regulations, adopting socially and ethically accepted business practices, reporting fully and honestly, and adding overall value. An organization's governance process is the established policies and procedures designed to meet those responsibilities. The process is directed by the board of directors, or equivalent governing body, and executive management. However, since the responsibilities are mostly ethical obligations, the success of the governing process hinges in the organization's ethical climate. Thus, the need exists for organizations to encourage ethical values.

PRINCIPLES OF CORPORATE CITIZENSHIP AND GOVERNANCE

Corporate governance is defined as the interactive and structural configuration—such as hierarchical or matrix formats—of personnel within an organization that are used by management to influence the behaviors, culture, and objective outcomes of the organization itself. The oversight of corporate governance thus requires framework considerations such as roles, responsibilities, and human resources to objectively monitor effectiveness and change the governance structure as needed. How an organization is governed is often a result of the culture within its ranks. Norms

such as rules, policies, SOPs, business systems, quality systems, and modes of communication can all influence how governance is executed and in turn how effective management can be.

To have an effective corporate citizenship and governance system in place, human resources should engage in the following:

- Create a code of corporate conduct and ethics so that all members of the firm know what behaviors are expected of them.
- Create a policy detailing how leaders and employees will be trained on the code, how any code violations should be reported, how whistle-blowers will be protected, how issues will be investigated, what consequences violators will face, and how reports will be tracked and documented.
- Ensure that leaders and board members uphold their fiduciary responsibility and always act with the best interests of the company in mind.
- Help spearhead or support environmental initiatives like reducing consumption and waste or using more eco-friendly supplies.
- Help spearhead or support activities that attempt to solve societal problems like poverty or a lack of access to clean water.

Employee Communications

ELEMENTS OF COMMUNICATION

Communication is defined as the practice of exchanging information, data, ideas, and opinions. There are many models that depict complex **communication processes**. However, almost all communications will include some variety of these fundamentals: source, sender, encoding, message, channel, receiver, decoding, and feedback. The **sender or source** chooses, creates, and encodes the message. The **receiver** decodes and interprets the message. In between, the message must be **transmitted** through some communication channel or medium like phone, text, email, video, or broadcast. Communication messages often pass through **noise barriers** such as environmental sounds, people speaking, traffic, and construction. Removing these barriers can decrease instances of misunderstanding and confusion. **Feedback** allows the model to be interchangeable, allowing for communication to flow both ways.

GENERAL COMMUNICATION TECHNIQUES
PLANNING COMMUNICATIONS

Delivering messages can be difficult, especially if the context is serious in nature. The message content should be tailored to fit the audience. This requires understanding the roles, expectations, and perspective of recipients. First, focus on eliminating any **barriers** or vague wording that may interfere with interpreting the message. Once the proper channel for delivery is selected, it may be important to focus on **nonverbal signals** and ensure that they coincide with the mood of the message content. Finally, messages should allow for **feedback** that will lead to follow-up discussions. If the message is complex in nature, such as a business change or new benefits offering, it may be critical to share repeated reminders and have open lines of communication to reduce confusion and ensure success.

ACTIVE LISTENING

Active listening is an important component of communication that requires paying close attention to what is being said. It often involves making eye contact and appropriately nodding to show engagement. To gain a better understanding, try to understand things from the speaker's point of

view, or visualize what he or she is saying. It is important to be considerate, avoid distractions or interruptions, and respond appropriately. Additionally, try to pick up on emotional cues beyond the literal words that are used. Even if the message differs from your own opinion, try to focus on accepting what the other person has to say rather than being critical. Make sure to fully hear what the other person is saying before formulating your own response. When compared to passive listeners, it has been noted that **active listeners** are more connected and conscientious.

COMMUNICATION TECHNIQUES FOR SPECIALIZED SITUATIONS

GIVING FEEDBACK

Feedback can be written or verbal and should be based upon factual data. Although the process can be emotional, it's important that feedback be constructive in nature, detailing the quality of someone's performance or conduct without judging on a personal level. Effective feedback should be delivered in a timely, consistent, and positively framed manner. If informal, feedback can be used to give advice or to provide clarity. If disciplinary, the feedback should also include required improvements to be made and potential consequences for not meeting the standard. When receiving feedback, take the time to carefully consider it and implement it as appropriate. The most important thing to remember about feedback is why it's being given: to facilitate an improvement.

FACILITATING FOCUS GROUPS

Focus groups can be used to investigate ideas, opinions, and concerns. **Focus groups** can be beneficial for clarifying supplemental research because they are relatively timely and inexpensive. The topic and objectives of the group should be clearly defined before potential participants are identified. Participants should be notified that their identities will be anonymous and that all information will be confidential. Once a **pool of participants** has been selected and separated into groups, a trained **facilitator** should be chosen, and a guide of discussion questions should be constructed. Most studies will contain three to 10 focus groups, each with five to 12 voluntary participants. A private location is ideal, and many discussions will last approximately 90 minutes. Finally, all collected information will be analyzed and reported.

FACILITATING STAFF MEETINGS

There are three core elements to a successful **staff meeting**: 1) invite all attendees to share a little, 2) focus on the group and any outcomes that might need adjustment or improvement, and 3) allow time for feedback in the decision-making process. Staff meetings are an excellent way to increase organizational communication and alignment, offering an open floor for staff to give feedback on recent messages or events. They are also a low-budget way to promote staff recognition, wellness programs, employee referral programs, and employee surveys. Moreover, staff meetings have a history of improving productivity, workplace conflicts, team synergy, and employee relations. It is important to consider religious holidays when scheduling staff meetings, seminars, or training events. For example, staff meetings scheduled on Ash Wednesday, Good Friday, Passover, Rosh Hashanah, or Yom Kippur might have low attendance.

COMMUNICATIONS MEDIA

Communication can be transmitted through a wide variety of **channels or media**, such as phone, email, face-to-face, reports, presentations, or social media. The method that you choose should fit both the *audience* and the *type* of communication. **Information-rich communication channels** include phone, videoconferencing, and face-to-face meetings or presentations. **Information-lean channels** include email, fliers, newsletters, or reports. If you are trying to sell a product or service, you might use a series of phone calls, face-to-face meetings, and presentations. This is because information-rich media are more interactive, which is more appropriate for complex messages that may need clarification. Rich and verbal communications should be used when there is time urgency,

18

immediate feedback is required, ideas can be simplified with explanations, or emotions may be affected. Lean and written communications should be used when you are simply stating facts or need information permanently recorded.

ENCOURAGING COMMUNICATION AND INVOLVEMENT

It is possible for a particular strategy to be used as both a communication strategy and an involvement strategy because, in many situations, the amount of employee involvement within an organization is closely related to the amount of employee communication. Strategies encouraging communication between employees and management will often allow employees to have more input in decision-making and ultimately allow employees to become more involved in operations as a whole. However, this does not necessarily mean that every strategy is both a communication strategy and an involvement strategy. In fact, a strategy allowing a manager to communicate important information to employees without allowing each employee to respond to or discuss the information may be considered a communication strategy, but it cannot be considered an involvement strategy. At the same time, a strategy allowing an individual to have more control over a particular task may be an involvement strategy without being a communication strategy, as it does not necessarily encourage an individual to communicate.

INVOLVEMENT STRATEGIES:

- Delegating authority refers to an employee involvement strategy in which an organization grants an individual the power to make decisions related to position. This strategy allows an individual to become more involved in the organization by allowing certain decisions to be made without receiving permission.
- An employee survey, also known as a climate survey, is an employee involvement strategy in which an organization gathers information about the priorities and concerns of employees by having them fill out and submit a form.
- A suggestion program is an employee involvement strategy in which an organization gathers ideas about how to control or eliminate problems by allowing employees to submit anonymous ideas. Suggestion programs usually use suggestion boxes, voice mail, etc.
- A committee, in this context, is a group of employees within an organization who work together to make decisions related to a particular concern of the organization. Employees may be assigned to a committee temporarily or permanently depending on the concern or activity the committee is designed to handle.
- An employee-management committee, also referred to as an employee participation group, is a group of employees who work with the supervisors and managers to make decisions related to a particular concern. Employees, supervisors, and managers may be assigned to an employee-management committee temporarily or permanently, depending on the specific concern or activity the committee is designed to handle.
- A task force is a group of employees who work together to determine the cause of a particular problem and identify a solution to the problem. Employees are usually assigned to a task force until the cause of a particular problem is solved.

COMMUNICATION STRATEGIES:

- A brown-bag lunch program is an employee involvement strategy in which an informal meeting is organized to discuss various concerns and issues. Brown-bag lunches are usually organized to take place during lunch to allow managers and employees to discuss issues and concerns in a relaxed setting.
- A department meeting is a formal gathering in which the employees, supervisors, and managers of a particular department discuss the various concerns and issues affecting that particular department. Department meetings usually take place on a regular basis.
- Town hall meetings, also known as all-hands staff meetings, are formal meetings in which all of the employees, supervisors, and managers within an organization attend a formal assembly to distribute and receive important information about the organization. Town hall meetings are usually conducted in a similar fashion to a large lecture and may or may not allow for effective two-way communication.
- An open-door policy is an employee involvement/communication strategy in which employees are encouraged to share information or suggestions with managers or supervisors by assuring them they will not be adversely affected by what they say. Open-door policies are designed to establish effective communication between managers, supervisors, and employees by removing barriers preventing or discouraging the discussion of important issues with supervisors or managers. The primary advantage of an open-door policy is that it allows the organization to identify problems and solutions that may have gone unnoticed without information from employees. One disadvantage is that in certain situations a manager or supervisor, in order to handle an issue that has been reported, may need to release information that will adversely affect an employee.
- The Management by Walking Around (MBWA) strategy is simply a communication and involvement method in which an organization encourages employee communication and involvement by making managers and supervisors readily available by walking around to check on the progress of each employee, discuss questions or concerns, and handle any problems the employee or the manager identifies. This strategy is straightforward and obvious because most managers and supervisors are required to monitor employees. However, managers and supervisors need to be reminded to "manage by walking around" because it is very easy get caught up in other activities and miss important issues that should have been identified and handled.

Ethical and Professional Standards

ETHICAL PRACTICE

TRANSPARENCY

Transparency can come in many forms within the workplace. Most employees appreciate it when management is transparent with information, such as healthcare costs and pay rates, or future changes, such as mergers or acquisitions on the horizon. **Transparency** may also be a tool for removing obstacles to diversity. Being transparent and openly communicating with staff during decision-making processes can also build employee trust and be leveraged as a recruiting or retention tool. The Internet provides job seekers with transparent information about a company's culture, benefits, average pay, and interview process.

CONFIDENTIALITY

Confidentiality is vital in human resources practices. Maintaining the confidentiality of all **employee records** is imperative. This may include social security numbers, birth dates, addresses, phone numbers, email, benefits enrollment, medical or leave details, earnings history,

garnishments, bank account information, disciplinary action, grievances, and employment eligibility data. When employee record information is requested for legitimate purposes, a written release signed by the employee should be obtained and kept on file. Examples of these requests might include bank loans, mortgage applications, or employment verification. Companies should also consider implementing **confidentiality or nondisclosure agreements** so employees are aware that databases, client lists, and other proprietary information must be protected and sharing these records will have serious consequences.

ANONYMITY

Anonymity is similar to confidentiality. It provides staff or participants the ability to partake in activities anonymously without their names being provided. Employers may have employees take a survey or evaluate their managers under anonymity to eliminate any fear of retaliation. Individuals may also report a complaint or immoral practice, such as harassment, to management and request anonymity so they are able to remain nameless. However, these complaints should be carefully investigated before being acted upon to ensure legitimacy.

PERSONAL INTEGRITY

Personal integrity comes from developing and sticking to an internal code of ethics that deems what is right and what is wrong. It is strengthened by choosing thoughts and actions that are based upon an individual's moral principles and personal values, as opposed to personal gain or popularity. Some values of **personal integrity** might include character traits like honesty, trustworthiness, kindness, courageousness, respect, and loyalty. Some examples of personal integrity might include: helping an elderly neighbor with yard work or home repairs, even when it might not be convenient. It is these behaviors that develop an individual's personal integrity and reputation. The stronger one's sense of personal integrity, the less likely he or she is to succumb to corruption.

PROFESSIONAL INTEGRITY

Professional integrity involves choosing actions that adhere to moral principles and an internal code of ethics. It originates from an individual's values of right or wrong and leads to behaviors that are honest, fair, kind, courageous, and respectful. Professional integrity avoids corruption or any potential conflicts of interest and develops professional credibility. It is also the proven virtue and quality of possessing high professional standards. Professional integrity and character have received increasing attention following corruption headlines about Jimmy Hoffa, Enron, Bernie Madoff, and even Martha Stewart. Moreover, leaders who demonstrate unyielding professional integrity frequently have a greater following of employees and customers.

ETHICAL AGENT

Ethics and compliance officers ensure that business is conducted in accordance with rules, legal regulations, and industry standards of practice. Additionally, an **ethical agent** makes moral judgments based on fundamental ethical principles that are rooted in their personal character, not based on a situation's potential gains. **Ethical dilemmas** occur when a corporation or individual is faced with a conflict of interest or actions that are blatantly wrong, deceptive, or may have uncertain consequences. Many ethical conflicts value profit over moral principles. Over the past few decades, ethics and business conduct have received increasing attention that has led to more stringent **compliance regulations**, like the Sarbanes-Oxley Act.

CONFLICTS OF INTEREST

A **conflict of interest** occurs when someone with a responsibility to act in the best interest of the company may also be in the position to derive personal benefit at the expense of the company. Some examples include:

- Utilizing company resources for personal financial gain
- Forming relationships or obligations that compromise objectivity when conducting duties
- Disclosing company information to interfere with bidding, negotiating, or contracting
- Exerting influence in business transactions that benefit the individual or a relative
- Traveling at vendors' or customers' expense
- Accepting gifts, services, or favors from company stakeholders

Conflicts of interest should be avoided. Clear policies should be in place, and all employees should be held to them.

PRIVACY PRINCIPLES

With technology now a part of every business transaction, it is essential that companies and employees adhere to strict confidentiality practices and **privacy principles**. From employee monitoring to asking interview questions, employers need to take care to avoid invading personal privacy. Legal regulations that inform best practices and internal privacy policies should be consulted regularly for guidance. On the other hand, companies should consider implementing **confidentiality or nondisclosure agreements** so employees are aware that databases, client lists, and other proprietary information must be protected and that the sharing of these records externally is strictly prohibited.

CODE OF CONDUCT

A **code of conduct** is a set of behavioral rules rooted in moral standards, laws, and best practices that a company develops, adopts, and communicates to employees. It outlines expected behavior as well as defines what behavior won't be tolerated. The document should also state what disciplinary actions employees could face if they violate the code.

Employee involvement in the development of a code of conduct will lead to greater employee buy-in and adherence. The code should be written in ambiguous language that can be applied to specific situations as they arise. Upon finalization, the code should be shared with all employees. Employees should then be required to sign a document acknowledging receipt and understanding of the new code.

> **Review Video: Ethical and Professional Standards**
> Visit mometrix.com/academy and enter code: 391843

HRIS and Data Reporting

HRIS/HCM SOFTWARE

Human resources information systems (HRIS) are software systems that contain employee profiles, workforce features, and reporting tools. Modules of an HRIS encompass many necessary modules including applicant tracking, time and attendance, payroll, benefits administration, and performance management. **Human capital management (HCM) systems** integrate features that might include document management, ways to provide policies or benefits summaries access, budgeting and forecasting, applicant tracking, succession planning, as well as engagement and

22

retention tools throughout the entire length of employment. Some also include learning and development modules. Both types of systems provide the benefit of employee self-service options that allow employees to take ownership of administrative tasks like updating personal information or compliance reporting.

BASIC CONCEPTS IN STATISTICS AND MEASUREMENT

DESCRIPTIVE STATISTICS

Descriptive statistics are used to summarize data that has been collected. **Descriptive statistics** can measure central tendency, dispersion, variability, frequency distribution, and proportions. The most common numerical descriptive statistic is the average or mean. The **mode** is the value of data that occurs most frequently. Other forms of descriptive statistics include frequency count, range, standard deviation, and correlation coefficient.

First the data is collected through primary methods such as surveys, observations, or experiments. Then, the data is analyzed or characterized by variable and presented using graphs or charts, such as the histogram. As samples get larger, the sample distribution often begins to appear more like the population distribution, which may result in a bell-shaped curve.

CORRELATION

A **correlation** is the relationship between two variables. There can be a positive relationship or a negative relationship. The strength of this relationship, or the **correlation coefficient**, is reflected as a range from –1.0 to 0 for negative correlations and 0 to 1.0 for positive correlations. The numbers closer to 0 represent a weaker relationship, whereas the numbers closer to –1.0 or 1.0 represent a stronger relationship.

REGRESSION ANALYSIS

Regression analysis is another statistical measurement that is used to find relationships among a set of variables. It is frequently used for predicting and forecasting. **Regression analysis** estimates or predicts the unknown values of one variable (dependent variable, labeled as Y) from the known or fixed value of another variable (independent variable, labeled as X). When there is only one independent variable to consider, a **linear regression** is used. When there is more than one independent variable to consider, a **multiple regression** is used. Regression analysis is also used to recognize which among the independent variables are related to the dependent variable and to what degree. There can be a **positive relationship** in which the line moves upward from the bottom left to the upper right. There can be a **negative relationship**, in which the line moves downward from the upper right to the bottom left. Finally, there can be **no relationship** in which plots are scattered all over.

RELIABILITY

Reliability refers to the consistency of a particular measure. A research tool is said to be **reliable** if it produces consistent and repeatable measures every time. For example, measuring tapes and stopwatches provide consistent and reliable measures. Surveys should be reliable if the questions are clear and straightforward, but ambiguous questions might return unreliable results.

VALIDITY

Validity refers to whether an instrument accurately measures what it is supposed to be measuring. The validity of a survey may be more difficult to interpret. For example, can a survey accurately measure company commitment or employee satisfaction? For an instrument to be deemed as valid, it needs to go through and pass rigorous statistical testing.

23

INTERPRETATION OF DATA AND CHARTS

Data interpretation involves drawing conclusions from data sets with the goal of answering a question and spurring meaningful action. Data can be qualitative or quantitative. **Qualitative data** is descriptive and focuses on categorizing concepts based on making observations, conducting interviews, or reviewing documents. **Quantitative data**, on the other hand, involves a numerical, statistics-driven approach, in which data is derived from surveys and other quantifiable media.

USING DATA TO SUPPORT A BUSINESS CASE

When human resource professionals present a business case to senior leadership, they must show a compelling need for the allocation of resources that they're requesting. They can accomplish this by incorporating relevant data into their business case. For example, if human resources wants to hire an additional maintenance technician per shift, they should include things like the average machine downtime (and the resulting cost of lost productivity) and how long the average repair ticket stays open. Additionally, human resources could add more descriptive data in the form of complaints from production management and current maintenance staff, who are experiencing major disruptions in productivity or are feeling overworked, respectively.

Change Management

GENE DALTON'S THEORY OF LASTING CHANGE

Many change efforts struggle to produce **lasting and sustainable results**. Although initial goals may be met, the ability to stick to the efforts or behaviors needed to prolong the success proves to be more difficult. **Gene Dalton** argued that change would not occur without a feeling of loss or pain to motivate it and that people will continue old patterns of behavior unless they feel a need for change. He also noted that those initiating and supporting organizational change should be perceived as trustworthy facilitators. Dalton developed four **focus areas** to support change efforts: generalized goals → specific objectives, former social ties → new relationships, self-doubt → heightened self-esteem, and external motives for change → internal motive for change.

LEWIN'S CHANGE MANAGEMENT MODEL

Kurt Lewin's theory of change describes three stages for planning change: unfreezing, change, and refreezing:

- **Unfreezing** is the first step. It occurs when current values, attitudes, and behaviors are challenged, and people understand the need for change.
- **Change** occurs during the action phase, whereby the situation is examined, and a new equilibrium is created. People develop new values, attitudes, or patterns of behaviors.
- **Refreezing** is the final step in which the change is stabilized, and new patterns are solidified. Refreezing requires that people experience positive consequences to strengthen their continuing commitment to the change process.

MCKINSEY 7-S MODEL

The McKinsey 7-S Model is frequently used in strategic planning and change management. The model is founded on the principle that each company has seven **elements** or key factors. Strategy, structure, and systems are more easily identified. Shared values, style, staff, and skills can be more difficult to describe and may be continuously changing. However, each element is interconnected

and may affect one another. The seven key elements of the McKinsey 7-S Model include the following:

1. **Strategy**—plan for competitive advantage and growth regarding business, products, and markets
2. **Structure**—structure of reporting hierarchy
3. **Systems**—everyday procedures and processes
4. **Shared values**—core concepts and work ethic, organizational mission, and goals
5. **Style**—leadership approach and operational culture
6. **Staff**—employee development and empowerment
7. **Skills**—competencies and capabilities

John Kotter's 8-Step Change Model

John Kotter's 8-Step Change Model identifies eight steps for implementing effective change:

1. **Create a sense of urgency**—examine the competitive market, identify threats or opportunities, articulate importance of speed, and make the case for change.
2. **Build a guiding coalition**—establish support from executives, and design a group with credibility and power to lead change efforts.
3. **Develop a shared vision and strategy**—create a plan to direct change efforts, and develop success metrics.
4. **Communicate the change vision**—readily and persistently communicate the new vision and strategy from the top down.
5. **Empower action**—eliminate obstacles, systems, or structures that undermine the new idea, and reward creativity.
6. **Generate short-term wins**—recognize and reward visible improvements in performance.
7. **Capitalize on momentum**—take advantage of small wins, reinvite those who have resisted, and become reenergized.
8. **Make the change stick**—continue to encourage new behaviors and leadership development.

> **Review Video: <u>Organizational Change Management Theories</u>**
> Visit mometrix.com/academy and enter code: 404217

Organizational Change Processes
Leadership Buy-In

Buy-in is support or endorsement for something. In the case of change, leadership buy-in is critical. Often, their support is necessary to get the change movement started because they may need to approve the use of resources or major modifications to business operations. If the change requires their endorsement, and they will not give it, then the change is defeated before it can get started. Additionally, leadership buy-in is necessary to champion the change across the organization. If the leaders believe in the effort, they can communicate their enthusiasm for it and model the new desired behavior, making it easier for the change to take root.

Building a Case for Change

One useful way to approach organizational change activities is the **action research model**. Once a problem has been identified, there are six basic steps that follow: data gathering, feedback of data to the target group, data discussions and diagnosis, action planning, action, and recycling. **Data gathering** involves collecting information about the problem from sources such as observations, interviews, surveys, and archived data. **Feedback of data to a target group** involves making the

gathered data openly available and sharing it with a group through presentations. **Data discussions and diagnosis** involve a roundtable conversation and analysis by the target group to diagnose a root cause and to explore alternatives or viable solutions. **Action planning** involves creating a plan to implement solutions, which may require outside parties. **Action** involves the execution of new changes. Finally, **recycling** involves reviewing and repeating the processes to ensure problems do not reoccur.

ENGAGING EMPLOYEES

For changes to be implemented successfully, the employees need to embrace them (or at least understand them). This can be accomplished by engaging them in the change process and ensuring that they remain engaged overall as employees. Engaging them in the change process includes asking for and using their feedback (when possible) before, during, and after the change. Doing this shows that the organization values their opinion and places an importance on collaboration and transparency. When employees can help shape the change, they are far more likely to go along with it. Additionally, when employees are truly engaged at work, they will have an easier time adapting to change (even if unpleasant) because of their strong emotional commitment to the company.

COMMUNICATING CHANGE

Provide clear communication to employees and all stakeholders as early as possible. Keep communications simple, and explain both the necessity and the timeline for the change. Let employees know what will be staying the same and proactively counter any negative reactions that can be anticipated. Develop opportunities for **two-way communications**. This provides employees with the chance to ask questions. Then, repeat communications, and explain how employees will be kept informed throughout the process to manage expectations. Finally, have leadership get involved to advocate for the change, and lead by example to keep morale high.

REMOVING BARRIERS

Human resource practitioners must be cognizant of any barriers to organizational change. Change actions can be thwarted by barriers such as staff attitudes or behaviors that discourage implementing new ideas, insufficient skills or technologies, and distances or obstacles between formal structures. These barriers can be eliminated by regularly communicating the rationale and timeline of the change, implementing new training programs or technologies, involving employee advocates in decision-making processes, and welcoming feedback from all levels.

ENSURING CHANGE MANAGEMENT IS SUCCESSFUL AND AVOIDING FAILURES

These tactics are recommended to accomplish a successful change effort:

- Have a change sponsor lead the initiative.
- Communicate a clear need for the change.
- Create a shared vision of the organization post change.
- Rally commitment or request participation from all involved.
- Integrate past systems, structures, policies, and procedures into the new normal.
- Monitor progress and benchmark results against other successful companies.
- Make change sustainable by having a clear plan and rewarding desired behavior.

Some important reasons that **change efforts fail** include the following:

- Change was not strategically aligned with organizational goals or mission.
- Change was not communicated meaningfully or was perceived as a superficial, quick fix.
- Change was unrealistic given the current economic and political environment.

26

- Change leaders were inadequate or lacked the necessary commitment.
- Measurable goals and timelines were not established.
- Resistance to the change thwarted change efforts.

FORCES AND KINDS OF ORGANIZATIONAL CHANGE

Forces of organizational change are much like the childhood game of Red Rover, in which you have all the kids on the driving forces of change team lock arms to form one line, all the kids on the forces resisting change team for another line, and each team sends one member at a time to run across and break through the opposing line. **Driving forces of change** might include internal forces such as new technology, desire for alternative work schedules, and new knowledge or values as well as environmental factors such as competition, customer demand, and available resources. **Forces resisting change** might include individual resistance, such as fear of the unknown or distrust of management, and organizational resistance, such as systems, relationships, or threat to power structure. Furthermore, additional time will be needed based upon the more uncertainty and complexity there is surrounding the change. **Developmental change** is a gradual improvement to create more efficient functions. **Transactional change** is a slow evolution toward new processes, products, or structure. **Transformational change** is the most radical upheaval and paradigm change to organizational structure that works best when planned in advance and is implemented gradually and systematically.

TARGETS OF CHANGE

The most common **targets of organizational change** include individual personality, dyads, groups, work teams, all organizational divisions, organizational structure, and organizational strategy. Individual personality, dyads, groups, and work teams all focus on targeting employee relationships. Interventions that target employee behavior are designed to a change strategy that eliminates conflicts and improves effectiveness. Targeting and designing change to all organizational divisions, organizational strategy, or organizational structure are often needs based due to lack of coordination, cooperation, cohesiveness, division of labor, departmentalization, span of control, eliminating product lines, or mergers and acquisitions.

Risk Management

Risk management refers to the process of identifying, analyzing, and prioritizing **risks or potential uncertainties** while developing strategies to protect the financial interests of a company. Risks or potential uncertainties may include workplace safety, workers' compensation, unemployment insurance, security, loss prevention, health and wellness, data management, privacy protection, project failures, and contingency planning. Depending upon the size of the company or severity of the threat, some or all of these areas might be assigned to human resources. The underlying goal of risk management is to mitigate the costs of these uncertainties as much as possible.

RISK TYPES

- Hazard risk involves potential liability or loss of property and is generally mitigated by insurance. Workplace accidents, fires, and natural disasters are examples of risk that fall into this category.
- Financial risk involves potential negative impacts to a firm's cash flow. A major customer not paying invoices on time is an example of this type of risk.

- Operational risk involves the impact to a firm's ability to function effectively and may include technology failures, process breakdowns, and human error.
- Strategic risk involves a firm's plans becoming outdated due to shifts in the economy, politics, customer demographics, or the overall competitive landscape.

RISK ASSESSMENTS

Risk assessments are a critical element of risk management. A **quantitative risk assessment** will allow the business to assign actual dollar amounts to each risk based on value, exposure, single loss expectancy, annualized rate of occurrence, and annualized loss expectancy. **Single loss expectancy** is measured when a value is placed on each asset, and the percentage of loss is determined for each acknowledged threat. The **annualized loss expectancy** can be calculated by multiplying the single loss occurrence and the annualized rate of occurrence. In these calculations, potential loss amounts are used to consider if implementing a security measure is necessary. Qualitative risk assessment, on the other hand, does not assign a defined monetary value to the risk. It uses descriptive statements to describe the potential impact of a risk, which can include a general reference to financial loss. For example, a major system breach would result in customer data being compromised, severe damage to the firm's reputation, and a significant financial blow to the organization due to handling the crisis, shoring up the system to prevent further issues, and responding to possible lawsuits by those affected.

HANDLING RISKS

The business has several options when a risk has been identified: accept the risk, retain the risk, avoid the risk, diminish or mitigate the risk, or transfer the risk. If the risk could be easily handled and doesn't pose a large threat to the organization, it may be wise to accept it. Preparing for it in advance could be a waste of time and resources. In addition, a firm might choose risk retention, or keeping the risk in-house, if doing so is financially prudent. Although not all situations allow for this, it may be wise to try and avoid larger risks. For example, if a firm believes a feature on its product isn't going to be functional for the product launch, it could decide to introduce it as an upgrade later or omit it entirely. If accepting the risk or avoiding it isn't possible, the company could decide to mitigate or diminish it. For example, if human resources thinks that workers will miss important changes to their benefits during open enrollment, they could offer training sessions and extra office hours to help employees understand their options. Finally, firms may be able to transfer, or share, some risks. When a business purchases an insurance policy of any kind, it is transferring risk to the insurer. A company could also transfer risk to suppliers with specific contract clauses.

EPLI

Employment practices liability insurance (EPLI) is a risk management tool used to share financial risk associated with employee lawsuits. EPLI is insurance purchased to protect against some of the legal costs faced if an employee brings a civil suit against the organization. There are many situations in which an employee may bring a lawsuit because of perceived rights violations. If the employee does, the organization will pay huge fees in legal costs, even if it wins the suit. EPLI can be extremely useful in covering these unexpected costs.

HARASSMENT TRAINING

Companies should complete regular **harassment training** because employers must exercise reasonable care to avoid and prevent harassment. Otherwise, employers may be found liable for the harassing behaviors of vendors, clients, coworkers, and supervisors. Harassment is defined as any demeaning or degrading comments, jokes, name-calling, actions, graffiti, or other belittling conduct that may be found offensive. Any form of **derogatory speech** can be considered harassment,

including neutral words that may be perceived in a vulgar or intimidating way. Furthermore, the Civil Rights Act of 1964 protects individuals from harassment on the basis of race, color, religion, sex, or national origin. More importantly, damages awarded under Title VII can total anywhere from $50,000 to $300,000, depending upon the size of the employer.

WORK-RELATED PROBLEMS OF ALCOHOLISM AND DRUG ABUSE

Shows like A & E's *Intervention* and recent news of the opiate epidemic address some of the many personal struggles for employees involved in or suffering from **alcoholism and drug abuse**. Moreover, these problems are not temporary, and many need help correcting these behaviors. Alcoholism is now a **protected disability** under the American with Disabilities Act. The act does not protect employees who report to work under the influence, nor does it protect them from the consequences of their actions or blatant misconduct. Problems caused by drug abuse are similar to those caused by alcoholism. However, additional problems associated with drug abuse are the likelihood of stealing, due to the expensive cost of the employee's habit, and its illegal nature. The Americans with Disabilities Act (ADA) does not protect current drug use as a protected disability.

DRUG-FREE WORKPLACE ACT

The Drug-Free Workplace Act of 1988 requires that government contractors make a good faith effort to ensure a drug-free workplace. Employers must prohibit illegal substances in the workplace and must create drug awareness trainings for employees. Any federal contractor with contracts of $100,000 or more must adhere to a set of mandates to show they maintain a drug-free work environment.

- Employers must develop a **written policy** prohibiting the production, distribution, use, or possession of any controlled substance by an employee while in the workplace.
- Employers are required to develop **standards of enforcement**, and all employees must receive a copy of the policy and understand the consequences of a violation.
- Employers need to implement **drug awareness trainings** to help employees understand the hazards and health risks of drug use.

Although drug testing is not required, it is intended that employers have some type of **screening** in place.

CAUTIONARY MEASURES WHEN DESIGNING DRUG TESTING PROGRAMS

Many employers utilize drug testing to screen applicants and, in some cases, current employees. Generally speaking, employers can legally require applicants to pass a **drug test** as a condition of employment or adopt programs that test active employees as long as the programs are not discriminatory. Due to the controversial nature, employers must be meticulously cautious when designing these programs to ensure practices will be upheld if brought to court. *Wilkinson vs. Times Mirror Corporation* established the following elements for testing programs:

1. Samples are collected at a medical facility by persons unrelated to the employer.
2. Applicants are unobserved by others when they furnish samples.
3. Results are kept confidential.
4. Employers are notified only if the applicant was passed or failed by a medical lab.
5. Applicants are notified of the portion they failed by the medical lab—some instances will provide applicants an opportunity to present medical documentation prior to the employer receiving results.
6. There is a defined method for applicants to question or challenge test results.
7. Applicants must be eligible to reapply after a reasonable time.

29

Qualitative and Quantitative Methods for Analytics

FINANCIAL ANALYSIS METHODS TO ASSESS BUSINESS HEALTH

Financial ratios can be broken down into relevant categories for management, stakeholders, and auditors. **Profitability ratios** analyze a business's ability to generate earnings in comparison to expense costs. **Liquidity ratios** measure the business's available cash or ability to pay off short-term debts. **Operational efficiency and employee productivity ratios** measure the efficiency of employees and business resources to generate a profit. **Leverage or capital structure ratios** assess how the business uses debt to finance operations. Although being able to calculate financial ratios is important, being able to interpret financial ratios is more valuable.

MARKETING AND SALES METRICS

Three of the most common sales and marketing business metrics are the number of customers or orders for the period, the average amount received for each order, and the gross profit margin. The **number of customers or orders** is an exact or estimated count of the number of people purchasing products from the company or the number of orders the company has received during a specific period of time. The **average amount received for each order** is the total amount in dollars received for a particular period divided by the number of orders. Finally, the **gross profit margin** is the total revenue for a certain period of time minus the cost of sales for that particular period divided by the total revenue for that period.

The number of customers or orders received is usually used to identify problems with current marketing and sales strategies. If the number of customers or orders for a specific period is significantly lower than previous periods, or the number of customers or orders is significantly lower than the numbers estimated from competitors, there may be a problem with the marketing strategy. For example, owners of a fast-food restaurant may decide to change their menu by adding and marketing healthier options to expand their customer base. If there is a sudden drop in the number of customers, the strategy is not working.

The average amount received per order is usually used to determine the effectiveness of marketing and sales strategies from the current customer base. The average amount received per order helps identify how much each customer is contributing to the organization's cash flow. This helps determine if the focus should be on expanding the customer base or encouraging the current customer base to spend more through marketing initiatives such as special sales, discounts, reward programs for frequent shoppers, and so on.

The gross profit margin is usually used to help determine whether a particular marketing or sales strategy currently in effect is profitable. For example, a fast-food restaurant chain may have instituted a new less-than-a-dollar menu and a marketing campaign focusing on this menu a year ago. Comparing the gross profit margin for the current year with the previous year is helpful in determining if the new campaign is increasing sales or if a new strategy is needed.

OPERATIONS AND BUSINESS DEVELOPMENT METRICS

Three of the most common operations and business development metrics used to measure performance are the number of activities, the opportunity success rate, and the innovation rate. The **number of activities** is an exact or estimated count of how many tasks the organization is attempting to do at one time. The **opportunity success rate** is the number of opportunities taken advantage of divided by the total number of opportunities available. Finally, the **innovation rate** is the gross revenue from new ideas, products, and services divided by the total gross revenue.

The number of activities is usually used to determine whether the company is taking on a larger workload than what it can normally handle. Multitasking is an important part of any enterprise, but it is important to identify how much work is too much. For example, if an old-fashioned toy manufacturer that prides itself for handcrafting toys wants to start building a large array of modern toys, they may find that it is not possible to expand without drastically increasing costs or eliminating other activities. This is because each old-fashioned toy takes a significant amount of time to construct, and the company may not be able to expand its modern toy-building activities without eliminating some of the old-fashioned toys from its product line.

Innovation rate is useful for developing a strategic plan because it helps determine if new ideas, products, and services are profitable. If the innovation rate is equal to or higher than competitors' rates, the current innovation strategy is appropriate, and the focus should be on designing products and services similar to those recently placed on the market. On the other hand, if the innovation rate is significantly lower than competitors' rates, a new innovation strategy should be implemented focusing on developing products and services not similar to those recently placed on the market. The innovation rate is not a measure of how innovative a company is but rather a measure of how profitable each group of new innovations has been for the firm.

INFORMATION TECHNOLOGY METRICS

Three of the most common information technology metrics an organization might use are the number of online orders, the availability of information resources, and the number of views per page or listing. The **number of online orders** is a count of how many orders have been placed by customers using the company's website. The **availability of information resources** is the percentage of time the company's servers, websites, email, and other technological resources are accessible at the time those resources are needed. The **number of views per page or listing** is a count of how many times customers have looked at a particular web page or online product.

The number of online orders placed using an organization's website can be useful for developing a strategic plan because it measures the effectiveness of the website. If the number of orders made online through the website or by email is equal to or greater than the number of orders placed through traditional means (such as in a store or by phone), the focus should be on maintaining or expanding online services. On the other hand, if the number of orders placed online is significantly lower than the number of orders placed through more traditional means, strategies should be implemented to improve online services. It is also useful to compare the number of online orders made through the website to the number of online orders made through websites belonging to competitors to determine the effectiveness of the website in relation to the rest of the industry.

The availability of the organization's information resources is an essential factor to consider for any organization's strategic plan because technology is useful only if it is working. If the computer systems, websites, email services, or other pieces of technology used by employees or customers are frequently inaccessible, the organization will not be able to function properly. Identifying problems with information technology (IT) systems and IT personnel minimizes future problems.

The number of views per page or views per listing for an organization's websites, ads, or other information resources is an important factor for an organization to consider during the strategic planning process because they measure the effectiveness of its websites and ads. If a listing receives a large number of views and results in many orders, it's performing well. However, if a listing is not receiving a large number of views, or it is receiving a large number of views but not resulting in many sales, website marketing and design should be rethought.

GENERAL BUSINESS AND ECONOMIC ENVIRONMENT METRICS

Three of the most common metrics related to the general business and economic environment an organization might use are the current number of competitors and the average number of new competitors entering the market per year, the organization's current market share, and the average income of customers in the target market. The **current number of competitors** is the number of other businesses within the same market. The **average number of new competitors** is the average number of businesses entering the same market during a year. The **current market share** is the percentage of the local or overall market the business controls or the percentage of the market with which the organization usually does business. The **average income of customers** in the target market is the amount an average customer would normally earn in a given year.

The current number of competitors in the market and the average number of new competitors entering the market per year is a useful set of statistics for organizations attempting to develop a strategic plan. The current number of competitors in the market measures how much competition is present in a particular market. The average number of new competitors entering the market per year is a good way to measure how that competition will change. In other words, these statistics help determine how much competition is in the market now and how much there will be in the near future. These statistics help in planning for the amount of competition likely to be faced and serve as a warning for potential problems in the market.

The organization's current market share is an important factor to consider during the strategic planning process because it measures success and growth in a particular market and compares that success and growth with competitors. As a result, the current market share is ultimately an indication of how the organization as a whole is performing in the current business environment for each specific market the organization is doing business in. If an organization's market share is continuing to grow or it is maintaining a large, stable market share, it is usually an indication that current strategies are working. However, if market share is beginning to decline or is stable, but low when compared to competitors, the firm needs to review its current marketing strategies.

The average income of customers in the target market can be an important piece of information to consider during the strategic planning process because it analyzes the current economic environment. Because the amount of money individuals within the target market earn can vary greatly, it is essential to ensure customers can afford to purchase the firm's products or services. For example, if a car dealer is attempting to sell a new car that costs $35,000, it will be much more difficult to convince someone who makes $40,000 a year to purchase the car than someone who makes $70,000 a year.

Talent Planning and Acquisition

Federal Laws and Regulations

DISCRIMINATION AND UNLAWFUL EMPLOYMENT PRACTICES

Discrimination refers to the process of making a decision about a particular individual or thing based on the specific traits that make the person or thing different from other individuals or things. Because the practice of discrimination is a type of decision-making, it is only illegal under certain conditions. Unlawful employment practices are specific business actions involving hiring, training, employee compensation, and other factors related to an individual's employment that are prohibited by law. These practices are specifically prohibited when they prevent individuals with certain characteristics from obtaining a position, performing the duties related to a position, or receiving all of the benefits and respect from the employer normally associated with the position.

The word *discrimination* by itself only refers to the practice of making a decision regarding a person or thing based on the characteristics of that particular person or thing, which is a practice most organizations perform legally on a daily basis. Discrimination is only unlawful if the employer's decision regarding a particular individual is based on a characteristic considered protected. For example, if an employer decides to only hire people under the age of 40, the employer is unlawfully discriminating against employees based on their age. On the other hand, if the employer decides to only hire people with a certain type of college degree and the college degree is required by law or the knowledge associated with that degree is necessary to perform the tasks related to that position, the employer is legally discriminating based on the individual's characteristics.

Disparate impact is a type of discrimination in which an employer institutes a policy that appears to be reasonable, but prevents individuals of a certain color, with certain disabilities, with a certain military status, of a certain national origin, of a certain race, of a certain religion, or individuals of a particular sex from receiving employment or any of the benefits associated with employment (such as promotions or pay). It refers to a policy that isn't motivated by bias, but is still unfair because it makes it more difficult for individuals of a certain group to receive the job or benefit. For example, a policy stating individuals applying for an office job must be at least 5'10" and weigh at least 185 pounds may create a disparate impact if it makes it more difficult for individuals belonging to one of the protected groups, such as women, to get the job. This type of discrimination was first identified by the Supreme Court in Griggs v. Duke Power Co.

Disparate treatment is a type of discrimination in which an employer deliberately treats an individual differently because of that individual's age, color, disability, military status, national origin, race, religion, and/or sex. It refers to any instance where an employer uses a different set of procedures, expectations, or policies than he would normally use simply because the individual belongs to a particular group. For example, a business that required female employees to follow a strict dress code while the male employees of the business could wear whatever they liked would be guilty of disparate treatment because of treating employees differently based on gender. This type of discrimination was first identified by Title VII of the Civil Rights Act.

EEOC

The Equal Opportunity Employment Commission (EEOC) was formed by Title VII of the Civil Rights Act to protect certain groups of individuals from unlawful discrimination. The EEOC is a federal agency designed to encourage equal employment opportunities, to train employers to avoid

33

practices and policies that could cause unlawful discrimination, and to enforce the laws included in the Civil Rights Act, Age Discrimination in Employment Act, and other anti-discrimination legislation. The EEOC attempts to obtain settlements from employers for actions that the commission deems to be discriminatory. If the employer will not settle with the EEOC, the EEOC will continue their attempt to enforce the law by filing a lawsuit against the employer on behalf of the victim of the discrimination.

TITLE VII

Title VII of the Civil Rights Act, which was originally passed in 1964 and amended in 1972, 1978, and 1991, is designed to prevent unlawful discrimination in the workplace. This section of the Civil Rights Act makes it unlawful to base decisions related to aspects of an individual's employment (such as the pay or benefits) on color, national origin, race, religion, and/or sex. Title VII also makes it unlawful for an employer to discriminate against individuals that are pregnant, about to give birth, or that have any similar medical condition. Title VII of the Civil Rights Act applies to any employer that has more than 15 employees. Exceptions include religious organizations (which can choose to only hire individuals within that religion or to consider individuals of that religion for employment before individuals of other religions), and Native American reservations (which can choose to hire or consider Native Americans living on or near a reservation for employment before other individuals).

ADEA

The Age Discrimination in Employment Act (ADEA), which was originally passed in 1967 and then later amended in 1991, is designed to prevent discrimination against individuals over the age of 39. This act makes it unlawful to base decisions related to an individual's employment (such as pay or benefits) on the age of the individual if that individual is at least 40 years old. This act applies to any business, employment agency, labor organization, or state or local government agency with more than 20 employees. Exceptions include individuals age 40 or over who do not meet the occupational qualifications required to perform the tasks reasonably necessary to the business's operations, termination due to reasonable cause, employment of firefighters or police officers, retirement of employees with executive positions, or tenured educators under certain conditions.

Under the Age Discrimination in Employment Act, any individual may waive the right to protection from age discrimination by signing a waiver of rights. To be legal, the waiver must be written in a clear and concise manner and state that the individual should consult with an attorney prior to signing the waiver. Secondly, the employee must be allowed at least 21 days to consider the terms of the waiver and at least 7 days to change his or her mind and terminate the waiver after signing. Finally, the waiver must offer consideration such as pay or benefits in addition to anything the individual would normally receive.

Under the Age Discrimination in Employment Act, early retirement or incentive programs encouraging individuals to leave the organization must meet certain requirements. First, the waiver must be written in a clear and concise manner, must state that the individual should consult with an attorney prior to signing the waiver, must allow the individual at least 45 days to consider the terms of the waiver, and must allow the individual to have at least 7 days to change his or her mind after signing. The employee must be informed of eligibility factors, time limits associated with the program, and the job titles and ages of each person who is eligible or has been chosen, and the ages of each person ineligible or has not been chosen to take part in the program.

ADA

The Americans with Disabilities Act (ADA), which was passed in 1990, is designed to prevent discrimination against individuals with disabilities. This act makes it unlawful to base decisions related to aspects of an individual's employment (such as pay or benefits) on whether or not the individual is disabled. This act specifically requires any business, employment agency, or labor organization with more than 15 employees to find or create a position the disabled individual will be able to perform as long as creating that position will not cause the business significant financial or operational harm. This act also requires the business, employment agency, or labor organization to ensure that the disabled individual has access to his or her place of employment unless making these changes will cause the business significant harm.

CRA OF 1991

The Civil Rights Act (CRA) of 1991 was designed to perform four primary functions. The first function is to establish specific rights which victims of discrimination may use to remedy the effects of discrimination. The second function of the CRA is to acknowledge and define the type of discrimination known as disparate impact. The third function of the CRA is to offer specific regulations and guidelines related to disparate impact cases. Finally, the fourth function is to expand on the discrimination laws and regulations that were established before the Civil Rights Act of 1991 to offer more protection against discrimination. It was primarily included to strengthen some of the equal opportunity laws seen as no longer offering enough protection due to rulings made by the Supreme Court after they had been passed.

The Civil Rights Act of 1991 made a number of changes to Title VII of the Civil Rights Act of 1964 including expanding the protection offered by Title VII to cover congressional employees, expanding the protection offered by Title VII to cover foreign locations owned and/or operated by American businesses, and creating a sliding scale for the maximum amount of damages for which a victim of discrimination could sue. It also granted individuals or organizations accused of discrimination the right to a jury trial if a civil suit is brought against that individual or organization, placed the burden of proof for disparate impact cases on the person alleging that they had been discriminated against, and granted individuals or organizations accused of discrimination the right to prove that a specific action or policy was necessary to the operation of the business and use that proof as a legal defense against accusations of disparate impact. The CRA also set guidelines defining specific actions that should be considered unlawful discrimination.

REHABILITATION ACT OF 1973

The Rehabilitation Act of 1973 is similar to the Americans with Disabilities Act (ADA) in that the Rehabilitation Act is designed to prevent discrimination against individuals with disabilities. However, the ADA expands the protections granted by the Rehabilitation Act which was only designed to prevent discrimination against individuals with disabilities if those individuals were seeking employment in federal agencies or with federal contractors that earned more than $10,000 a year from government contracts. Employers were not required under the Rehabilitation Act to make the organization's facilities accessible to individuals with disabilities so there was no legal remedy for an individual that was employed, but unable to access his or her place of employment due to disabilities.

VEVRAA

The Vietnam Era Veteran's Readjustment Assistance Act (VEVRAA) is designed to prevent discrimination against veterans. This act makes it unlawful for federal contractors or subcontractors with $25,000 or more in federal contracts or subcontracts to discriminate against someone based on the fact that the individual is a veteran. It also requires federal contractors or

subcontractors meeting these requirements to list open positions with state employment agencies and requires these employers to institute affirmative action plans for veterans. However, in order for this act to apply, the veteran must have served for more than 180 days with at least part of that time occurring between August 5th, 1964 and May 7th, 1975, or the veteran must have a disability or group of disabilities that are rated at 10 percent or more and be eligible for compensation from the Department of Veteran Affairs, or the veteran must have served on active duty for a conflict with an authorized campaign badge.

IRCA

The Immigration Reform and Control Act (IRCA) is designed to prevent discrimination based on nationality. This act makes it unlawful for an employer to base employment on an individual's country of origin or citizenship status as long as the individual can legally work within the United States. This act also makes it unlawful for an organization to intentionally hire individuals that cannot legally work in the United States and requires the completion of the I-9 form for all new employees. This act specifically requires the employer to obtain proof of the employee's eligibility to work in the United States for the I-9 form, but the employee must be allowed to provide any document or combination of documents considered acceptable by the IRCA.

DISCRIMINATION CLAIMS AND LAWSUITS

A discrimination claim must be made within a certain length of time from the time that the specific discriminatory act occurs. If the individual is filing in a state with an equal employment opportunity enforcement agency, the claim must be filed within 300 days of the incident. If the individual is filing in a state that does not have an equal employment opportunity enforcement agency, the claim must be filed within 180 days of the incident. If the discrimination claim is not filed within the appropriate time limit, the Equal Employment Opportunity Commission (EEOC) will not investigate the claim.

A discrimination claim must first be filed with the Equal Employment Opportunity Commission (EEOC). If the EEOC establishes enough evidence to prove unlawful discrimination, the EEOC will attempt to reach a settlement. If the EEOC cannot reach a settlement, they may file a lawsuit on the victim's behalf. If the EEOC determines there is not enough evidence, the individual has 90 days to file suit. Otherwise the individual forfeits the right to file any lawsuit related to that specific act of discrimination.

The Civil Rights Act of 1991 establishes a sliding scale for the total amount of compensatory and punitive damages an individual can receive from a discrimination suit. This sliding scale is based on the number of employees in the organization. The maximum amount an individual can be awarded increases as the size of the organization increases. If the individual is suing an organization with 15 to 100 employees, the maximum they can receive is $50,000. If the individual is suing an organization that has between 101 and 200 employees, the maximum is $100,000. If the individual is suing an organization 200 employees to 501 employees, the maximum is $200,000. Finally, if the individual is suing an organization with more than 500 employees, the maximum is $300,000. However, it is important to note that these limits apply **only** to compensatory and punitive damages.

MERITOR SAVINGS BANK V. VINSON

The Supreme Court case known as Meritor Savings Bank v. Vinson recognized sexual harassment as a form of unlawful discrimination. The case was brought against Meritor Savings Bank by Mechelle Vinson because the bank's vice president had created a hostile work environment through a series of repeated unwelcome sexual advances and acts. Prior to this case, the protections offered by Title

VII of the Civil Rights Act of 1964 for discrimination based on sex had been related solely to economic or other tangible discrimination. However, after the Meritor decision, any disparate treatment that causes a hostile work environment for a member of a protected class constitutes a form of unlawful discrimination.

PREGNANCY DISCRIMINATION IN EMPLOYMENT ACT OF 1978

There are two main clauses of the Pregnancy Discrimination in Employment Act of 1978. The first clause applies to Title VII's **prohibition against sex discrimination**, which also directly applies to prejudice on the basis of childbirth, pregnancy, or related medical conditions. The second clause requires that employers treat women affected by pregnancy the **same as others** for all employment-related reasons and similarly in their ability or inability to work. In short, the Pregnancy Discrimination in Employment Act makes it illegal to fire or refuse to hire or promote a woman because she is pregnant, force a pregnancy leave on women who are willing and able to perform the job, and stop accruing seniority for a woman because she is out of work to give birth.

VOCATIONAL REHABILITATION ACT

The Vocational Rehabilitation Act was intended to increase occupational opportunities for disabled individuals and to prohibit discrimination against "handicapped" persons. The **Rehabilitation Act** applies to federal government contractors and subcontractors holding contracts or subcontracts of $10,000 or more. Contractors and subcontractors with greater than $50,000 in contracts and more than 50 employees must develop written affirmative action plans that address hiring and promoting persons with disabilities. Although there are regulations that protect those engaged in addiction treatment, this act does not protect against individuals who currently suffer with substance abuse that prevents them from performing the duties of the job or whose employment would constitute a direct threat to the safety and property of others.

UGESP

The Uniform Guidelines on Employee Selection Procedures (UGESP), which were passed in 1978, are actually a collection of principles, techniques, and procedures designed to help employers comply with federal anti-discrimination laws. The primary purpose of these guidelines is to define the specific types of procedures that may cause disparate impact and are considered illegal. The UGESP relates to unfair procedures that make it much less likely that an individual belonging to a protected class would be able to receive a particular position.

GRIGGS V. DUKE POWER CO. (1971)

Prior to the 1964 Civil Rights Act, Duke Power Co. segregated employees by race. Once the act passed, the company started requiring a high school diploma and a certain score on an IQ test to qualify for any positions above manual labor. As a result, many African Americans could not obtain the higher-paying jobs. This 1971 case determined that employers must be able to demonstrate that position requirements are actually linked to being able to perform the work. It also determined that employers may be charged with discrimination, even if they did not intend to discriminate. This is known as disparate impact.

PHILLIPS V. MARTIN MARIETTA CORP. (1971)

Linked to the 1964 Civil Rights Act, this case ruled that a company cannot refuse to employ women with young children if they employ men with young children unless there is a legitimate business necessity.

EXECUTIVE ORDERS

An executive order is a written declaration made by the President of the United States establishing a policy for enforcing existing legislation. Executive orders are legally binding and are treated as law if the order remains in the Federal Registry for more than 30 days. Executive order 11246, which was published to the Federal Registry in 1965, states that federal contractors are not only required to avoid employment discrimination, but are also required to take steps to ensure equal opportunities are available to individuals belonging to protected classes. This executive order established the concept of affirmative action and required federal contractors with more than $10,000 in government contracts during a single year to implement affirmative action plans and federal contractors with $50,000 or more in contracts and 50 or more employees to file written affirmative action plans with the Office of Federal Contract Compliance Programs (OFCCP.)

Originally, Executive Order (EO) 11246 only applied to employment discrimination based on an individual's color, national origin, race, or religion. However, EO 11375, EO 11478, EO 13152, and EO 13279 expanded the number of groups that were covered. EO 11375 made it unlawful to discriminate based on sex; EO 11478 made it unlawful to discriminate based on disabilities or age if that individual is over age 40; EO 13152 made it unlawful to base discrimination on parental status; and EO 13279 exempted federal contractors who were religious or community organizations providing services to the community from the need to adhere to the policies.

AAPs

Written Affirmative Action Plans (AAPs) were first established by Executive Order 11246. The main purpose of an AAP, as established by a revision to 41 CFR Part 60-2 made in late 2000, requires the establishment of a series of goals related to equal employment opportunities. An AAP includes a list of action-oriented programs, an availability analysis of employees from protected classes, a section that designates the individual responsible for the organization's AAP, a job group analysis, an organizational profile, placement goals, a system for internal audits and reports related to analyzing barriers to equal employment opportunities, and a utilization/incumbency analysis of the number of protected individuals employed by the company compared to the number of protected individuals available.

The availability analysis of an Affirmative Action Plan (AAP) includes information related to the number of individuals belonging to a protected class within a certain area that could be hired to fill a particular type of position. It is a report of the estimated number of individuals for one of the protected classes externally available through the hiring process or internally available for a particular type of job from another department within the organization. The job group analysis of an AAP includes information related to the structure of job groups within the organization. Each job title is separated into groups of related jobs and then the number of employees is determined within each group. The report must also determine the appropriate Equal Employment Opportunity category code associated with each job group.

The utilization analysis of an Affirmative Action Plan (AAP), also referred to as an incumbency analysis, includes information comparing the number of available individuals belonging to a protected class within a certain area with the number of individuals belonging to a protected class actually hired for a particular group of jobs. This report usually consists of a chart showing the percentage of the local labor pool in a protected class within each job group compared with employees actually hired. The analysis of equal employment opportunity barriers of an AAP determines the monitoring procedures in place to identify the effectiveness of affirmative action plans. It establishes the specific system of internal audits and reports. This ensures problems are continually identified and eliminated.

The placement goals section of an Affirmative Action Plan (AAP) is a list of specific objectives to improve problems identified by the AAP by the various analyses, audits, or reports conducted. Usually, placement goals are necessary if the utilization/incumbency analysis indicates that the percentage of individuals employed by belonging to a specific protected class is less than 80% of the percentage belonging to the group of individuals with the highest percentage. For example, an organization that had 300 white applicants and hired 100 white employees and had 200 African-American applicants and hired 50 African-American employees would have hired 33% (100/300) of the white employees available and 25% (50/200) of the African American employees available. This organization would need to set placement goals for the organization because 25% is not equal to 80% or 4/5 of 33% (33% * 80% = 26.6%).

The action-oriented programs section of an Affirmative Action Plan (AAP) should establish the specific procedures, policies, and plans the organization intends to use to meet placement goals or to fix problems identified by internal audits or reports. The information included in this section must provide a detailed explanation of the procedural plans for making changes to the employment system and provide specific deadlines for procedural implementation and progress. It is also essential that the procedures and plans included are different from plans introduced in previous years that have failed to deliver desired results.

The designation of responsibility section of an Affirmative Action Plan (AAP) is a list of names and titles of managers and HR professionals responsible for AAP implementation, monitoring, and remediation. It is also important in identifying which professionals will perform each task.

The organizational profile section of an AAP expands the information included in the job group analysis. It contains information about the pay assigned to each job title within a specific job group, the number of males and females holding each job title, and the number of individuals of each ethnicity holding each job title. The primary purpose of this section is to identify areas of large differences in pay between people of different races or genders.

EMPLOYEE POLYGRAPH PROTECTION ACT OF 1988

The **Employee Polygraph Protection Act of 1988** was designed to protect individuals seeking employment from being required to submit to polygraph tests. This act specifically forbids private employers from basing hiring decisions on polygraph tests unless the individual is seeking a position involving pharmaceuticals, working in an armored car, or serving as a security officer. This act does not apply to any government agency or federal contractor or subcontractor with Federal Bureau of Investigation, national defense, or national security contracts. If an employer requires a polygraph test and the position is not related to one of these areas, the company can be fined up to $10,000.

USERRA

The **Uniformed Services Employment and Re-Employment Rights Act (USERRA) of 1994** is applicable to all employers. USERRA forbids employers from denying employment, reemployment, retention, promotion, or employment benefits due to service in the uniformed services. Employees absent in services for less than 31 days must report to the employer within eight hours after arriving safely home. Those who are absent between 31 and 180 days must submit an application for reemployment within 14 days. Those who are absent 181 days or more have 90 days to submit an applicant for reemployment. Employees are entitled to the positions that they would have held if they had remained continuously employed. If they are no longer qualified or able to perform the job requirements because of a service-related disability, they are to be provided with a position of equal seniority, status, and pay. Moreover, the **escalator principle** further entitles returning

employees to all of the seniority-based benefits they had when their service began plus any additional benefits they would have accrued with reasonable certainty if they had remained continuously employed. Likewise, employees cannot be required to use accrued vacation or PTO during absences. USERRA requires all healthcare plans to provide **COBRA coverage** for up to 18 months of absence and entitles employees to restoration of coverage upon return. Pension plans must remain undisturbed by absences as well. However, those separated from the service for less-than-honorable circumstances are not protected by USERRA.

WARN Act

The **WARN Act** applies to employers with more than 100 full-time workers or more than 100 full- and part-time workers totaling at least 4,000 hours per week. The WARN Act requires that employers provide a minimum of 60 days' notice to local government and affected workers in the event of a plant closing that will result in job loss for 50 or more employees during a 30-day period and mass layoffs that will result in job loss for greater than 33 percent of workers or more than 500 employees during a 30-day period. There are few situational exceptions to the WARN Act, including natural disasters and unforeseeable business circumstances.

Planning Concepts and Terms

SUCCESSION PLANNING

Succession planning is a method of planning how management and executive vacancies will be filled so a company has highly trained replacements available to fill available vacancies. First, determine what the requirements are for key positions and create profiles that outline responsibilities. The experience, education, career progress, and future career interests of managerial candidates should also be reviewed. Then, the performance of prospective managers should be assessed to determine whether they are promotable or not and identify developmental objectives to prepare for advancement opportunities. Performance should be evaluated based upon traditional goals and standards. Developmental objectives might include seminars, training programs, special projects, or temporary assignments.

WORKFORCE PLANNING

Because the specific skills and knowledge needed to perform tasks vary from organization to organization, from department to department, and from position to position, workforce planning is essential. The needs of an organization can change as size or environment changes, making it important to identify available human resources and human resources for future needs.

Some of the most common activities an organization might perform in the workforce planning process include conducting staffing forecasts, establishing staffing goals and objectives, conducting job analyses, and establishing plans to meet staffing goals and objectives. Many organizations begin by conducting a staffing forecast, which refers to any analysis determining how staffing needs might change. Once an organization has conducted a staffing forecast, the organization may set specific staffing goals and objectives describing current and future positions to fill. After staffing goals and objectives are established, each position is analyzed to determine specific qualifications needed. Finally, a plan is established to find and hire individuals to fill these positions.

FORECASTING METHODS

The two main types of forecasting methods an organization might use to evaluate changing labor needs are qualitative forecasting methods and quantitative forecasting methods. Qualitative forecasting methods include any forecasting method based on the opinions or analyses of managers or experts in the industry. Quantitative forecasting methods are based on actual data, such as past

trends or employee to output ratios. The difference between the two types is that qualitative forecasting is based on knowledge and opinion and quantitative forecasting is based on statistics or mathematical data.

The most common qualitative forecasting methods include management forecasts and a variety of techniques associated with expert forecasting. Management forecasts determine future staffing needs by asking managers of each department to discuss staffing needs at a meeting or to submit reports. Expert forecasting methods (such as the Delphi method) seek the opinion of experts outside the organization. This allows information to be obtained about the effects of changes in the industry or changes from a variety of sources. That information is then formed into a report about possible changes in staffing needs.

Some of the most common quantitative forecasting methods include historical ratios analyses, trend analyses, turnover analyses and probability models. A ratio analysis is a type of analysis comparing current employment ratios (such as the number of employees required to produce a certain number of products) with past ratios to determine if staffing needs might change in the future. Trend analyses compare a single current employment variable (such as the number of employees) with a past employment variable, rather than comparing two ratios. Turnover analyses examine the rate employees leave the organization during a given period compared to previous turnover rates. Probability models allow the organization to chart and predict data related to changes in the organization.

The two most important factors to consider when deciding which forecasting method to use are how far in the future the organization is attempting to plan and if the organization needs to change at a steady rate. Qualitative methods are usually effective for short-term forecasts or for constantly changing staffing needs, while quantitative methods are more effective for long-term forecasts in organizations that have staffing needs that change at a steady rate. Most organizations need both short-term and long-term forecasts.

LONG-TERM FORECASTING TECHNIQUES FOR PLANNING EMPLOYMENT NEEDS

Long-term forecasting often covers a time frame of 2–10 years and is reviewed on an annual basis for adjustment. There are many techniques for **long-term forecasting** such as unit demand, probabilistic models and simulations, or trend projections and regression analysis. One example of the **probabilistic forecasting** is a Markov analysis, which tracks the movement of employees among different job classifications to forecast the movement among departments, operating units, salary levels, or from one category to another. **Expert opinions** may also be considered. The **Delphi technique** consists of having experts provide their best estimates of future needs based on questionnaires and interviews. An intermediary will collect results and provide a summary or report to the experts. If an expert feels differently than the findings of the group, he or she is asked to justify his or her views so the intermediary can revise and redistribute reports.

JOB ANALYSIS

A job analysis is an essential part of any workforce planning process because it identifies specific skills and knowledge required to meet staffing goals and objectives. It also identifies the specific skills and qualifications required to meet the strategic goals and objectives set for the organization as a whole. A job analysis allows the organization to not only identify which tasks need to be performed, but also breaks those tasks into specific skills, traits, and knowledge that would qualify an individual to perform each task appropriately.

The three main components an organization identifies during a job analysis include job descriptions, job competencies, and job specifications. A job description is a detailed breakdown of

41

all tasks, specific skills and knowledge needed for a particular position. Job competencies are a detailed list of all broad skills and traits (such as leadership ability) needed for a particular position. Job specifications are detailed descriptions of all specific qualifications (such as experience or education) an individual must have to perform the task.

ATTRITION

Attrition, or **restrictive hiring**, is the act of reducing the workforce by not replacing individuals who leave an organization. Only absolutely essential roles that are critical to strategic business success are filled. Typically, attrition is used to avoid layoffs during times of financial burden. A **hiring freeze** is the least painful way to reduce labor costs. A *"hard" freeze* means that all open positions will remain open indefinitely, whereas a *"soft" freeze* means that only nonessential roles will remain open.

STAGES OF HUMAN RESOURCE PLANNING

Human resource planning systems should support an organization's business plans. Businesses must have the precise blend of knowledge, skills, and abilities among employees. **Human resource planning** can be separated into three forecasting periods: short range (less than one year), middle range (two to five years), and long range (five to 10 years). **Short-range planning** involves projecting workforce staffing requirements. **Middle-range planning** involves a mix of both short- and long-term forecasting. **Long-range planning** requires more strategic analysis and environmental scanning. The supreme test of a human resource planning system is whether it provides the right number of qualified employees at the right time.

Current Market Situation and Talent Pool Availability

ANALYTICAL STEPS FOR EVALUATING LABOR SUPPLY AND DEMAND

Human resource practitioners must understand and follow the ever-changing labor market and talent supply, which can be influenced by the state of the economy and competitors, technology, new regulations, and other factors. Strategic workforce planning evaluates the ability to sustain future needs so the organization can function accordingly. There are four analytical steps in **workforce planning**:

1. The **supply model analysis**, which reviews an organization's current labor supply
2. The **demand model analysis**, which estimates future business plans and objectives
3. The **gap analysis**, which compares the variances in the supply and demand models to identify skill surpluses and deficiencies
4. The **solution analysis**, which focuses on how to tackle gaps in current and future staffing needs through recruiting, training and development, contingent staffing, or outsourcing

DEMOGRAPHIC FORCES THAT INFLUENCE THE LABOR MARKET

There are a number of demographic forces that influence the labor market; a few of the most notable include birthrates, education, immigration, and participation rates. Since the baby boomers, **birthrates** have stayed relatively low, and many are anticipating a shortage of skilled workers in the United States now that the baby boomers are preparing for retirement. Moreover, **educational disparity** is increasing despite the number of high school students going to college. Dropout rates have increased, limiting job opportunities for a large percentage of the workforce due to increasing technologies. Those who do pursue an education are seeking more advanced professional trainings and degrees. Additionally, many **immigrants** provide large applicant pools at both ends of the spectrum. Many Hispanic workers from Mexico and Central America have fled to the United States due to difficult economic and political reasons and provide farmhands or harvesting assistance in

42

much of the Southwest. Employers might seek and provide immigration assistance to those highly skilled in areas like technology, science, and medicine. Finally, the **participation rates** for men and women have changed dramatically in the past century. Male participation rates have declined in every age group, whereas female participation rates have increased in every age group.

Staffing Alternatives

INTERNAL AND EXTERNAL SOURCING APPROACHES

Sourcing candidates can be done both internally and externally. Recruiting **internal candidates** allows the employer to encourage loyalty and evaluate past performance and is generally less expensive. *Job posting* notifies employees of available positions. *Job bidding* allows qualified employees to apply for opportunities. Methods of recruiting **professional employees** and clerical or sales professionals can vary immensely. *Referrals* are often touted for being relatively quick and inexpensive while returning high-quality candidates. *Online job posting* reaches the largest audience, but it can be time-consuming to review the number of applications. *Employment agencies* are viable resources for locating executive or highly skilled candidates, fulfilling temporary needs, or evaluating performance prior to extending an employment offer through temp-to-perm opportunities. However, employers should consider that the average fee charged by employment agencies falls between 10 and 25 percent of the employee's annual salary. *College recruiting* can return a large pool of professional candidates, whereas vocational schools and associations are usually good sources for technical or trade skills. Other external recruiting sources include job fairs, social media, and state workforce websites.

OUTSOURCING

Outsourcing is the process of contracting with outside specialists to perform selected human resource functions. Businesses may **outsource** some or all of their human resource functions, such as payroll, benefits, or recruiting. The specialists who conduct human resource functions in this relationship are not employees of the business but most likely employees of the company providing the outsourcing service. The value of outsourcing is that it allows managers to focus on more core business matters and decisions while the legal reporting and responsibilities often fall to the company performing the tasks. However, outsourcing can be expensive to implement.

TEMPORARY OR CONTRACT WORKERS

Sometimes, employers may have a temporary need for contingent or contract workers. The **Department of Labor regulations** provide a few regulations for identifying temporary workers. First, the individual assignment for these workers must be either seasonal or intermittent in nature and not exceed one year of employment. Furthermore, temporary workers are not eligible for transfer or promotion. If temporary workers are hired through a staffing agency, they are often classified as employees of either the company or the staffing agency. As such, these workers are eligible for unemployment insurance and workers' compensation. Moreover, nonexempt workers must be paid at least the federal minimum wage and are eligible for overtime provisions under the **Fair Labor Standards Act (FLSA)**.

Interviewing and Selection Techniques

INTERVIEWS

After making it through the résumé and job application review round, and possibly a phone screening, the applicant advances to the interview phase of the selection process. Some reasons for

conducting interviews are to obtain information about the applicant, to sell and provide information about the company, and to build relationships.

There are many different types of interviews. A **structured, or patterned, interview** allows the interviewer to ask a series of prepared questions and may even contain a list of multiple-choice answers. In a **semi-structured interview**, the interviewer follows a guide of prepared questions, but can ask follow-up questions to evaluate qualifications and characteristics. Situational interviews that gauge responses to hypothetical problems and behavioral interviews that question previous or anticipated behavior are frequently semi-structured in nature. An **unstructured, or nondirective, interview** is more conversational and allows more freedom so the applicant may determine the course of the discussion. To be successful, the interviewer should listen carefully without interruption.

Due to technological advancements and the rise of telecommuting, the number of **virtual interviews** has increased. These may involve the candidate sitting in front of a webcam and answering recorded questions or both the candidate and the interviewer speaking in real time from their respective locations. These interviews are often less expensive and more convenient and can provide both personality and standardized evaluations.

Sometimes interviews involve many parties. **Group interviews** involve multiple candidates, whereas **panel interviews** and **board interviews** involve multiple interviewers. Finally, candidates may be required to go through additional screening, such as preemployment testing, a physical examination, drug testing, a background investigation, academic achievement verification, and/or reference checking.

There are two main disadvantages associated with a selection interview. First, it can be heavily affected by the interviewer's own biases. Regardless of how much experience or training an interviewer has, preconceived ideas of a particular candidate or a particular type of candidate can influence the evaluation. Second, even the best planned interview can be rendered useless when intelligent applicants, wanting to cast themselves in the best possible light, control the interview. Further, when the interviewer does not ask the right questions, the applicant may appear to be a viable candidate even though he or she lacks the necessary skills or traits to do the job.

SELECTION PROCESS

The **selection process** is sequential and includes a series of steps; each systematically screens out unsuccessful individuals who will not continue to the next round. The order of steps is often organized based upon a cost/benefit analysis, with the most expensive steps at the end of the process. Steps of the selection process may include introductory screening, questionnaires, initial interviews, employment testing, final interviews, selection decisions, reference checks, drug testing, post-offer medical exams, and placement. The **two basic principles of selection** that influence the process of making an informed hiring decision are 1) past behaviors and 2) reliable and valid data. Past behavior is the best predictor for future behavior, and knowing what was done in the past may be indicative of future actions. **Reliable data** is consistently repeated, whereas **valid data** measures performance.

USES OF JOB ANALYSIS

Equal Employment Opportunity Commission (EEOC) guidelines encourage employers to prepare written job descriptions listing the essential functions of a job. Some of the major uses of **job analysis** include the following:

- Human resources planning, to develop job categories
- Recruiting, to describe and advertise job openings
- Selection, to identify skills and criteria for selecting candidates
- Orientation, to describe activities and expectations to employees
- Evaluation, to identify standards and performance objectives
- Compensation, to evaluate job worth and develop pay structure
- Training, to conduct needs assessments
- Discipline, to correct subpar performance
- Safety, to identify working procedures and ensure workers can safely perform activities
- Job redesign, to analyze job characteristics that need to be addressed in job redesign
- Legal protection, to identify essential functions that must be performed and protect the organization against claims

APPLICANT TRACKING SYSTEMS

An applicant tracking system (**ATS**) can be particularly useful for organizations that perform high-volume recruiting on a consistent basis, but they can be valuable to businesses of all sizes. Despite the initial cost, most medium to large businesses use an ATS due to the time it can save from reviewing thousands of resumes or automating new hire paperwork. New, cloud-based systems may integrate with social media or popular job boards and receive automatic updates that eliminate the need for pricy servers and onsite specialists. Additionally, an ATS is a positive first impression for applicants because it can make the process easier and save time on their end.

> **Review Video: Applicant Tracking System**
> Visit mometrix.com/academy and enter code: 532324

Moreover, an ATS can allow you to do the following:

- brand your company with a career page
- modify or set up standard templates
- save forms for compliance or reporting
- push employee information to a payroll or human resource module
- collect data and metrics for reporting and strategic review

Candidate and Employee Testing Processes

METHODS FOR SELECTION ASSESSMENT

Selection methods and tools are an essential part of an organization's hiring process because the goal is to find groups of acceptable employees and then choose the best candidate from that group. However, even if an organization has located a suitable group of potential employees, it can be extremely difficult for an interviewer to separate the most qualified individual from the rest of the group based on applications and résumés alone. As a result, it is necessary to have a set of well-defined selection tools and methods that are both valid and reliable.

45

Eliminating unqualified candidates saves money and time and focuses resources on those individuals most suited for each position. The screening tools most commonly used include employment applications, résumés, and interviews. **Employment applications** include any form designed by an employer requiring an individual to give personal information, previous experience, education, and so on. **Résumés** are usually one to two pages and list experience, education, and references qualifying an individual for a particular position. Résumés are not usually a premade form to be filled out but rather a document designed and written by the individual seeking employment.

PREEMPLOYMENT TESTS

Two of the most common types of preemployment tests are aptitude tests and in-box tests. An **aptitude test** is an examination designed to determine if an individual has the basic knowledge to perform the tasks associated with a particular position. For example, an aptitude test for a bank teller might consist of a series of basic math problems related to specific banking activities (e.g., determining an account balance after several deposits and withdrawals).

During an **in-box test**, also called an in-basket test, the individual must determine the appropriate way to handle particular problems. For example, a person applying for a position as head bank teller might be asked to describe the appropriate way to handle a check deposited into the wrong account.

The two main advantages associated with preemployment tests are that they allow the organization to have more control over the information gathered and they make it easier to gather information in a consistent way. Preemployment tests comprise premade questions that assess an individual's ability to use specific skills and areas of knowledge. The results will either support or refute the information gathered during the interview. Preemployment tests provide consistent results as long as each applicant takes the exam under the same conditions.

There are some disadvantages associated with using a preemployment test. First, it is easy to unintentionally cause a disparate impact to a protected class if questions are not relevant to the position for which the individual is applying. A series of poorly worded or irrelevant questions may make it more difficult for members of a particular group of people to get the job, which may make the organization legally liable. Second, preemployment tests do not allow for flexibility because the same questions are asked of every applicant. An interviewer is able to ask questions specifically related to each individual applicant, whereas a preemployment test cannot.

ASSESSMENT CENTERS

An **assessment center** is a standardized system of tests designed to gauge candidates' knowledge, skills, abilities, and behaviors in relation to the position for which they are being considered. The assessment center may include interviews, psychological tests, simulations of scenarios typical to the role, and other forms of measurement. A firm employing this screening approach may use live raters. However, technological advances, such as objective computerized tests, have made it possible to rate candidates without human intervention, resulting in a more cost- and time-effective process.

CONCERNS WITH USING BEHAVIORAL OR PERSONALITY ASSESSMENTS IN THE HIRING PRACTICE

When evaluating the potential use of behavioral or personality assessments in the hiring process, human resource practitioners should focus on what they are trying to achieve and research options carefully to ensure they are not **unethical** or violate any employment regulations. If human

resources decides to use such assessments, they must ensure that they are designed specifically for making employment decisions and that they have undergone rigorous reliability and validity testing.

ENSURING VALIDITY AND RELIABILITY OF SCREENING AND SELECTION METHODS

One reason valid and reliable screening tools are important is to avoid unintentionally causing a disparate impact to a particular group of individuals by using screening measures that are not necessarily related to the actual position. Because disparate impact is unlawful discrimination, an organization using questionable screening procedures may unintentionally open itself to liability. Another reason valid and reliable screening tools are important is to ensure the employee hired for a position is suitable. When a screening procedure does not relate to the position or provides inconsistent information, highly qualified candidates might be eliminated.

A good rule of thumb is if the procedure used to gather information from the applicant does not actually assess the basic qualifications of the job or the information is not relevant to the specific position being applied for, the procedure is probably inaccurate or unfair. A valid screening tool should provide information that is well-defined, relevant, and job related.

The three main types of validity a human resources professional may employ to determine if a screening or selection tool is valid are construct validity, content validity, and criterion validity. **Construct validity** assesses the specific traits shown to indicate success for a particular position. It must test for specific characteristics shown to be indicators of job performance. **Content validity** assesses the skills and knowledge necessary to perform the tasks associated with a particular position. **Criterion validity** is used to predict how an individual will behave in the workplace based on written or verbal test scores.

The two types of criterion validity a human resources professional may evaluate to determine if a screening or selection tool is valid are concurrent and predictive validity. **Concurrent validity** indicates that the individual currently possesses the desired trait or will behave in the desired fashion. For example, a test might be considered valid if test scores indicate the individual remains calm in stressful situations, as indicated by a stressful situation the organization places the individual into at the time of the test. **Predictive validity** indicates that the individual will possess the desired trait or will behave in the desired fashion at some point in the future.

EMPLOYER CONSIDERATIONS REGARDING PRE-EMPLOYMENT BACKGROUND CHECKS

Many employers will conduct **pre-employment background checks** on candidates to ensure that employees have sound judgment and are unlikely to engage in improper conduct or don't have a criminal record. Human resource departments often order credit checks or criminal record searches through online service providers and then review results. However, drug screening may either be administered by staff or conducted at a local or national site. The **Fair Credit Reporting Act**, like many legal regulations, requires that employers not only notify applicants that they administer background checks, but applicants must also sign a written release consenting that the employer may receive their personal information. Furthermore, when implementing a pre-employment background check, employers must consider if doing so may be discriminatory and validate the business necessity. Many states have joined the 'Ban the Box' movement, which prohibits employers from asking about an applicant's criminal history at the time of application. If an offense is found, employers are urged to consider the severity of the offense, the amount of time since the offense, and if the offense is related to the nature of the job.

Verbal and Written Offers and Contracts

SUCCESSFUL NEGOTIATIONS

Negotiation is a vital technique for every business professional. New or expired contracts and changing behaviors require skillful **negotiations**. Human resource practitioners must know how to handle negotiations to successfully avoid conflicts, improve relations, secure pay rates, and evaluate contracts. It is paramount to note that negotiations are only possible when all parties are open to compromise and finding solutions that are mutually satisfying.

Some tips for successful negotiation might include: be prepared, listen carefully, be flexible, be patient, be alert, be persuasive, be considerate, be professional, be respectful, remain confident, keep communications honest, encourage taking steps forward, manage expectations, always have an alternative plan, think outside the box to find creative solutions, remain task oriented, strive to build relationships, avoid delays, and review details.

IMPROVING NEGOTIATIONS

Once a candidate has been selected, the salary must be **negotiated** before a formal offer can be made. An employee agreement often includes the first day of work, starting salary, company benefits, and other terms or conditions. The following techniques may be used to improve negotiations:

1. Consider the interests and expectations of both parties.
2. Plan a negotiation strategy that addresses minimum requirements and discussion points.
3. Be creative. Include low-cost incentives such as people, culture, and time off, as well as opportunities for growth and development.
4. Address compromises or trades and avoid making biased concessions to encourage fairness. Think, "If we give you this, we will expect that in return."
5. Know your limitations and when to walk away. Allow time for contemplation.

WRITTEN EMPLOYMENT CONTRACTS

Many details may be explained in **written employment contracts**. The contract should summarize what is being offered, rate of pay, benefits, perks, expectations regarding performance, probationary periods, and proprietary information. Written employment contracts will frequently include some combination of these elements:

- **The length of the contract** - if agreement is for a specified period of time
- **Duties and responsibilities** - if not included in a job description
- **Career opportunities** - succession planning or likelihood of advancement
- **Compensation** - hourly or salary rate and sign-on bonus inclusions
- **Benefits and bonus incentives** - commissions, bonus potential, or stock options
- **Restrictive covenants** - limitations such as confidentiality and noncompete disclosures
- **Severance payments** - if employees can expect any promised pay at the end of an assignment
- **Dispute resolution** - arbitration requirements and payment of legal fees
- **Change of control** - in the event of a merger or acquisition

> **Review Video: Written Employment Contracts**
> Visit mometrix.com/academy and enter code: 407808

48

New Employee Orientation Processes

APPROACHES TO ONBOARDING

EMPLOYEE ORIENTATION

An employee orientation, also known as an on-boarding program, is a program designed to help employees become effective members of the organization. The first step is to ensure that all resources necessary for performing the job are available. Tools and workspace should be set up before the employee's first day on the job in addition to a formal explanation regarding the organization's mission, objectives, and values. The individual's specific position and department can then be addressed by introducing co-workers and supervisors, showing the individual around the facilities, explaining the department's rules, guidelines, and goals, and by identifying places to find help.

There are many approaches to **onboarding** newly hired employees, from the interview through orientation and a 90-day review. However, all companies do things a bit differently, and the size or engagement from the welcoming committee will vary every time. A majority of the responsibility will fall upon human resources in most cases, but the hiring manager and information technology often share some responsibilities as well. Here are a few steps that might appear on an onboarding checklist for office personnel:

- **Phone interview**—a brief 10- to 30-minute screening of applicants (human resources)
- **Live interview**—more in-depth discussion often lasting one to three hours (human resources/hiring manager)
- **Offer letter**—formal written offer to finalist (human resources)
- **Computer access**—workstation set up with email, phone, and systems access (information technology)
- **Keys, equipment, and business cards**—order/log equipment usage (operations)
- **Welcome email**—introductory email welcoming new hires, tips for success (human resources)
- **Federal paperwork**—employment eligibility, tax forms (human resources)
- **Company paperwork**—handbook, policies, nondisclosure agreements, benefits acknowledgments (human resources)
- **Orientation**—thorough company and policy overview, required training (human resources/hiring manager)
- **Position overview and mentor/training**—buddy assignment, job expectations, process manual (hiring manager)
- **Introductions**—site tour, staff introductions, icebreaker questionnaires or games (human resources/hiring manager)
- **30-/60-/90-day reviews**—summary of how the new hire is assimilating into the new role (human resources/hiring manager)

Internal Workforce Assessments

WORKFORCE ANALYSIS

A workforce analysis is required in most affirmative action plans. This analysis results in a **workforce profile** that conveys the talent, knowledge, and skills of the current workforce. The first step is conducting an examination of the **demographics** in the current workforce. Then, a **gap and risk analysis** can be performed to determine any vulnerability. Anticipated changes to how work is performed and how advances in technology can have an effect are documented. Finally, future

talent needs can be forecasted. Workforce profile data can be obtained voluntarily or through publicly reported statistics and census results. Workforce profiles calculate employee traits such as age, experience level, average education in the field, as well as status changes as active, full time, part time, or temporary. These might be reported per department, salary band, or as a whole.

Transition Techniques for Corporate Restructuring

MERGERS AND ACQUISITIONS

Mergers and acquisitions are actually similar in many ways, as both terms refer to a type of structural change in which two organizations join together to form a single organization. However, it is important to realize that the two terms are not exactly the same, as each term actually refers to a different way in which an organization's structure changes. A merger refers to a situation in which two or more organizations agree to "merge" into a single organization because both organizations will benefit from the merger. An acquisition, on the other hand, refers to a situation in which an organization purchases enough of another organization's stock to "acquire" control of the organization's operations. This can actually be an important difference to keep in mind because all of the organizations involved in a merger must agree to the merger in order for the merger to take place, while all the organizations involved in an acquisition do not necessarily need to agree to the acquisition in order for the acquisition to take place.

APPROACHES TO RESTRUCTURING

RESTRUCTURING DURING MERGERS AND ACQUISITIONS

Human resource and change management professionals are often called upon to provide consultation during **mergers and acquisitions**. This involvement should start at the beginning and carry throughout the integration. Human resource experts ordinarily investigate factors like employee benefit plans, compensation programs, employment contracts, and organizational culture. Experience and many studies have shown that issues with people and culture are the most frequent cause of failure in most mergers and acquisitions. Human resource departments must play an active role in these transitions, and there should be a unified purpose and message from each of the previous units. These steps have been established for joining two companies:

1. Develop a workforce integration project plan.
2. Conduct a human resource due diligence review.
3. Compare benefits programs.
4. Compare the compensation structures.
5. Develop a compensation and benefits strategy for integrating the workforce. Any reduction in pay or benefits must be explained and justified relative to the strategy or economic conditions. It's best to minimize changes and act quickly.
6. Determine leadership assignments.
7. Eliminate redundant functions. The best people should be retained, and the remainder should be laid off, with careful consideration given to avoid adverse impact and Worker Adjustment and Retraining Notification (WARN) Act violations.

RESTRUCTURING THROUGH DOWNSIZING

Restructuring through downsizing happens when a firm needs to reduce the number of layers of management to increase efficiency or respond to changes in corporate strategy. This downsizing can occur via layoffs or early retirement agreements.

CONDUCTING A LAYOFF OR REDUCTION IN FORCE

The following are the steps for conducting a layoff or reduction in force:

1. Select employees for layoff using seniority, performance, job classification, location, or skill.
2. Ensure selected employees do not affect a protected class to avoid adverse or disparate impact.
3. Review compliance with federal and state WARN Act regulations, which require employers to provide 60 days' notice to affected employees while specifying whether the reduction in force is permanent or for a specified amount of time.
4. Review compliance with the Older Workers Benefit Protection Act that provides workers over the age of 40 the opportunity to review any severance agreements that require their waiver of discrimination claims. The act allows a consideration period of 21 days if only one older worker is being separated and 45 days when two or more older workers are being separated. They also must receive a revocation period of seven days after signing the agreement. Additionally, they must be informed of the positions and ages of the other employees affected by the layoffs so that they can assess whether or not they feel age discrimination has taken place.
5. Determine if severance packages including salary continuation, vacation pay, employer-paid Consolidated Omnibus Budget Reconciliation Act (COBRA) premiums, outplacement services, or counseling might be available to affected employees.
6. Be empathetic, have tissues, ensure that all required documentation is available to the employee, and review all information in detail when conducting meetings with employees.
7. Inform the current workforce by communicating sustainability concerns, methods used to determine who would be selected for the reduction in force, and commitment to meeting company goals and objectives to maintain morale and productivity.

RISKS AND ALTERNATIVES TO A LAYOFF OR REDUCTION IN FORCE

Most importantly, remember that it could be considered illegal retaliation to consider any past grievances, complaints, claims, or leave requests in the selection process if a reduction in force is necessary. To ensure fairness and avoid risk exposure, **selection criteria** should include measurable data such as seniority, merit or skill set, full- or part-time status, location, job categories, or prior disciplinary actions. Reductions in force are commonly due to financial strains on the organization. Thus, the goal is to reduce human capital costs by a percentage or specified dollar amount. Some measures that can be introduced as an **alternative to a reduction in force** include eliminating overtime, freezing or reducing compensation, introducing reduced work hours, cutting perks, increasing employees' share of benefit costs, and imposing a hiring freeze.

OFFSHORING

Offshoring is a process similar to outsourcing because it refers to hiring an individual or company located in another country to perform a task the organization would normally perform domestically. Usually, organizations hire offshore, overseas, or in a different country because it can be more cost effective. Offshoring differs from outsourcing because it is possible to have an offshore division that is actually a part of the organization.

DUE DILIGENCE

The due diligence process refers to a series of activities that each organization involved in a merger or acquisition must conduct before the merger or acquisition actually takes place. These activities are related to gathering, reviewing, and distributing legal, financial and operational information for each organization involved in the merger or acquisition. The information that must be gathered and provided to the other organizations involved in a merger or acquisition

include employment and financial documents, employee policies and procedures, information related to legal concerns such as current legal disputes or recent fines and violations, information related to contracts and licenses that the organization currently holds, information related to recent or ongoing labor/union concerns and other similar information. This information is primarily designed to provide each organization involved in the merger or acquisition with a detailed idea of exactly where each organization stands at the time of the merger or acquisition.

DIVESTITURES

A divestiture is the opposite of an acquisition (just as divestment is the opposite of investment), whereby a company separates a portion of itself (such as a division or subsidiary) in a form of restructuring. Companies that initiate a divestiture typically seek to remove a business line that is unrelated to its core operations or is simply a poor fit requiring inordinate management attention. A subsidiary that operates in an aging business with modest growth prospects may be sold or spun off in order to focus on more promising opportunities. Alternatively, the divestment may be required by a regulatory authority, such as in compliance with an antitrust adjudication. Three of the common forms of divestiture include the following:

- Sell-off—In this form, a company sells the net assets of a division or the stock of a subsidiary outright in exchange for some form of consideration. The selling company relinquishes all ownership interest in the divested entity.
- Spin-off—A company that distributes assets to existing shareholders in the form of the stock of a new company is said to have created a spin-off. The existing shareholders thus become the new owners of the divested entity.
- Equity Carve-Out—In this form, a company engages in a sell-off but retains some portion of ownership or control of the removed entity, either by retaining some portion of existing stock or reserving a portion of a new public offering.

Metrics to Assess Past and Future Staffing Effectiveness

TALENT ACQUISITION METRICS

Organizations of all shapes and sizes should regularly review recruiting processes and try to make them more efficient. When evaluating recruitment efforts, it is important to consider these two main metrics: the average cost per hire and the average time to fill.

$$Time\ to\ fill = \frac{Total\ Days\ Elapsed\ Since\ Job\ Posted}{Number\ of\ Hires}$$

$$Cost\ per\ hire = \frac{(External\ Costs\ +\ Internal\ Costs)}{Number\ of\ Hires}$$

Human resource professionals should also ensure that their job ad spend is effective.

FOUR-FIFTHS RULE AND ADVERSE IMPACT ANALYSIS

The EEOC defines **adverse impact** by the **four-fifths rule** as follows: "A selection rate for any race, sex, or ethnic group which is less than four-fifths (4/5 or 80 percent) of the rate for the group with the highest rate will generally be regarded by the federal enforcement agencies as evidence of adverse impact."

Let's say that Alpha Company requires a previously outlined exam for specified positions. Two hundred applicants took this exam, including 124 Caucasian males and 57 Latino males, and only

108 passed. Of the 108 who passed the exam, there were 72 Caucasian males and 28 Latino males. The four-fifths rule may now be used to determine if the exam used by Alpha Company has an adverse impact. Caucasian males had the highest pass rate at 58.06 percent, and four-fifths of that rate is 46.45 percent. Latino males had a 49.12 percent pass rate, which is greater than 46.45 percent. Thus, we can conclude that the exam presented by Alpha Company does not have an adverse impact. However, if the four-fifths rule had determined adverse impact, the burden of proof would fall upon Alpha Company to convince the courts that the exam was a) job related for the specified positions and b) consistent with business necessity.

Learning and Development

Theories and Applications

MAIN KINDS OF LEARNING AND BEST PROCESSES

There are three main types of learning, each with different suitable training methods. If teaching **motor responses**, such as physical acts that involve muscle groups, a training method that involves exploration, demonstration, activity practice, and corrective guidance works best. If teaching **rote learning**, such as memorization, a training method that involves familiarity, patterns or associations, repetition, and timely feedback works best. If teaching **idea learning**, such as operant conditioning or learning complex ideas, a training method that involves sequential concepts, with practice or exhibition, progressive mastery, and reinforcement at each step works best.

EMPLOYEE DEVELOPMENT METHODS

A few methods of employee development include the following:

- **Literacy training**: basic education programs offered by companies such as English-as-a-second-language training, how to interpret engineering designs, or how to make basic computations
- **Competency training**: teaching skills, abilities, and behaviors essential for executing responsibilities effectively and successful performance
- **Mentoring**: when a more experienced individual teaches valuable job skills and provides encouragement or emotional support
- **Attitude change**: group communications through lectures, video presentations, or similar methods to accomplish increased customer service, diversity training, ethical behavior, or harassment training.

ON-THE-JOB TRAINING METHODS

On-the-job techniques are used more frequently due to the lesser cost and immediate production compared to off-the-job trainings, which are designed more for education and long-term development.

Some **on-the-job training techniques** include the following:

- **Job-instruction training** is the most popular method of training, involves introductory explanation and demonstration or shadowing before given the opportunity to try alone.
- **E-learning** is generally on-demand training (sometimes learners can log on live) that can be taken anywhere with an internet connection at a time that's convenient for the learner. E-learning modules can cover a range of topics such as company policies, job-related how-tos, and more. E-learning is extremely cost-effective. The main drawback is that those watching a recording can't provide or receive any real-time feedback.
- **Apprenticeships** are a process of working alongside and under the direction of a skilled professional, such as trade electricians, plumbers, and carpenters.
- **Internships, cooperative education, and assistantships** are similar to apprenticeships but are often paired with colleges or universities.

- **Job rotation and cross training** involve a rotating series of job assignments in departments for specified periods of time to expose individuals to a number of skills and challenges.
- **Coaching and counseling** act as providing an identifiable and virtuous model, setting goals, providing timely feedback, and providing reinforcement and encouragement.

OFF-THE-JOB TRAINING METHODS

A few **off-the-job techniques** include the following:

- **Independent study**: people self-motivated to take individual responsibility toward learning and attempting to train themselves by reading books, taking courses, or attending seminars
- **Corporate universities**: where employees attend classes taught by corporate trainers, executives, and consultants
- **Vestibule training**: similar to on-the-job training but occurs in a separate training area identical to the actual production area
- **Lecture**: an efficient way to transfer large amounts of information to a large audience

MANAGEMENT AND LEADERSHIP DEVELOPMENT

Management development is ensuring individuals have all the knowledge, skills, and abilities necessary to manage effectively. **Leadership development** is ensuring individuals have all the knowledge, skills, and abilities necessary to lead effectively. Management development is designed to teach an individual how to ensure each function is carried out as expected, whereas leadership development is designed to teach an individual how to predict change within the business environment, identify the way the organization needs to change to meet those needs, and encourage other individuals to meet the changing needs of the organization.

Adult Learning Processes

PRINCIPLES OF LEARNING

Research from both operant conditioning and social cognitive theory suggest **principles of learning** that are critical to the architecture of training programs. These principles of learning include the following:

- **Stimulus**—should be easily perceived and meaningfully organized in a local or systematic way
- **Response**—providing students with opportunities for practice and repetition
- **Motivation**—reinforcements to facilitate extrinsic rewards, intrinsic satisfaction, and active participation
- **Feedback**—performance feedback is necessary for learning, change, and knowledge of results
- **Transfer**—occurs when students can apply the knowledge and skills learned to their jobs

BLOOM'S TAXONOMY OF LEARNING

Learning occurs at different levels. **Bloom's taxonomy of learning** is sometimes reflected as a pyramid containing six **domain levels**. **Knowledge** forms the base of the pyramid and is the stage in which learners can recall previously learned facts. Learners then graduate to the **comprehension stage**, in which they are able to grasp the meaning of the material. The **application stage** comes next. In the application stage, learners can apply information to solve problems in new situations. Following application is the **analysis stage**, in which learners are capable of understanding the context and structure of material. The tip of the pyramid comprises synthesis and evaluation. During the **synthesis stage**, learners are capable of drawing from existing knowledge or sources and processing to form conclusions. Finally, at the **evaluation stage**, learners are capable of judging the value of materials.

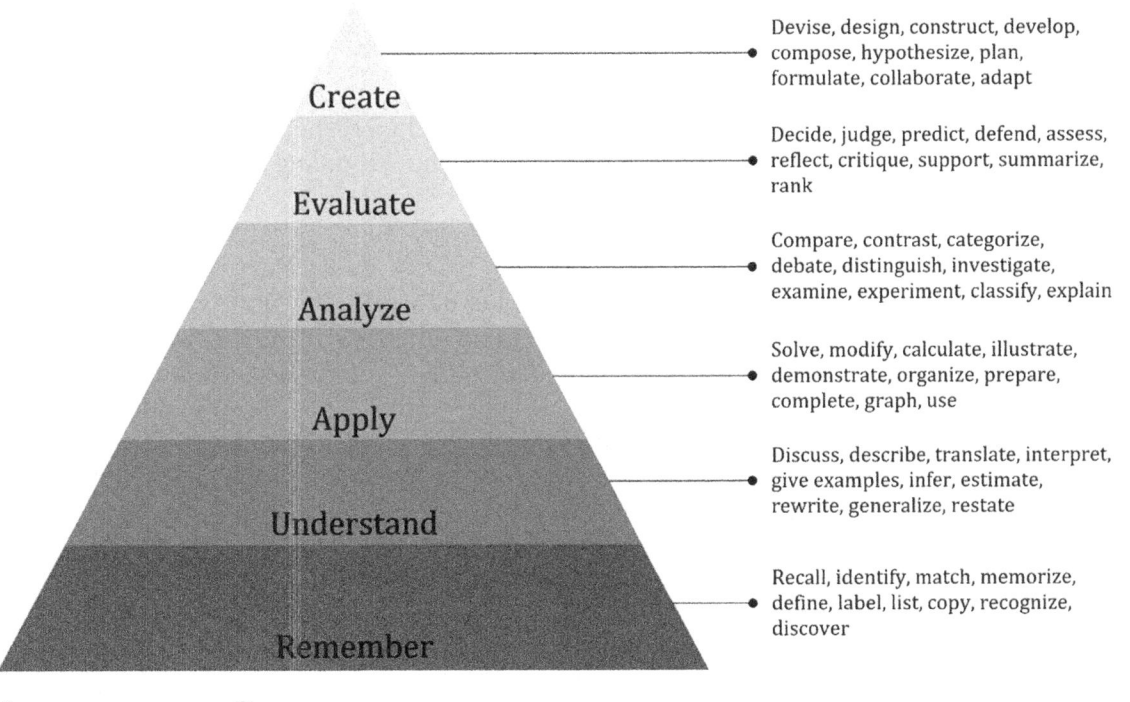

Create	Devise, design, construct, develop, compose, hypothesize, plan, formulate, collaborate, adapt
Evaluate	Decide, judge, predict, defend, assess, reflect, critique, support, summarize, rank
Analyze	Compare, contrast, categorize, debate, distinguish, investigate, examine, experiment, classify, explain
Apply	Solve, modify, calculate, illustrate, demonstrate, organize, prepare, complete, graph, use
Understand	Discuss, describe, translate, interpret, give examples, infer, estimate, rewrite, generalize, restate
Remember	Recall, identify, match, memorize, define, label, list, copy, recognize, discover

ANDRAGOGY AND PEDAGOGY

Andragogy and pedagogy are both sciences of how individuals learn. **Andragogy** is the study of how adults learn and focuses on making it easier to teach adults. **Pedagogy**, on the other hand, is the study of how children learn and focuses on making it easier to teach children. They are different fields because studies have found that children and adults learn in different ways. An instructor who understands these differences is able to identify the most effective teaching methods. However, there is a noteworthy debate as to whether there is a great deal of difference between pedagogy and andragogy.

MALCOLM KNOWLES'S ASSUMPTIONS OF LEARNERS

According to Malcolm Knowles, there are five assumptions typically made about adult learners. The first assumption (motivation) is that they are internally motivated to learn by understanding why they need to learn. The second assumption (self-concept) is that they want to direct their own learning. The third assumption (adult experience) is that they want to apply what they already know as they learn and use their experience to help others learn. The fourth assumption (readiness) is that they are willing to learn if what they learn will help them in some way. The fifth assumption (orientation) is that they learn so they can apply knowledge to current rather than future problems.

TRAINING VS. EDUCATION AND EXPLICIT KNOWLEDGE VS. TACIT KNOWLEDGE

Although both training and education programs enable people to acquire new knowledge, learn new skills, or conduct behaviors in a new way, they are distinct and different processes. **Training** can be described as the more narrow acquisition of specific knowledge or skills. Most training

programs try to teach students how to perform a particular activity for a specific job. **Education** is broader and attempts to provide students with general knowledge that may be applied to a variety of settings. Distinguishing between two kinds of knowledge can assist with the design of training and education programs. **Explicit knowledge** can be formalized, communicated, or found in job specifications and manuals. **Tacit knowledge** is personal, based upon past experience, and is more difficult to explain to others.

LEARNING STYLES

A **learning style** refers to the way an individual learns most effectively. Because each person learns information differently, some teaching methods are more effective than others. The three main learning styles are auditory, tactile, and visual. Training programs need to be designed to take different learning styles into consideration so participants will learn the material as efficiently as possible.

> ### Adult Learning Processes and Theories
> Visit mometrix.com/academy and enter code: 638453

An **auditory learner** learns most effectively by hearing information rather than seeing it or using it. They usually learn most effectively by hearing descriptions or instructions such as lectures, group discussions, demonstrations of a particular sound (such as an alarm that might indicate a problem with a piece of machinery) or by listening to themselves read aloud.

A **tactile learner** learns most effectively by touching or using something rather than hearing it or seeing it. They usually learn most effectively by using a new tool or process, by actually being able to touch or move an object, or by physically applying the information in a controlled situation. They will have difficulty learning through verbal instructions (lectures or explanations) and visual methods (reading a handout). Learning activities include practicing techniques, role-playing, simulations, and other activities that allow the individual to learn through a hands-on approach.

A **visual learner** learns most effectively by seeing information rather than hearing or using it. They learn most effectively by seeing the information on a flashcard, chalkboard, handout, or book; seeing a representation in a picture or diagram; watching videos or presentations; or taking detailed notes and then rereading those notes. They have difficulty learning through verbal instruction (lectures and explanations) or by performing a task without written instructions or handouts.

Instructional Design Principles and Processes

ADDIE MODEL

The ADDIE Model is a set of instructional design guidelines commonly used by organizations to develop human resource development (HRD) programs. This model consists of five separate steps and each step is identified by one of the letters in the term ADDIE. *A* represents the *Analysis* step, the first *D* represents the *Design* step, the second *D* represents the *Development* step, *I* represents the *Implementation* step, and *E* represents the *Evaluation* step. Each step of the model establishes a basic set of guidelines and procedures an individual or organization can follow to develop a training or instructional program piece by piece. This procedure is commonly used in human resource development because it is a simple, but effective way of creating a training program. The ADDIE model can also be applied to a variety of fields and is not limited to training programs.

Analysis is the first step described by the ADDIE Model. The problem to solve is defined in detail, and specific goals and objectives (along with the knowledge, skills and abilities required) are identified. The process is usually started by asking questions about why the program is being developed, how it will be used to improve performance or eliminate performance problems, etc.

Design is the second step described by the ADDIE Model. In this step, a plan is designed to achieve the goals and objectives set forth in the analysis phase. A series of documents is created describing strategies to use to solve the problem, improve overall performance, etc. Strategies must be identified which will provide the knowledge, skills, and abilities necessary to achieve the goal.

Development is the third step described by the ADDIE Model. In this step, a series of tools (activities, exercise, handouts, etc.) are developed to carry out strategies identified during the design step. Instructional guides are also developed which will help each skill trainer understand the procedure for teaching specific information employees need to know.

Implementation is the fourth step described by the ADDIE Model. In this step, the materials created during the development stage are put into action. Most organizations will begin this phase by testing through a pilot program to allow problems to be identified and changed before the program is implemented. The program is put into action once the program is functioning as expected.

Evaluation is the fifth and final step described by the ADDIE Model. Although evaluation occurs as adjustments are made throughout the model, this step refers to an ongoing evaluation of the results of the program. Determinations are made regarding the achievement of goals and if additional programs need to be added.

NEEDS ANALYSIS

It is important for an organization to perform a needs analysis before designing a training program for several different reasons. First, an organization should accurately identify problems. Second, even if a particular problem is known prior to the analysis, it can be difficult to identify the cause of that problem. Third, and most importantly, it is impossible to design an effective training program without first identifying the specific knowledge, skills, and abilities required to achieve goals or required to correct a problem. A needs analysis can be an essential part of the training development process because it helps to identify and detail problems so possible solutions can be found.

There are a variety of steps that might be taken during a needs analysis, but most begin by collecting data related to the performance of each part of the organization. This information is usually gathered from surveys, interviews, observations, skill assessments, performance appraisals, etc. Once this information is collected, problems are identified within specific areas of the organization and solutions proposed. Advantages and disadvantages of each solution are then identified and the plan chosen that seems to provide the greatest benefit for the lowest cost.

Techniques to Assess Training Program Effectiveness

KIRKPATRICK'S FOUR-LEVEL LEARNING EVALUATION MODEL

It's important to analyze the effectiveness of training programs so you don't waste resources. Donald Kirkpatrick introduced a **four-level training evaluation model** for planning, evaluating,

and preserving. The four levels of the evaluation model include 1) reaction, 2) learning, 3) behavior, and 4) results:

- **Reaction**: measures how people react to the training, often a survey upon completion that asks for feedback or satisfaction levels on the subject, the material, the instructor, and so on
- **Learning**: measures what objectives people have learned from the training program (could be in the form of a questionnaire, assessment, etc.)
- **Behavior**: measures how far the performance or behavior of people that received the training has changed and observes how they apply what has been learned to their environment
- **Results**: analyzes noticeable effects of training, such as changes in production, efficiency, and quality

COST/BENEFIT ANALYSIS

Although training and development programs should be viewed as an extremely valuable capital investment, they should also provide measurable returns. Simple calculations can be used to measure the costs and benefits of training. **Costs** should include both direct costs (e.g., materials, facilities, etc.) and indirect costs (e.g., lost production time). The overall costs of training and development programs might contain staff hours, program materials, hardware or software, videos, and production losses such as training time and respective salaries. **Benefits** of training should be evaluated according to how well the training will increase productivity, advance product quality, reduce errors, improve safety, or reduce operating costs. One calculation for measuring training is the cost per trainee, in which the total cost of training is divided by the total number of trainees. Regardless, the long-term benefits of training should outweigh the costs, and this can be determined through a **cost/benefit analysis**. There are creative adjustments that can be used to reduce training costs. The size of training classes can be increased, and materials can be reused when not violating copyrights. Expenses can be further eliminated by making training available online or using videoconferencing.

THE LEARNING CURVE

A learning curve is a representation of the rate at which an individual learns. It is referred to as a curve because the rate changes over time. Learning curves are useful tools for instructors, human resource professionals, managers, and other individuals who are overseeing training or evaluating training programs. Sudden changes in the learning curve may indicate a new training program is working effectively or that a change in the work environment is slowing the learning process.

A **negatively accelerating learning curve** is the most common type of learning curve. Negatively accelerating learning occurs when an individual rapidly acquires information in the beginning and

then makes smaller successive achievements as time progresses. Some examples of this learning behavior include everyday tasks such as walking, talking, or riding a bike.

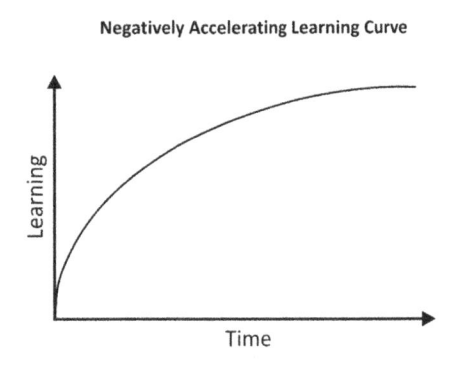

Some people are slow to pick up and absorb material in the beginning, then everything gradually "clicks," and they are able to ramp up learning speed. This would be a **positively accelerating learning curve**. Positive accelerating learning curves are most common when the material is highly complex, when the individual doesn't have the standard background, or when motivation or confidence is low to start.

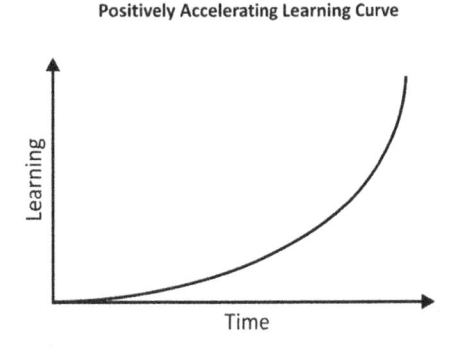

A combination of positively accelerating in the beginning and negatively accelerating down the road creates an **S-shaped learning curve**. S-shaped learning curves occur most frequently when an individual is learning a new problem-solving task. Initially, there will be a gradual success, then rapid comprehension, followed by a slowdown to "polish" the new skill. A period in which no learning takes place and performance remains stagnant is often referred to as a **plateau**.

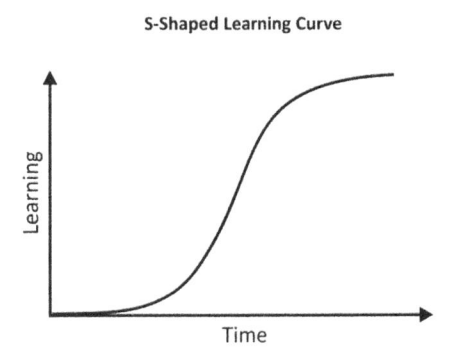

60

Organizational Development

Organizational development (OD) is a customized process to guide management on implementing changes. Its goals include: fostering employee awareness and alignment with the organization's goals, increasing communications and cooperation, developing a problem-solving environment, and encouraging participation. According to social psychologist, Kurt Lewin, there are three main phases in OD: unfreezing, change, and refreezing.

The unfreezing phase is about preparing employees for the change by promoting the reasons for it, how it will be implemented, and its expected results. Various methods, such as announcements, meetings, and bulletins, may be used to accomplish this. To assess, or diagnose, employees' attitudes about the change, managers may check for changes in absenteeism, speak individually with employees, provide a questionnaire, and observe their behavior. The change phase is about correcting issues that may impede the process of change. There are various interventions that may be used to achieve this. The refreezing phase is about resolving unexpected problems, assessing the effectiveness of the change process, and doing follow-up checks.

The change phase is about correcting issues that may impede the process of change. This is achieved through intervention at individual, group, and organizational levels. One individual intervention includes having employees incorporate their personal goals in their career plans and showing them how the organization's success will help them achieve their own personal success. Another individual intervention is aimed at developing employees' problem-solving and leadership skills, which nurtures a better understanding of the need for change.

Group interventions include clarifying job roles and duties on interdependent tasks, and to provide team building environments. According to statistical data, team building is the most effective OD intervention. One example of an organizational intervention is to reveal the results of a company-wide survey so that employees may compare their personal feelings with others'.

MOTIVATION THEORIES
EXTRINSIC VS. INTRINSIC MOTIVATION

Motivation is what propels someone to behave in a certain way.

Extrinsic motivation is derived from external factors. People can be externally motivated by money, gifts, and recognition.

Intrinsic motivation is derived from thoughts and beliefs a person has within. People can be internally motivated by the feeling of achievement, the excitement of learning something new, or by their competitive nature.

TAYLOR'S SCIENTIFIC MANAGEMENT

Frederick Taylor ran a series of experiments within a manufacturing setting to better understand the nature of work. He found that people could be motivated by their working conditions and noted that employers should provide adequate safety measures, lighting, and tools to do the work. Further, he concluded that employees will change their behavior when they know they are being observed.

SKINNER'S OPERANT CONDITIONING

B. F. Skinner concluded that motivation is based on extrinsic factors such as reward and punishment. Employers can influence behavior through positive reinforcement or negative

61

reinforcement, which results in employees acting in certain ways to receive prizes or to avoid discipline.

MCCLELLAND'S ACQUIRED NEEDS THEORY

David McClelland saw motivation as primarily intrinsic and said that it arose from three main needs: achievement, affiliation, and power. The need for achievement involves embracing challenges, being goal oriented, and taking calculated risks. The need for affiliation involves wanting to belong, yearning to be liked, and focusing on collaboration over competition. The need for power involves wanting to influence others, being competitive, and striving to attain a high status. Employees could be motivated by a blend of these needs. For example, an employee may be achievement oriented and still want to be liked.

LOCKE'S GOAL-SETTING THEORY

Dr. Edwin Locke developed a goal-setting theory for motivation in the 1960s. His research concluded that employees are driven by explicit, measurable **goals** that are challenging but attainable. Locke suggested that if the employees take part in **collaboratively** setting the goals and objectives, they will be more vested in attaining them. However, those who have an internal drive may be more likely to succeed. He also noted that providing **feedback** to employees is critical. Locke tied goal setting to task performance because it energized employees and assisted them with handling specific situations that arose. Finally, Locke stated that attaining the goal should provide both intrinsic and extrinsic **rewards** that result in employee satisfaction.

VROOM'S EXPECTANCY THEORY

Victor Vroom's expectancy theory assumes that rationality will drive employees toward the option that provides *maximum pleasure* and *minimal pain*. Although he noted that performance strength may be determined by an individual's personality, knowledge, experiences, skills, and abilities, Vroom believed that increased effort would eventually lead to better performance as long as employees have the necessary tools to get the job done. Moreover, employees will be motivated if they believe that favorable performance will return a desired reward, which will satisfy an important need and thus make the effort worthwhile. There is a calculation that reflects the **expectancy theory**: *Expectancy x Instrumentality x Valence = Motivation*. **Expectancy** is the belief that one's best efforts will yield good performance. **Instrumentality** is the belief that the good performance will yield a particular result. **Valence** is the value of an outcome to a given employee. (This will fluctuate as not all employees are motivated by the same things at the same time.) If any of the multipliers are low, then motivation will be low.

ATTRIBUTION THEORY

The attribution theory was first introduced by Fritz Heider and further developed by Bernard Weiner. It identifies ability, effort, task difficulty, and luck as the most important factors for achieving success. This theory can help identify the root causes of an individual's behavior or performance. **Attribution** consists of **three stages**: 1) behavior observation, 2) determining if the behavior is deliberate or consistent, and 3) concluding if the behavior is due to internal or external factors. The **locus of causality** identifies outcomes based upon internal controls such as ability and effort as well as external factors such as task difficulty and luck. The **locus of stability** identifies outcomes based upon fixed, stable factors such as ability and task difficulty as well as variable factors such as effort and luck. Correctly identifying the source or rationale behind an employee's behavior can help leaders effectively motivate them.

SELF-DETERMINATION THEORY

This theory identifies three core intrinsic motivators: autonomy, competence, and relatedness. **Autonomy** in this context focuses more on self-initiation and regulating one's behavior toward task selection, organization, and completion. **Competence** involves the mastery of skills required to complete the work and interact with the environment effectively. **Relatedness** involves attachment to and a sense of belongingness within a group. Leaders should give employees the opportunity to make decisions about their work, sharpen their skills, and connect with others in the organization whenever possible. Doing so will increase their internal drive and promote psychological wellness.

JOB CHARACTERISTICS MODEL

Hackman and Oldman found that the following job characteristics affect job performance and satisfaction: task identity, task significance, skill variety, autonomy, and feedback. Task identity is when employees can see how their roles affect the entire organization so that they no longer feel like they operate in isolation. This knowledge can lead to greater job satisfaction. Task significance is when employees can understand the larger impacts of their work on other people or society, which can also lead to greater job satisfaction. Skill variety is when employees can use many different skills in their work, which reinforces that the job is important. Autonomy is when employees receive their manager's trust and have leeway in decision-making. This empowerment typically leads to higher levels of employee engagement and job satisfaction. Feedback is when employees receive commentary on their performance, enabling them to improve or encouraging them to stay the course. Regular feedback can also lead to higher levels of employee engagement and job satisfaction.

Coaching and Mentoring

COACHING

Coaching in business is a method of training in which an experienced individual provides an employee with advice to encourage his or her best possible performance and career. Having a strong **coaching culture** among strategic goals often leads to increased organizational performance and engagement. Coaching is a personal, one-on-one relationship that takes place over a specific period. Coaching is often a technique used in performance management, but it can be applied to many business objectives. For example, coaching may be used to prepare individuals for new assignments, improve behavior, conquer obstacles, and adapt to change. Coaching might also be used to support diversity initiatives, such as generational differences, behavioral styles, or awareness and inclusion.

MENTORING

Mentoring is a career development method in which a new or less experienced employee is paired with an experienced leader for guidance. **Formal mentoring programs** need to be measurable and integrated into the culture, without being seen as a rigid, forced system. These programs typically establish goals at the onset and track progress throughout. Similar to coaching, mentoring is a partnership relationship that takes place over a specific period—and both need a customized approach that fits the receiver. However, mentoring carries a history of recognition for having considerable impact with the power to positively transform career trajectory. Successful mentors are able to support, encourage, promote, and challenge while developing deep connections. Mentoring can also happen more informally where the mentee looks up to and takes the advice of the mentor without there being defined goals or objectives. This happens naturally, and often the people involved don't know the mentor–mentee relationship existed until later reflection.

Employee Retention

CAUSES OF ABSENTEEISM AND TURNOVER

Absenteeism is when employees miss work temporarily. **Turnover** is when employees leave permanently.

Poor morale, frustration, and conflict are some factors that lead to absenteeism and turnover. **Involuntary absenteeism and turnover** are caused by situations beyond the employee's control, such as illness, family concerns, relocation, layoffs, and terminations. **Voluntary absenteeism and turnover** occur when employees have a choice and intentionally miss work or resign. Absenteeism can be further categorized as planned absences, unplanned absences, intermittent absences, or extended absences. Employees may also permanently leave their jobs for higher-paying work, better benefits, a promotion, to start a business, or for other reasons.

RETENTION AND TURNOVER METRICS

Retention Rate: (number of employees who were employed for entire measurement period / number of employees at start of measurement period) x 100

Turnover Rate: (number of employees who left during the measurement period / average number of employees during the measurement period) x 100

EMPLOYEE RETENTION PROGRAMS

An employee retention program is a set of policies, procedures, and practices designed to encourage employees to stay with the organization. This program can be an essential part of a staffing strategy because it decreases employee turnover, which is especially important for positions that are difficult and costly to replace. An employee retention program may offer extra benefits or compensation (such as vacation time and bonuses), which can help the organization retain key staff and function effectively.

EMPLOYEE LIFECYCLE PHASES

- Recruitment: initial phase that encompasses the entire process of finding and acquiring new talent, from creating job descriptions through onboarding a new hire
- Integration: subsequent phase of getting the recent hire fully acclimated and functioning well in his or her assigned role
- Development: third phase when employee grows as a professional via training programs, promotion opportunities, and so on
- Departure: last phase of the employment relationship when the employee leaves the organization and human resources processes him or her out of company systems

Total Rewards

Federal Laws and Regulations

FLSA

The **FLSA of 1938,** also known as the Wagner-Connery Wages and Hours Act, or the Wage Hour Bill, sets minimum wage standards, overtime pay standards, and child labor restrictions. The act is administered by the Wage and Hour Division of the Department of Labor. FLSA carefully separates employees as exempt or nonexempt from provisions, requires that employers calculate **overtime** for covered employees at one and one-half times the regular rate of pay for all hours worked in excess of 40 hours during a week, and defines how a workweek should be measured. The purpose of **minimum wage standards** is to ensure a living wage and to reduce poverty for low-income families, minority workers, and women. The **child labor provisions** protect minors from positions that may be harmful or detrimental to their health or well-being and regulates the hours minors can legally work. The act also outlines requirements for employers to keep records of hours, wages, and related payroll items.

> **Review Video: US Employment Compensation Laws**
> Visit mometrix.com/academy and enter code: 613448

MINIMUM WAGE

The Fair Labor Standards Act (FLSA) established regulations designed to prevent employees from receiving substandard wages, and also established the federal minimum wage. The federal minimum wage is the lowest amount an employer can pay any nonexempt employee for each hour of work. An employee will be considered exempt from this provision if the individual receives a weekly salary of at least $455, if the employee works in a profession not covered by the FLSA or a profession identified as exempt from the minimum wage provision of the FLSA, or if the employer has received special permission to pay less than the minimum wage as part of a Department of Labor program.

There are two situations in which an organization may need to pay an employee more than the federal minimum wage. First, if the individual has worked more than 40 hours in a single week and is in a position covered by the Fair Labor Standards Act, he or she is entitled to overtime pay for each additional hour over 40 hours. Secondly, when the minimum wage for the state in which the organization's employees are located is higher than the federal minimum wage. However, most states have their own list of exemptions and requirements so that a particular organization may be part of an industry covered by the Fair Labor Standards Act, but not by the regulations set by state law.

OVERTIME

The Fair Labor Standards Act established regulations designed to prevent employees from receiving substandard wages, especially related to overtime pay. It defines overtime pay as 1 and ½ times the regular wage normally received and establishes that overtime pay must be paid to any nonexempt individual working more than 40 hours in a single week. The number of hours an individual has worked in a given week does not include hours paid for vacation time, sick leave, paid holidays, or similar pay received when work is not actually performed. Certain states may have overtime regulations in addition to those established by the Fair Labor Standards Act.

ON-CALL

The Fair Labor Standards Act established regulations designed to prevent employees from receiving substandard wages especially related to on-call pay. This regulation requires an employer to pay regular wages if the employee is required to wait at the job site ready to perform work as it becomes available. This must be paid to the employee even if the individual is not actually performing work as he or she waits. However, this regulation does not apply to individuals who are on-call at any location other than the job site.

CHILD LABOR

The Fair Labor Standards Act established child labor regulations designed to prevent children from entering the workforce before they are mature enough to do so, from working in hazardous environments, from working for long periods, and from working instead of attending school. These regulations prohibit employers from hiring anyone under the age of 14 unless the individual is working for a parent or for a farm and from hiring individuals under the age of 18 for any kind of work deemed hazardous by law. These regulations also prevent individuals under the age of 16 from working in any manufacturing or mining-related job, working during school hours, working more than 3 hours a day or 18 hours a week during a school week or 8 hours a day and 40 hours a week during a non-school week, and working before 7:00 a.m. or past 7:00 p.m. during the school year or working before 7:00 a.m. or past 9:00 p.m. during the summer.

EQUAL PAY ACT

The **Equal Pay Act**, which was passed in 1963, prevents wage discrimination based on gender. It requires an employer to provide equal pay to both men and women performing similar tasks unless the employer can prove that there is an acceptable reason for the difference in pay, such as merit, seniority, quantity or quality of work performed, and. This act also establishes the criteria that must be considered to determine whether a particular position is similar. This includes the effort necessary for the tasks related to the position, the level of responsibility associated with the position, the skills required to perform the position, and the working conditions associated with the position.

LILLY LEDBETTER FAIR PAY ACT OF 2009

This law overturns the 2007 Supreme Court decision in the *Ledbetter v. Good Year Tire & Rubber Co.* case, which ruled that the statute of limitations to make a discriminatory pay claim was 180 days from the first discriminatory paycheck. The Lilly Ledbetter Fair Pay Act of 2009 results in the statute of limitations restarting with each discriminatory paycheck. The act applies to all protected classes and covers both wages and pensions. Due to the scope of the act, employers could face claims years after an employee has left the company. This act was designed to make employers more proactive in resolving pay inequities.

ERISA

ERISA was passed in 1974 to protect employees who are covered under private pensions and employee welfare benefit plans. ERISA ensures that employees receive promised benefits and are protected against early termination, mismanaged funds, or fraudulent activities. ERISA mandates that employers adhere to eligibility requirements, vesting requirements, portability practices, funding requirements, fiduciary responsibilities, reporting and disclosure requirements, as well as compliance testing. Most employees who have at least 1,000 hours of work in 12 months for two consecutive years are eligible to participate in **private pension plans**. Employees have the right to receive some portion of employer contributions when their employment ends. Employees must be allowed to transfer pension funds from one retirement account to another. Sufficient funds must be available from the employer to cover future payments. Employers must appoint an individual to be

responsible for seeking ideal portfolio options and administering pension funds. Employers must adhere to extensive reporting requirements, provide summary plan documents, and notify participants of any changes. Employers are required to complete annual minimum coverage, actual deferral percentage, actual contribution percentage, and top-heavy testing to prevent discrimination in favor of highly compensated employees.

FEDERAL WAGE GARNISHMENT LAW

The **Federal Wage Garnishment Law of 1968** imposes limitations on the amount of disposable earnings that may be withheld from an employee's income in a given pay period to satisfy a **wage garnishment order** for failure to pay a debt. The law restricts the amount that can be withheld to 25 percent of an employee's disposable weekly earnings or an amount that is 30 times the FLSA minimum wage, whichever is less. However, overdue payments to the IRS, child support in arrears, and alimony payments are a few exceptions that allow for more significant amounts to be withheld. Employers must immediately begin income withholdings upon receipt of a garnishment order, and funds must be sent to the respective agency within seven days. Failure to do so could impose hefty fines and penalties for the employer. There are certain protections for employees, whereby employers may not take disciplinary action or discriminate due to the receipt or obligation to comply with wage garnishment orders.

FMLA

The FMLA of 1993 is a federal regulation that provides employees the right to a maximum limit of 12 weeks of **unpaid leave** each 12-month period for the specified care of medical conditions that affect themselves or immediate family members. To be eligible for FMLA leave, an employee must have worked for a covered employer for the preceding 12 months and for a minimum of 1,250 hours during that time. All private employers, public or government agencies, and local schools with 50 or more employees within a 75-mile radius must adhere to the regulations. Qualifying events covered under FMLA include the following:

- The birth or adoption of a new child within one year of birth or placement
- The employee's own serious health condition that involves a period of incapacity
- An ill or injured spouse, child, or parent who requires the employee's care
- Any qualifying exigency (such as arranging childcare, tending to legal matters, and attending military ceremonies) due to the employee's spouse, child's, or parent's active-duty foreign deployment.
- The care of an ill or injured covered service member as long as the employee is a spouse, child, parent, or next of kin. In addition, time to care for military personnel or recent veterans has been expanded to 26 weeks in a 12-month period.

The FMLA has undergone some significant amendments, and human resource practitioners should be aware of the following:

- If a company fails to denote an employee's leave as FMLA leave, the employee may be eligible to receive compensation for any losses incurred.
- Prior to 2008, all FMLA disputes required Department of Labor or legal intervention. Now, employees and employers are encouraged to work any issues out in-house to avoid the cost of litigation.
- Light duty does not count toward FMLA taken.
- FMLA covers medical issues arising from preexisting conditions.
- Due to their unique scheduling, airline employees are eligible for FMLA after 504 or more hours worked during the preceding 12 months.

COBRA

The **Consolidated Omnibus Budget Reconciliation Act (COBRA) of 1986** requires that all employers with 20 or more employees continue the availability of **healthcare benefits coverage** and protects employees from the potential economic hardship of losing these benefits when they are terminated, working reduced hours, or quit. COBRA also provides coverage to the employee's spouse and dependents as qualified beneficiaries. Events that qualify for this continuation of coverage include the following:

- Voluntary or involuntary termination for any other reason than gross misconduct
- Reduction in hours that would otherwise result in loss of coverage
- Divorce or legal separation from the employee
- Death of the employee
- The employee becoming disabled and entitled to Medicare
- The dependent no longer being a dependent child under plan rules (older than 26)

Typically, the employee and qualified beneficiaries are entitled to 18 months of continued coverage. There are some instances that will extend coverage for up to an additional 18 months. Coverage will be lost if the employer terminates group coverage, premium payments are not received, or new coverage becomes available.

HIPAA

The **Health Insurance Portability and Accountability Act** (HIPAA) was passed in 1996 to provide greater protections and portability in healthcare coverage. Some individuals felt locked into current employer plans and feared that they would not be able to obtain coverage from a new employer plan due to preexisting conditions. Some of the **key HIPAA provisions** are preexisting condition exclusions, pregnancy, newborn and adopted children, credible coverage, renewal of coverage, medical savings accounts, tax benefits, and privacy provisions. Employees who have had another policy for the preceding 12 months cannot be excluded from coverage due to a preexisting condition or pregnancy or applied to newborn or adopted children who are covered by credible coverage within 30 days of the event. **Credible coverage** involves being covered under typical group health plans, and this coverage must be renewable to most groups and individuals as long as premiums are paid. **Medical savings accounts** were created by Congress for those who are self-employed or otherwise not eligible for credible coverage. Individuals who are self-employed are also allowed to take 80 percent of health-related expenses as a deduction. Finally, HIPAA introduced a series of several regulations that impose **civil and criminal penalties** on employers who disclose personal health information without consent.

> **Review Video: What is HIPAA?**
> Visit mometrix.com/academy and enter code: 412009

MHPA

The Mental Health Parity Act (MHPA), which was passed in 1996, is designed to prevent health plan providers from setting limits on mental health benefits that are stricter than the limits the provider has set for other health benefits. This act prohibits a health plan provider from setting a financial cap on the amount the health plan provider will pay for mental health benefits if that cap is lower than the cap the provider has set for other benefits. This act applies to any health plan provider providing coverage for an employer with at least 51 employees, but only if the regulations set by this act will not result in a 1% or greater increase in the costs of the provider. It is also important to note that health plan providers are not required to offer mental health benefits and providers may set other limits related to mental health coverage as long as there is no specific payout limit.

PPACA

The **Patient Protection and Affordable Care Act** (PPACA) is a comprehensive healthcare law that was passed in 2010 to establish regulations on medical services, insurance coverage, preventative services, whistle-blowing, and similar practices. A few key provisions of PPACA include the following:

- **Individual mandate**— required all individuals to maintain health insurance or pay a penalty; however, it was removed from the statute effective tax year 2019
- **State healthcare exchanges**—provides individuals and families a portal in which they can shop through a variety of plans and purchase healthcare coverage
- **Employer shared responsibility**—requires that employers with more than 50 employees provide affordable coverage to all employees that work 30 or more hours per week or pay a penalty
- **Affordable coverage**—does not allow employers to shift the burden of healthcare costs to employees and imposes a penalty for employees who obtain government subsidies for coverage
- **Flexible spending accounts (FSAs)**—imposes a cap on pretax contributions to flexible spending accounts, health reimbursement arrangements (HRAs), and HSAs
- **Wellness incentives**—allows employers to provide premium discounts for employees who meet wellness requirements
- **Excise tax on "Cadillac" plans**—will impose excise tax on employers that provide expensive coverage beginning in 2022
- **W-2 reporting requirements**—requires employers to report the cost of coverage under employer-sponsored group health plans on each employee's W-2 form
- **Summary of benefits coverage**—requires insurance companies and employers to provide individuals with a summary of benefits coverage (SBC) using a standard form
- **Whistle-blower protections**—amends the FLSA to prohibit employers from retaliating against an employee who applies for health benefit subsidies or tax credits

NATIONAL FEDERATION OF INDEPENDENT BUSINESS V. SEBELIUS (2012)

Opponents of the PPACA argued that certain provisions of the law, such as the individual mandate, were unconstitutional. The court ultimately ruled that PPACA was constitutional, and it remained intact until President Trump reversed the individual mandate effective 2019. Other elements of the PPACA legislation are still currently in place.

OWBPA

The Older Worker Benefit Protection Act (OWBPA), which was passed in 1990, is an amendment to the Age Discrimination in Employment Act designed to prevent employers from unfairly refusing benefits to individuals over a certain age. This act prohibits an employer or benefit plan administrator from preventing participation or continuing to participate in a benefits program due to age if the individual is covered by the Age Discrimination in Employment Act. It establishes that an employer may only set a maximum age limit or reduce an individual's benefits due to age in situations in which the age limit or age-related reduction can be shown to significantly reduce the costs associated with implementing the benefit plan. The act also specifically establishes that an employer may implement a plan or system based on seniority as long as the plan does not require an individual to leave the program after a certain age.

REA

The Retirement Equity Act (REA), which was passed in 1984, is an amendment to the Employee Retirement Income Security Act (ERISA) designed to establish a number of benefit plan regulations in addition to those originally established by ERISA. These regulations are designed to protect spouses from losing their benefits after a plan participant's death or after a divorce, but also include regulations to strengthen the protections offered by ERISA. Protections established by REA include regulations prohibiting benefit plan administrators from considering maternity/paternity leave as a break in service regarding the right to participate in a plan or become vested in a plan, regulations that require pension plans to automatically provide benefits to a spouse in the event of the plan participant's death unless a waiver has been signed by both the spouse and the participant, and regulations that lowered the age at which an employer has to allow an individual to participate in a pension plan.

PENSION PROTECTION ACT

The Pension Protection Act, which was passed in 2006, is an amendment to the Employee Retirement Income Security Act (ERISA) designed to protect individuals from pension plans that do not have enough funding to pay out all of the retirement benefits promised to employees. This act requires any employer establishing a pension plan to make contributions in amounts large enough to ensure the plan is not underfunded and requires employers to offer at least three investment options in addition to the employer's own stock if the employer's stock is offered as part of a benefit plan. This act also allows employers to include employees in an organization's 401(k) program with or without the permission of the individual as long as the individual has the right to opt-out of the plan.

OASDI

The Old Age, Survivors, and Disability Insurance (OASDI) program, which was established by the Social Security Act (SSA) of 1935, offers benefits to employees that have retired or become disabled. This program requires employees to pay a percentage of their income to the federal government and requires employers to match the contributions made by their employees. As employees contribute to the fund, they will accumulate Social Security credits and may receive up to four Social Security credits a year based on the amount paid into the fund. If an individual becomes completely disabled for a period of at least five consecutive months or retires at age 62 or older, he/she is entitled to receive a portion of previous earnings from the Social Security program. To receive retirement benefits from social security, the individual must have at least 40 credits before retiring.

> **US Employment Compensation Laws**
> Visit mometrix.com/academy and enter code: 613448

Compensation Policies, Processes, and Analysis

The concept known as **total rewards** refers to all of the compensation and benefits received for performing tasks related to each position. It is important to have an effective total rewards program for two main reasons. First, it encourages employees to join and then stay with the organization. Second, there are legal concerns associated with the minimum amount of compensation an individual can receive for a certain amount of work, making it essential to consider these concerns to avoid unnecessary fines or litigation. When taking total rewards into account, the whole of an employee's compensation can be seen, not just monetary compensation.

TYPES OF REWARDS

The two main types of rewards used to compensate employees are monetary and nonmonetary. **Monetary compensation** is any tangible reward provided as payment for work, including salary and wages, paid sick days, paid vacation time, retirement plans, and stock options. **Nonmonetary compensation** is any intangible reward provided to encourage an individual to perform work, including better assignments, employee-of-the-month awards, flexible scheduling, and special privileges.

An organization can issue monetary compensation to employees through direct or indirect compensation. Direct compensation is any monetary compensation paid directly to the employee, including salary or wages, bonuses, overtime, or special pay. Indirect compensation is monetary compensation paid to a third party on the employee's behalf or paid without the employee having to perform work, including health insurance, paid sick days, paid vacation time, retirement plans, and stock options.

> **Review Video: Total Rewards and Compensation**
> Visit mometrix.com/academy and enter code: 502662

PHILOSOPHY

A total rewards philosophy is developed to clearly state reward goals and how those goals will be achieved. Identifying this philosophy is necessary to determine if the rewards are reflecting the values and goals of an organization or if they need to be modified.

The two types of total reward philosophies are entitlement philosophies and performance-based philosophies. An **entitlement philosophy** issues rewards based on the length of time a particular employee has been with the organization. It assumes an individual is entitled to certain rewards because of seniority or length of time in a specific position. Entitlement philosophies encourage individuals to stay with the organization but do not necessarily encourage effective performance. A **performance-based philosophy**, on the other hand, issues rewards for good performance.

STRATEGY

A **total rewards strategy** is a plan used to design a total rewards program. It is based on the organization's total rewards philosophy and is primarily designed to establish the framework for the allocation of program resources. It refers to the ways resources are used to encourage individuals to work for the organization without exceeding limits.

There are a variety of factors to consider when designing an effective total rewards strategy. The four main factors include the competitive environment, the economic environment, the labor market, and the legal environment. The **competitive environment** is the effect competition has on the ability to allocate resources to the total rewards program. For example, if competitors are offering a specific product at a price that is far lower, the organization may need to reduce the amount of funds allocated to its total rewards program to afford a price reduction. The **economic environment** refers to the effect the economy has on the cost of labor. For example, as the cost of living increases, the cost of labor will usually increase as well. The **labor market** is the availability of skilled employees and the **legal environment** refers to taxes and regulations.

Job Analysis and Evaluation

It is important to conduct a job evaluation during the total rewards planning process for two major reasons. First, a job evaluation identifies the positions most important to success so rewards can be

71

assigned appropriately. Second, it determines whether there should be a difference in pay between two positions. For example, a secretary and an administrative assistant with the same skills and performing similar jobs should receive equal pay even though they have different titles.

A **compensable factor** is a specific characteristic of a position used to determine the value of that position. They are specific job requirements that are considered important, and individuals are compensated based on their ability to meet these requirements. Compensable factors are commonly used during a job evaluation to compare the requirements of a variety of different positions. Some of the most common compensable factors relate to knowledge, skills, and abilities. These factors include characteristics related to a particular position such as experience required, level of education required, level of responsibility required, and knowledge of specific technology or processes required.

The two main types of job evaluation techniques used to determine the value of a particular position are nonquantitative techniques and quantitative techniques. **Nonquantitative techniques**, also referred to as **whole job methods**, are used to evaluate the skills and abilities associated with a particular position and assign it a value based on whether it requires more or less skill than other jobs within the organization. **Quantitative techniques**, also referred to as **nontraditional techniques** or **factor-based methods**, are techniques of assigning a specific value to each factor in a series of compensable factors identified as important. The organization can then evaluate each position, determine how many compensable factors are required for the position, and can assign a value to the position by using a mathematical formula.

The three most common nonquantitative job evaluation techniques are the classification method, the pricing method, and the ranking method. The **classification method** separates positions into categories based on tasks. Each category is then listed in order of its importance and assigned pay based on its importance. The **pricing method**, also known as the slotting method, assigns a value to a position equal to the value of a similar position or category that already exists. Finally, the **ranking method** ranks each position from lowest to highest based on how the skills and abilities required to perform the position compare with those associated with other positions.

The most common quantitative job evaluation techniques are the factor comparison method and the point factor method. The **factor comparison method** identifies a series of compensable factors and establishes a ranking system to measure how much of a particular compensable factor, such as education, is required for a particular position. Each factor ranking is assigned a specific dollar value, and the value of the position is determined by adding the total dollar value for the rank of each factor required for the position. The **point factor method** is similar, but it assigns a point value to each factor instead of a dollar value, and the pay for the position is determined by comparing the total amount of points to a chart.

Job Pricing and Pay Structures

PAY STRUCTURES

A **pay structure** is the compensation system an organization uses to determine the appropriate base pay for positions by separating each job into categories based on value to the organization. The pay structure is an essential part of any organization's total rewards program because it establishes a guide for appropriate hourly wages or salaries. Specific base pay minimums and maximums for each category are well-defined and allow firms to avoid arbitrarily assigning pay.

Creating a pay structure can vary greatly, but most organizations begin the process by conducting a job evaluation for each position. Once all positions are evaluated and assigned a value, they are categorized based on their value to the organization. The organization will usually gather information from salary surveys to determine the market median for each category and wages an individual would receive at the midpoint of a similar pay category for another organization. Finally, using all of this information as a guide, a pay range is developed for each category.

PAY LEVELS AND PAY BANDING

Some compensation structures break out pay grades or ranges into separate **levels** or **bands** so the company can maintain pay equity and stay within budget. This is done by conducting a job analysis and grouping titles into families. For example, those that fall into the first pay grade may have a pay band of $20,000 to $35,000, the second pay grade may have a band of $30,000 to $50,000, and the third pay grade may have a band of $50,000 to $100,000. Jobs may also be evaluated and ranked based upon overall responsibilities and worth to the organization. Although pay bands are broken out based upon job duty and skill level, it is important to recognize whether the company tends to lead, lag, or match current market rates. Matching or leading the market is best for recruitment and retention. The sizes of pay bands tend to grow as you move up the managerial ladder, with executives having the largest pay levels.

BROADBANDING

Broadbanding is a type of pay structure design in which an organization creates a small number of broadly defined pay grades into which all jobs are separated, for example, general staff, management, and executives. Organizations usually choose to use a broadbanding approach to encourage teamwork and eliminate problems arising from perceived differences in status between different pay grades. The focus is on performance rather than activities related to achieving promotions.

Non-Cash Compensation

WORKERS' COMPENSATION

Workers' compensation provides employees with coverage of medical expenses and a continuation of income for individuals who sustain work-related injuries. The basic concept makes compensation and expenses the employer's responsibility without liability or fault to the employee, assuming that the employee has adhered to reasonable safety precautions. Each state administers its own **workers' compensation** per state and federal laws. There are **three types of benefits** awarded to employees: medical expenses, wage replacement payments, and death benefits. The wage replacement payments are often calculated based upon an employee's average weekly wages and become available after a waiting period. Costs are determined by an experience rating based upon an employer's claim history.

> **Review Video: US Employment Compensation Laws**
> Visit mometrix.com/academy and enter code: 613448

UNEMPLOYMENT COMPENSATION

Unemployment compensation is a national program that is regulated by the IRS as the **Federal Unemployment Tax Act (FUTA)** to provide workers with short-term sustenance while they are looking for new employment. Employers pay FUTA as a payroll tax at a rate of 6.2 percent. Although a majority of the administration is held at the state level, the federal government also administers the programs. FUTA applies to all employers who either employ one or more employees or pay

wages greater than $1,500 in any quarter of a calendar year. Employees typically receive about half of their former weekly wages; however, each state regulates the amount and duration of benefits. Eligibility requirements require that individuals be available and readily seeking new employment opportunities, which they must record and present upon request. The company costs vary depending upon the employer's experience rating, which is based on prior claims receiving payments.

CAFETERIA PLANS

IRS section 125 defines a **cafeteria plan** as a defined employer plan providing participants the opportunity to receive certain benefits on a pretax basis. Funds allocated to these benefits are not included as wages for state or federal income tax purposes and are generally exempt from Federal Insurance Contributions Act (FICA) and FUTA. Qualified benefits under these plans might include the following:

- **Medical healthcare coverage**—plans may include some or all portions of physician services, office visits and exams, prescription drugs, hospital services, maternity services, mental health, physical therapy, and emergency services.
- **Dental coverage**—plans may include some or all portions of routine exams, cleanings, X-rays, fluoride treatments, orthodontic services, fillings, crowns, and extractions.
- **Dependent care**—plans may cover some or all portions of on-site childcare, allowances and flexible spending for childcare, day-care information, or flexible scheduling.
- **Short-term disability**—this provides partial income continuation to employees who are unable to work for a short period of time (three to six months) due to an accident or illness.
- **Long-term disability**—this provides partial income continuation to employees who are unable to work for long periods of time (greater than three to six months) due to an accident or illness.
- **Group-term life insurance and accidental death or dismemberment**—this provides financial assistance to an employee or his or her beneficiaries if the employee has an accident that results in the loss of limbs, loss of eyesight, or death. The cost of group plans is frequently lower than individual plans, and payments are based upon the employee's age and annual salary.

DISABILITY INSURANCE

Disability income insurance is divided into two categories: short-term disability (STD) and **long-term disability (LTD)**. These private insurance plans replace a portion of employees' wages if they are out of work due to an injury or illness. Contrary to workers' compensation, the injury or illness does not need to be work related to qualify for STD or LTD. Many employers offer disability insurance benefits on a fully paid, partially paid, or ancillary basis. Employers should check state regulations to determine if they are required to provide partial wage replacement insurance coverage to eligible employees. STD typically runs for 90 to 180 days, providing employees with 60 to 75 percent wage replacement following a short waiting period. LTD kicks in after STD is exhausted. Depending on the plan, the LTD coverage may last 24–36 months or run until employees can return to work (whether for the same company or a new one) or until they are old enough to collect retirement or they are able to collect social security disability.

EMPLOYEE WELLNESS PROGRAMS

Many companies have begun to implement **employee wellness programs** to encourage employees to take preventative measures and avoid illness and accidents. The level of employee wellness programs varies greatly. Some may include physical examinations to assess health and health

education to teach nutrition or healthy habits, whereas others might be intended to assist with smoking cessation, but almost all employee wellness programs will include some element of weight management. Moreover, the Patient Protection and Affordable Care Act allows employers to **reward** employees for participating in wellness programs, such as covering a higher percentage of premiums for employees who comply with wellness program requirements like having annual physical examinations and attending trainings. However, rewards should be based only upon participation and not achieving health objectives.

EMPLOYEE ASSISTANCE PROGRAMS

Employee assistance programs (**EAPs**) help employees with personal problems, such as seeking guidance through a substance abuse problem and obtaining counsel referrals during a marital separation. An EAP may be categorized as a **welfare plan** and obligated to file reports with the Department of Labor and IRS if it provides counseling for substance abuse, stress, anxiety, depression, or similar health and mental problems. Moreover, these programs may be required to comply with reporting and disclosure requirements of the **Employee Retirement Income Security Act (ERISA)**. EAPs must adhere to strict guidelines to avoid legal risks regarding privacy, malpractice, or coercion.

FAMILY AND FLEX BENEFITS PROGRAMS

In recent years, employees have come to expect benefits that promote work–life balance and support families. To that end, an increasing number of employers offer telecommuting, flex time, and compressed work week options to help workers juggle all of life's different demands. In addition, many workplaces now offer benefits like paid parental leave and designated lactation rooms, making it easier on new parents. Additionally, some employers have started offering paid caregiver leave, which allows workers to care for parents and other relatives without worrying about their paychecks.

ESOP

An **employee stock ownership plan** (ESOP) is created by establishing a trust into which the business makes contributions of cash or stock that are tax deductible. Employees are then granted with the ability to purchase stock or allocate funds into individual employee accounts. The stock is held in an **employee stock ownership trust (ESOT)**, and the business can make regular contributions, typically up to 25 percent of its annual payroll. ESOPs became popular because it is believed that employees who have an ownership interest in the business will work more diligently and also have a vested interest in its efficiency and profitability. Although this logic is debatable, many studies have shown that ESOPs actually do motivate employees and support business growth.

Methods to Align and Benchmark Compensation and Benefits

SALARY SURVEYS

A salary survey is an assessment of the compensation and benefits currently offered by organizations in a particular labor market. It is a collection of information related to how each organization encourages employees to work in the current economic environment. These surveys are usually conducted by individuals or third-parties outside the organization and are an essential part of a total rewards planning process because they identify changes in the current labor market that may impact effectiveness.

The three most common types of salary surveys are commissioned surveys, government surveys, and industry surveys. A commissioned survey is prepared from outside the organization. Because

these surveys are expensive, they are used to obtain very specific information related to the labor market. A government survey is prepared by a government agency such as the Bureau of Labor Statistics and usually accomplished without cost to the organization. However the information is normally less specific than the information included in other types of surveys. An industry survey is prepared by the members of a particular industry. They are relatively inexpensive and provide more specific information than government surveys.

WAGE COMPRESSION

Wage compression occurs when an employee is hired at the same or higher wage than existing employees with more experience already in that position. It can also occur when line level employees earn close to what management earns. It is important to avoid wage compression because it leads to employees becoming dissatisfied and unmotivated because of the perceived arbitrary nature of pay decisions. Wage compression can happen in several ways, such as external hires expecting more of a pay bump to change jobs than a normal, internal annual increase (typically less than 4 percent), and companies may be willing to offer inflated salaries in a tight labor market. To combat wage compression, human resources can use strategies such as reviewing existing staff salaries prior to hiring a new employee (and making adjustments if necessary) and promoting from within whenever possible, which should result in a lower salary than hiring externally.

COMPA-RATIO

A compa-ratio is a mathematical formula used to compare a specific employee's pay with the pay at the middle of the pay range. A **compa-ratio** is expressed as a percentage and can be determined by dividing the employee's base salary by the midpoint salary for the employee's pay range (*base salary/midpoint salary = compa-ratio*). For example, if an individual is in a pay grade that ranges from $25,000 to $45,000 a year and the individual receives $30,000 a year, the midpoint of the range is equal to ($25,000 + $45,000)/2 or $35,000, and the compa-ratio is equal to $30,000/$35,000, which is equal to 0.857 or 85.7 percent. Compa-ratios are primarily used to compare an employee's current pay with the pay of other employees in similar positions to determine whether the individual is receiving a fair amount considering seniority, performance, and so on.

CALCULATING PIECE RATES

Piece rates calculate the amount of compensation an employee receives for conducting a specified unit of work. A worker who produces multiple products at different rates would need overtime calculated using a combined weighted average to find the regular hourly rate of pay. First, multiply each rate by the total hours worked, then divide the sum by the total hours worked to find the **blended hourly rate**. This method is industry standard best practice for compliance with **FLSA**. For example, if a worker produced 60 pieces at a rate of $9.00 per piece over 40 hours and another 40 pieces at a rate of $6.00 per piece over 10 hours, the hourly rate for this worker would be $7.80 (60 pieces times $9.00 per piece plus 40 pieces times $6.00 per piece equals $780, divided by 50 hours equals $15.60 per hour). Then, earnings would be calculated as follows:

Regular time = 40 hours × $15.60 = $624.00

Overtime = 10 hours × $23.40 = $234.00

Weekly earnings = $858.00

USING BENCHMARKING TO DESIGN COMPENSATION INITIATIVES

When organizations and compensation professionals need to make pay decisions or determine whether internal rates are competitive with the industry, most will rely upon **benchmarking** of both internal and external peer groups. Benchmarking is a tool for measuring and comparing current practices or processes against **competition** so that any gaps may be addressed. For example, making changes to incentive plans may be a tough sell. If your business practice involves not providing employees with a bonus plan, benchmarking data might support new initiatives by showing that many in your industry do provide bonus incentives. Thus, not providing this incentive could jeopardize performance or risk losing top performers. However, it is important to consider organizational structure, size, location, industry, and other factors. Compensation rates in San Francisco will differ greatly from rates in Omaha, and smaller companies often pay less than large, national entities.

USING REMUNERATION SURVEYS TO ENSURE COMPETITIVENESS

Competitive compensation structures are not only equitable and motivating, but they should also be legal, be cost-benefit effective, and provide security. The most readily available **remuneration surveys** are those conducted by government agencies, such as the Bureau of Labor Statistics (BLS) and wage surveys conducted by private organizations. Government surveys may include local, state, or federal data. BLS regularly publishes reliable data findings on occupational earnings and benefits of blue- and white-collar jobs. Furthermore, professional organizations, journals, and associations may perform sophisticated surveys to obtain remuneration data of top managers, supervisors, and entry-level workers. Some popular publications are *Forbes's* CEO compensation report or those compiled by wage survey companies like PayScale or Towers Watson. However, the U.S. Justice Department has stated that human resource professionals cannot conduct salary surveys on their own. Doing so violates the Antitrust Safety Zone guidelines. Professionals should consider that these surveys frequently consider varying components of compensation, such as base pay, incentives, and benefits.

Benefits Programs

PENSIONS OR RETIREMENT PLANS

Pensions and company retirement plans fund an individual's retirement by providing deferred payments for prior services. These accounts may be funded by the employer through a variety of means. Retirement benefits are accumulated by the total amount contributed plus interest and market earnings. These **defined contribution benefit plans** are the traditional company-provided plans, such as 401(k)s, 403(b)s, Simplified Employee Pensions (SEPs), SIMPLEs, and IRAs. A defined contribution benefit plan requires separate accounts for each employee participant, and funds are most often contributed by both the employee and the employer. Some employers will implement an auto-enroll policy in which new employees are automatically enrolled and minimum contributions to the plan are withheld from payroll. The contribution rates may even automatically increase on an annual basis. However, the **Pension Protection Act of 2006** provides employees with a 90-day window to opt out of these plans and recover any funds contributed on their behalf.

SOCIAL SECURITY

The Social Security Act was first implemented to force workers into saving a fraction of earnings for retirement and making employers obligated to match those funds. These funds are now withheld as

a portion of the **Federal Insurance Contributions Act (FICA) payroll taxes** and regulated by the IRS. The benefits have since been extended to cover four types of **insurance benefits**:

1. **Old age or disability benefits**—for workers who retire or become unable to work due to disability, based upon eligibility requirements
2. Benefits for dependents of retired, disabled, or deceased workers—paid to certain dependents
3. **Lump-sum death benefits**—paid to the worker's survivors
4. **Medicare**—healthcare protection provided to individuals age 65 and older, consisting of Parts A, B, and D

HEALTHCARE INSURANCE PLANS

There are many forms of healthcare insurance plans, and the increasing cost of insurance has forced employers to absorb additional costs, pass more costs to employees, or find affordable alternatives. **Fee-for-service plans** allow employees to decide what services they need from any provider; fees are paid by both the employee and the employee's benefits plan through deductibles and co-insurance. **Preferred provider organization (PPO) plans** allow insurers to contract with providers of the employees choosing with lower fees and better coverage for providers within the organization; fees are paid by deductibles, co-insurance, and co-payments. **Health maintenance organization (HMO) plans** emphasize preventative care through fixed costs regardless of the number of visits, but primary care physicians (PCPs) must refer others, and no other providers are covered; fees are paid by deductibles, co-insurance, and co-payments. **Point of service (POS) plans** are similar to PPO plans with certain elements (PCP referrals) of HMO plans; fees are paid by deductibles, co-insurance, and co-payments. **Consumer-directed health plans** provide tax-favored accounts, such as an FSA or an HSA, to pay for medical expenses, and may allow employees to see any provider of their choosing. However, these plans carry high deductibles and may have low or no co-insurance after deductible is reached.

FSA

A flexible spending account (FSA) is a special account in which an individual can put money in to pay for certain out-of-pocket, non-covered health care costs. FSA users don't have to pay taxes on this money. This means the insured can save an amount equal to the taxes he or she would have paid on the money set aside. Money is placed in the account by the enrollee tax free and is taken out tax free or as tax deductible to pay for qualified medical expenses. FSAs are available only with job-based health plans. Employers and the employees themselves can make contributions to the FSA. Individuals cannot use FSA funds on insurance premiums. FSAs are set up by the employer, but funds can be added by either the employer or employee. FSAs can be used to reimburse an enrollee's—or his or her dependent's—medical, dental, and vision expenses. Funds in FSAs can be used to cover expenses related to prevention diagnosis and treatment of medical illnesses.

Eligible medical care expenses are defined by the IRS and include costs that relate to disease deterrence, diagnosis, or treatment. Expenses for solely cosmetic reasons generally are not expenses for medical care and are not reimbursable. These include procedures and services such as liposuction or Botox treatments and are therefore not eligible under an FSA. Ineligible expenses also include contact lenses and personal trainers, for example. Eligible expenses do, however, include things like service or guide animals and acupuncture. Employees can also open dependent care FSAs, which allow them to use pretax dollars to pay for dependent care, like day care.

The IRS determines FSA contribution limits annually. The main drawback to the FSA is that it requires careful budgeting as there is a lose-or-use provision attached to the benefit. If employees

do not use the funds within an account during the given plan year, they may lose the money. Exceptions to this are when the employer opts to offer a grace period (granting an additional 2.5 months to use the funds) or a carryover provision (limited to $500). Employers are not required to offer either and can offer only one of the two. They may also offer a run-out period, which gives employees an additional 90 days to make claims for reimbursement.

HSA

The health savings account (HSA) is an individual, tax-advantaged account, and funds can be deposited by both the employee and employer. The funds added to this account are then used to pay medical expenses not covered by the high deductible health plan (HDHP), including the deductible. An HDHP is a health insurance plan that meets federal guidelines in three benefit areas—deductible, out-of-pocket maximum, and first-dollar coverage. These amounts are adjusted each calendar year by the IRS.

Health Savings Accounts (HSAs) have been growing steadily in popularity since their introduction in 2003 as part of the Medicare, Prescription Drug, Improvement and Modernization Act. This health insurance product consists of two parts: the individual HSA and an HDHP. The HDHP is like a traditional health plan, but its unique feature is that it has higher deductibles giving the insured a higher financial stake and financial incentive in healthcare decisions. Federal law says individuals can open an HSA only if they are enrolled in an HDHP and are not enrolled in other forms of low-deductible health insurance.

The HSA offers a triple tax advantage. The money is not taxed going into the account. If the money is invested and increases in value, those gains are not taxed. And, withdrawals are not taxed so long as employees use them for qualified medical expenses. In addition, an HSA does not have any use-or-lose provision, and funds may be carried over from year to year. Like an FSA, however, there is an annual contribution limit, which the IRS announces each year.

LEAVE PLANS AND APPROACHES
PTO POLICIES

There are many different **paid time off** (PTO) policies across different businesses, industries, and geographic locations. Many of these all-encompassing PTO plans are available only to full-time employees. Whereas many companies recognize eight to 10 fixed holidays, some companies have implemented policies that provide employees with floating holidays. Trends have shown an increase in organizations of all sizes adopting a collective in which vacation, personal, sick, and sometimes holiday days are kept in a **single pool** of PTO. Many employees and employers report that having flexibility in time-off plans leads to greater employee engagement and retention. However, as more states are imposing sick time regulations, recent trends reflect a number of organizations moving back to traditional buckets of separate vacation and sick time. Additional consideration should be given to state regulations for **termination payouts**. Some states do not require employers to pay out accrued sick time, but many consider PTO pools equivalent to vacation during terminations, so employers must pay out any accrued balances. Companies must also determine whether employees will be gifted with a bank of time immediately or at a predetermined time versus **accrued**. Policies should provide details about carryover provisions and if negative balances are allowed. Having an attractive and well-administered PTO policy can give employers an advantage against growing competition for talent, evolving legal regulations, and an increasingly diverse workforce.

HOLIDAYS AND OTHER PAY FOR TIME NOT WORKED

Whereas the average number of **paid holidays** is around eight per year, most businesses will recognize the following six U.S. holidays: New Year's Day, Memorial Day, Independence Day, Labor Day, Thanksgiving Day, and Christmas Day. Additionally, a majority of employers will pay a set number of days for bereavement and jury duty for eligible employees. However, employees may be required to provide documentation. Other instances in which employees might be paid for time not worked include reporting time guaranteed for minimal work, union activities, and time to vote.

UNPAID LEAVE

When employees have exhausted all of PTO options and needs to take time away from work, the employer may allow them to take an unpaid leave. This leave may be classified as a personal leave or a work sabbatical. Criteria to qualify and rules that govern the leave will depend on individual firm policies. Policies will need to address items such as how to apply for the leave, length of leave allowed, benefits continuance, the employee's right to return to the same role, the process to return from a leave, and more.

Employee and Labor Relations

General Employee Relations Activities and Analysis

EMPLOYEE MISCONDUCT INVESTIGATIONS

The investigation process usually begins when a complaint is received or if it is determined there is reasonable cause to investigate an employee's conduct. The organization should identify exactly what is being investigated, what sort of evidence is needed to prove or disprove the misconduct, who should be interviewed during the investigation, and which questions need to be asked to gather the necessary evidence. Next, the organization needs to interview the person making the complaint, the individual the complaint is against, and any other employees who have relevant information. Finally, the organization should come to a decision and take the appropriate action.

WEINGARTEN RIGHTS

In *National Labor Relations Board (NLRB) vs. Weingarten*, the Supreme Court established the right of employees to have **union representation** at investigatory interviews in which the employee must defend conduct or behavior. If an employee believes that discipline or other consequences might follow, he or she has the right to request union representation. However, management does not need to inform an employee of their **Weingarten rights**. It is the employee's own responsibility to know and request representation. When requested, management can a) stop questioning until a representative arrives, b) terminate the interview, or c) ask the employee to voluntarily relinquish his or her rights to representation. The company does need to inform the representative of the interview subject, and the representative does have the right to counsel the employee in private and advise him or her what to say.

GRIEVANCES

A grievance is a work-related complaint or formal dispute that is brought to the attention of management. However, in nonunion environments, grievances may encompass any discontent or sense of injustice. **Grievance procedures** provide an orderly and methodical process for hearing and evaluating employee complaints and tend to be more developed in union companies than in nonunion companies as a result of labor agreement specifications. These procedures protect employee rights and eliminate the need for strikes or slowdowns every time there is a disagreement.

Disagreements may be unavoidable in situations where the labor contract is open to interpretation because negotiators cannot anticipate all potential conflicts. **Formal grievance procedures** increase upward communication in organizations and make top management decisions more sensitive to employee emotions. The first step to resolving grievances is for a complaint to be submitted to the supervisor or written and submitted to the union steward.

If these parties cannot find resolution from there, the complaint may be heard by the superintendent or plant manager and the industrial relations manager. If the union is still unsatisfied, the grievance can be appealed to the next step, which may be arbitration if the company is small. Large corporations may have grievance committees, corporate officers, and/or international union representatives who will meet and hear grievances. However, the final step of an unresolved dispute will be **binding arbitration** by an outside third party, where both parties come to an acceptable agreement.

PREVENTING RETALIATION CLAIMS

To prevent retaliation, employees must believe that a) complaints can be easily presented without a lot of hassle, embarrassment, or paperwork; b) complaints will be assessed by a fair and impartial third party; and c) they will not be mistreated or terminated for submitting complaints or pressing for resolution. The final protection is necessary for the success of both union and nonunion **grievance procedures**, although union employees typically have more protections than nonunion employees because their labor agreement is written and enforceable by collective action. However, federal regulations such as the Sarbanes-Oxley Act and Whistleblower Protection Act now include safeguards for employees who have witnessed or stumbled upon illegal or immoral actions and make the information known to the public. Employers can also follow a number of best practices to **avoid retaliation**, such as these:

- Treat all complaints seriously and similarly.
- Allow the employee a chance to be heard, investigate the claim, collect evidence or witness statements, and treat all cases as though they might result in arbitration.
- Review the labor agreement carefully, and follow any required procedures.
- Examine all information prior to making a final determination.
- Avoid any unnecessary delays, and clearly communicate the conclusion.
- Correct the problem if the company is in the wrong.

Federal Laws and Procedures

NLRA

The **NLRA** was passed by Congress in 1935 after a long period of conflict in labor relations. Also known as the **Wagner Act**, after the New York Senator Robert Wagner, it was intended to be an economic stabilizer and establish collective bargaining in industrial relations. Section 7 of the NLRA provides employees with the right to form, join, or assist **labor organizations** as well as the right to engage in **concerted activities** such as collective bargaining through representatives or other mutual aid. Section 8 of the NLRA also identifies five **unfair labor practices**:

1. Employers shall not interfere with or coerce employees from the rights outlined in Section 7.
2. Employers shall not dominate or disrupt the formation of a labor union.
3. Employers shall not allow union membership or activity to influence hiring, firing, promotion, or related employment decisions.
4. Employers shall not discriminate against or discharge an employee who has given testimony or filed a charge with the NLRA.
5. Employers cannot refuse bargaining in good faith with employee representatives.

TAFT-HARTLEY ACT

Because many employers felt that the NLRA gave too much power to unions, Congress passed the **Labor Management Relations Act** in 1947. Also known as the **Taft-Hartley Act**, the act sought to avoid unnecessary strikes and impose certain restrictions over union activities. The act addresses **four basic issues**: unfair labor practices by unions, the rights of employees, the rights of employers, and national emergency strikes. Moreover, the act prohibits unions from the following:

- Restraining or coercing employees from their right to not engage in union activities
- Forcing an employer to discriminate in any way against an employee to encourage or discourage union membership

- Forcing an employer to pay for work or services that are not needed or not performed
- Conducting certain types of strikes or boycotts
- Charging excessive initiation fees or membership dues when employees are required to join a union shop

LANDRUM-GRIFFIN ACT

The government exercised further control over union activities in 1959 by the passage of the **Labor Management Reporting and Disclosure Act**. Commonly known as the **Landrum-Griffin Act**, this law regulates the **internal conduct of labor unions** to reduce the likelihood of fraud and improper actions. The act imposes controls on five major areas: reports to the secretary of labor, a bill of rights for union members, union trusteeships, conduct of union elections, and financial safeguards. Some key provisions include the following:

- Granting equal rights to every union member with regard to nominations, attending meetings, and voting
- Requiring unions to submit and make available to the public a copy of its constitution, bylaws, and annual financial reports
- Requiring unions to hold regular elections every five years for national and every three years for local organizations
- Monitoring the management and investment of union funds, making embezzlement a federal crime

> **Review Video: US Employment Law: Employee and Labor Relations (NLRA)**
> Visit mometrix.com/academy and enter code: 972790

NLRB

The National Labor Relations Board (NLRB) is a federal agency that protects the right of employees to choose whether they want to be represented by a union or not and is designed to handle activities related to investigating and preventing employers and unions from taking part in unfair labor practices. The National Labor Relations Board can take a number of actions related to employer unfair labor practices including requiring employers to rehire or return positions to employees that were affected by an unfair labor practice, requiring employers to resume negotiations with a union, and disbanding unions that are controlled by an employer. The NLRB may also take a number of actions related to union unfair labor practices including requiring unions to refund membership fees with or without interest to union members that have been charged unreasonable fees, requiring unions to resume negotiations with an employer, and requiring unions to accept the reinstatement of any employee if the union specifically discriminated against that employee.

NLRB VS. WEINGARTEN (1975)

This case resulted in union employees being able to request coworker presence at investigatory meetings that may involve disciplinary action. In 2000, the NLRB expanded this protection to nonunion employees. These are known as **Weingarten rights**.

LECHMERE, INC. VS. NLRB (1992)

This case determined that nonemployee union organizers may solicit employees on private company property if no other reasonable alternative to contact employees exists. This preserves the employees' right to organize.

Norris-LaGuardia Act

The Norris-LaGuardia Act, which was passed in 1932, protects the right to unionize. This act grants employees the right to form unions and initiate strikes. In addition to granting the right to unionize, this act also prohibits the court system from using injunctions to interfere with any nonviolent union activity and prohibits employers from forcing employees to sign "yellow-dog" contracts. A "yellow-dog" contract is any contract that prohibits an employee from joining a union or any contract that requires an employee to agree to be terminated if it is discovered that he/she is a member of a union or intends to become a member of a union.

Human Relations, Culture, and Values

Human Relations Management Theory

The human relations management theory is the most modern of the management approaches. The theory is based on the concept that the people performing the jobs have needs that should be considered equal to or above the needs of the organization. Some big names in human relations management are Fritz Roethlisberger and Elton Mayo, who conducted the "Hawthorne studies" that analyzed the correlation between employees' satisfaction and safety/comfort with successful and productive work. The studies focused on employees, who seemed to work better while being studied; however, when the study was over, they went back to their old working habits. The conclusion was that employees worked better when they were being paid attention to. This showed management personnel that by considering their employees' needs, overall productivity would improve. Two related theories include Maslow's hierarchy of needs and Herzberg's motivation-hygiene theory.

Maslow's hierarchy of needs (based on Abraham Maslow's theory that people experience problems when their needs are not met) can be illustrated by a pyramid. At the top is self-actualization and fulfillment of potential. Next, in order, are esteem (self-esteem as well as esteem by others), then social acceptance, security (from harm, job loss, etc.), and finally physiological comfort (safety from hunger, thirst, cold, etc.). Maslow theorized that the more these needs are met, the more likely the person is to be a well-centered individual. This theory relates directly to human relations theory in that a management that considers its employees' needs and attempts to meet as many as possible is likely to produce the most efficient, happy workers.

> **Review Video: Maslow's Hierarchy of Needs EXPLAINED**
> Visit mometrix.com/academy and enter code: 461825

Herzberg's motivation-hygiene theory is based on the idea that people are influenced by both positive rewards (motivation) and negative repercussions (which he called hygiene factors). He felt that motivation comes from within each employee, and that negative factors come from those things outside the employees' control (such as things controlled or influenced by supervisors or others in a company). Dissatisfaction results from poor working conditions, work relationships, salary issues, company policies or procedures with which the employee disagrees, poor supervision, bad relations with coworkers, etc. Motivation occurs when the employee feels responsible, has a chance to advance, enjoys his/her work, feels accomplished, and is rewarded for a job well done through some sort of recognition.

CULTURAL INTELLIGENCE

Cultural intelligence is a measure of one's capability to interact suitably with people from other cultures and to behave appropriately in multicultural situations. It involves the following:

- **Motivational drives**: personal interests and confidence in multicultural situations
- **Knowledge and attitudes**: learning and accepting how cultures are similar or different
- **Cognitive or strategic thinking**: awareness and ability to plan for multicultural interactions
- **Behavioral actions**: talent for relating and working with others of differing backgrounds

Learning about one's own culture is vital to cultural intelligence because it provides a more objective model when gaining familiarity about other cultures. Exploring diverse cultural values and expectations may help address insecurities and introduce new attitudes or behaviors that appreciate differences. Some considerations when comparing cultures may be how relationships are viewed, local laws, societal norms, and so on. **Cultural intelligence** is much more than knowing what kinds of gifts are appropriate, when to bow, and which nonverbal gestures to avoid. Cultural intelligence can be increased by learning a different language, attending a holiday celebration, or spending time in a cultural setting different than your own while sincerely asking questions about habits, attitudes, and beliefs. The key is to always concentrate on valuing and showing respect for others.

CULTURAL NORMS, VALUES, AND DIMENSIONS
HALL MODEL OF ORGANIZATIONAL CULTURE

The Hall model, developed by Edward T. Hall, investigates cultural relationships and separates them into two classes: high contrast and low contrast. **High-contrast relationships** tend to last longer and have more defined patterns of behavior or boundaries of entry, such as families, religious congregations, or on-campus relations. In high-contrast environments, there may be more implicit communications, body language interpretation, shared values, and a great deal of commitment. **Low-contrast relationships** tend to be short term and require more rules and structure, such as a cafeteria line or making your way through a large, international airport. In low-contrast environments, there may be more explicit communications, diverse beliefs, and limited commitment. It should be noted that every culture will demonstrate a combination of both high- and low-contrast interactions.

HOFSTEDE MODEL OF CROSS-CULTURAL DIFFERENCES

The following are the six values identified by the Hofstede model of cross-cultural differences:

1. **Power distance** is the social acceptability of power distinctions, such as rich versus poor. In *lower-power distance societies,* high-power distance is regarded as undesirable, and inequalities are kept to a minimum. In *high-power distance societies,* power differences or castes are generally accepted, and those of particular status receive privileges.
2. **Uncertainty avoidance** is the acceptability of ambiguity and the unknown. Societies that practice *strong uncertainty avoidance* attempt to avoid risk and impose structure. Societies that practice *low uncertainty avoidance* view risk as unavoidable and are more tolerant to ambiguity.
3. **Individualism versus collectivism** is the relationship between society as a whole and the individual. *Individualistic cultures* believe in self-reliance and acting in the best interest of the individual. Power is more evenly distributed, and economic mobility is attainable. *Collective cultures* believe in cohesiveness and are loyal to the best interests of the entire group. Power is contained within the in group, and economic mobility is limited.

85

4. **Masculinity versus femininity** is the societal perception of the value of typical male and female traits. *Low-masculinity societies* accept the blending of male and female roles and tend to favor traits like cooperation and modesty. *High-masculinity societies* accept clearly defined gender roles, and traits like achievement, assertiveness, and competition are championed.
5. **Long-term orientation versus short-term normative orientation** describes a society's propensity to remain traditional or change with the times. Low-scoring societies are skeptical of change and hold steadfast to their norms. High-scoring societies are likely to prepare for the future.
6. **Indulgence versus restraint** is whether a society values fun and gratification or regulation. Those societies that favor indulgence allow members to give in to their desire for enjoyment. Those that favor restraint suppress these desires.

SCHEIN'S MODEL OF ORGANIZATIONAL CULTURE

Edgar Schein developed his well-known **model of organizational culture** in the 1980s. Many of Schein's studies indicate that culture is rooted with the CEO and developed over time. The model separates culture into three core layers: 1) artifacts, 2) values and beliefs, and 3) underlying assumptions. The first layer, **artifacts**, is the most visible. This includes the vision and mission, office dress codes, and generally accepted behaviors. Employee **values**, thought patterns, and organizational goals make up the second layer. The deepest layer is the **underlying assumptions**, ideologies, and perceptions of the organization. These cannot be easily measured but can greatly affect the organizational culture.

TROMPENAARS' MODEL OF ORGANIZATION CULTURE

Fons Trompenaars designed a model of organizational culture that divides people and cultures into seven dimensions:

- **Universalism versus particularism**—what's more important (rules vs. relationships)?
- Individualism versus communitarianism—who comes first (me vs. community)?
- **Specific versus diffuse**—how much separation (work/life balance vs. work/life blend)?
- **Neutral versus affective**—what's appropriate (reason vs. emotion)?
- **Achievement versus ascription**—do we need to prove status or title (accomplishments vs. identity)?
- **Sequential time versus synchronous time**— how do we work (focused vs. multitasking, punctual vs. flexible schedule)?
- **Internal direction versus outer direction**—what's in control (autonomy vs. circumstance)?

BEST PRACTICES FOR MANAGING GLOBALLY DIVERSE WORKFORCES

Diversity fosters the potential for more perspectives, creative ideas, and innovation. **Inclusion** involves realizing and accepting the benefits and competitive advantage to be had when everyone feels welcome and respected. This environment can be developed with openness, cultural sensitivity, and equal support. Human resource practitioners can advocate for a diverse and inclusive workplace by reflecting how it can align with business objectives. Building diverse teams can improve problem-solving and productivity and may increase customer satisfaction by providing better representation of an employer's stakeholders. Once buy-in has been gained from upper management, a **diversity committee** can collaborate to design and communicate initiatives.

Human resources practitioners should identify if there are any areas of concern or need in the organization. Do current employees fairly represent the available talent pool? Human resources

should work to address any unconscious biases or prevailing attitudes in policies or practices that do not support diversity initiatives. Human resources practitioners can further support diversity by drawing attention to and eliminating discriminatory perspectives or prejudices. They should train managers how to fairly and consistently conduct interviews and to supervise employees from various backgrounds. Moreover, providing appropriate **accommodations** to employees in need can increase safety, efficiency, and team morale.

Human resource practitioners should create programs that outline and reinforce organizational core values and ensure that employees who embody those values are recognized and rewarded. Training programs can educate managers and employees about work values, regardless of national origin or home culture. **Behavioral norms** that are consistent with company values can then be cultivated.

Human resource departments need to adjust their strategies when the **company structure** evolves to international, multinational, or global levels. This might involve learning about new cultures, religious customs, foreign labor laws, safety regulations, union activity, or economics. Knowledge of expatriation, repatriation, and global compensation are additional assets for human resource practitioners. Some companies may choose to seek consultation with a local specialist in payroll laws and taxation to assist in-house human resources.

INTERACTIONS AND CONFLICTS OF PROFESSIONAL AND CULTURAL VALUES

Research suggests that one's home national culture has a greater impact on thought processes and behaviors than the culture of the current organization. As such, if the cultural values of one's home nation and the cultural values of one's workplace aren't in alignment, conflict may arise. Because organizations are becoming much more diverse and globally dispersed, this type of conflict is common. The conflict may arise due to differences in things like communication style, perceptions of hierarchy, decision-making processes, the need for physical space, adherence to timelines, and many others. Leaders need to develop their cultural intelligence and work with these differences to reduce conflict. They can also try to facilitate constructive conflict, where employees and leaders collaborate through their cultural differences.

Methods for Analyzing Employee Attitudes, Opinions, and Satisfaction

FOCUS GROUPS

Focus groups can be used to glean employee views and concerns. They may be used to assess a new benefit plan or organizational change. Most **focus groups** contain five to 12 voluntary **participants**, with three to 10 groups in total. Participants should be informed about the subject of the focus group, about who will benefit, and that the information will be kept confidential. Participants may be selected at random or through the use of certain applicable filters. Focus group organizers should ensure that power differentials within the group are avoided. It's also important to involve participants from various levels of staff so they can fully represent the affected population. A neutral **facilitator** should be chosen to lead the discussion and ask open-ended, guided questions. Following the meeting, collected data should be analyzed and reported.

STAY INTERVIEWS

A **stay interview** is a purposeful yet casual conversation between an employee and a company leader regarding the employee's propensity to leave the organization. The leader will ask the employee questions such as the following:

- What keeps you in your current role?
- What might cause you to leave the company?
- What's important to you professionally?
- What can I do to improve your overall work experience with the firm?

The objective is to increase the employee's engagement and prevent turnover.

SURVEYS

Employee surveys can be valuable when examining employee engagement levels and job satisfaction. These surveys, whether created externally or internally, may be completed on a number of websites and platforms. Employee participation should be voluntary and anonymous. If they want to participate, employees should be provided with time during the workday to complete the survey. The survey should be available long enough to give all departments and shifts ample time to participate.

Many third-party vendors and national agencies conduct regular surveys and publish statistics. Human resource practitioners should benchmark their own survey results against these results or those of similar organizations before presenting findings to the executive leadership team. Generalized survey results and plans to address concerns raised should be shared with the employees as soon as practically possible after the survey period ends. **Employee engagement** should be analyzed on a regular basis, and survey results should be kept on file for data comparison over time. Moreover, survey items should be measured against organizational **key performance indicators (KPIs)** like quality, productivity, and customer satisfaction.

Diversity and Inclusion

APPROACHES TO AN INCLUSIVE WORKPLACE

First, identify any areas of concern. An internal workforce should reflect the available labor market. Examine the corporate culture and communications to ensure that they advocate for a diverse and inclusive workplace. Review or amend policies and practices to support an inclusive culture. Focus on the behavioral aspects, how people communicate, and how people work together. Are all perspectives respected and input from all positions valued? Address any areas that might not welcome protected classes or disabilities. Then brainstorm approaches and ideas for an **inclusive workplace**. Once a **diverse culture** is established, target recruiting efforts to reach a broad audience. Some ideas may include college recruiting, training centers, career fairs, veteran's offices, and state unemployment offices or career centers. Set business objectives for areas that can be improved upon, document what changes will be implemented, and review progress.

DIVERSITY TRAINING

Although we most often think of diversity as the inclusiveness of minorities, diversity may also embrace a robust variety of traits such as generation, gender, sexual orientation, race, ethnicity, language, religious background, education, or life experiences. Diversity is the ability to consider and value the perspectives of all people. It is important for human resource practitioners to recognize that everyone has both conscious and unconscious biases. **Diversity and inclusion training** supports establishing a nonjudgmental and collaborative workforce that is respectful and

sensitive to differences among peers. Additionally, it can teach humility and self-awareness. Training program methods may be extensive or address specific gaps. Moreover, diversity and inclusion training may introduce new perspectives to the workforce, promoting creativity and innovation.

> **Review Video: Diversity and Inclusion**
> Visit mometrix.com/academy and enter code: 990195

MANAGING A MULTIGENERATIONAL WORKFORCE

Human resource practitioners must learn how to manage a **multigenerational workforce**. We currently have baby boomers nearing retirement, Generation X gaining experience, and millennials becoming leaders in the workforce. Soon, Generation Z will join in the workforce. How can employers address the management needs of this multigenerational workforce and their diverse sets of values? The most obvious change in values is the **loyalty factor** of each generation. Baby boomers began their careers believing they might have only a few employers over the course of their working years, whereas Generation X workers are more likely to change employers frequently to gain experience and better salaries. Millennial and Generation Z workers show the least amount of loyalty to their employers. Instead, they want to define their own careers and work their way. Millennial workers are more **entrepreneurial**, and Generation Z workers are anticipated to flood the **freelance markets**. Work/life balance and the chance to make a difference are valued more in the younger workforce. In return, they bring more tech savvy, social media branding, and adaptability. Millennial workers desire constant **feedback**; annual reviews will not do. Weekly or even daily one-on-one meetings will help motivate millennial workers and provide them with favored inspiration and direction. Millennials want plenty of learning opportunities and a manager who is concerned with their **career growth**. Coaching, mentoring, and on-the-job training are attractive qualities for this generation. Millennials flourish when they have freedom for creative expression and clear areas of responsibility.

DEMOGRAPHIC BARRIERS ENCOUNTERED IN TODAY'S WORKPLACE

The Civil Rights Act prohibits **sex or religious discrimination** regarding any employment condition, including hiring, firing, promotional advancements, transfers, compensation, or admissions into training programs. The condition in which many women experience subtle forms of discrimination that limit their career advancement is referred to as the **glass ceiling**. It encompasses a host of attitudinal and organizational barriers that prevent women from receiving information, training, encouragement, and other opportunities to assist in advancement. The Civil Rights Act does not protect sexual orientation, but other legal actions at the federal level have come to protect those attracted to or married to the same sex in recent years. The EEOC has ruled that **gender identity discrimination** can be asserted as claims of sex discrimination under existing law. Preferential treatment for any particular gender or religious quality is strictly prohibited unless there is a bona fide occupational qualification. Customer preference is not a defense against discrimination to appearances that deviate from the norm, such as a Muslim woman wearing a hijab (headscarf), Rastafarian dreadlocks, Jewish sidelocks, or a Sikh's turban and uncut hair.

SUPPORTING A LGBTQ WORKFORCE

There has been increasing attention on the rights of the **lesbian, gay, bisexual, transgender, and queer (LGBTQ) community** in the past few years. Many states have expanded civil rights to include **LGBTQ discrimination protection** for sexual orientation of employees and applicants. In most cases, gender identity is also protected. Presidents Obama and Trump have both enforced **workplace regulations** for the LGBTQ community; ensuring a work environment free from harassment and oppression has never been more important. There are a few states that have not

89

joined in the fight for LGBTQ equality. However, employers should remain vigilant in adhering to local regulations and accommodating LGBTQ needs, which may require the availability of benefits for domestic partners or a unisex restroom for transgender workers.

WORKPLACE ACCOMMODATIONS
ACCOMMODATIONS FOR DISABILITIES

If a job candidate or employee is disabled, but otherwise qualified, the employer must make reasonable workplace accommodations. For the accommodation to be reasonable, it must not cause the employer undue hardship. Some examples of disability accommodation are making the building more accessible (via ramps, elevators, redesigned restrooms, etc.); altering work duties, location, or schedule; ordering assistive equipment (like a screen magnifier or standing desk); modifying policies, performance assessment tools, or training materials, and more. Human resources should create a policy detailing how accommodation requests should be made, how they will be evaluated, and what appeals process exists if the request is denied.

ACCOMMODATIONS FOR RELIGION

Employers must accommodate job candidate or employee sincerely held religious beliefs so long as doing so doesn't cause the company undue hardship. Possible religious accommodations include allowing time off for religious holidays and having different dress and grooming rules. Human resources should create a policy detailing how accommodation requests should be made, how they will be evaluated, and what appeals process exists if the request is denied.

ACCOMMODATIONS FOR VETERANS AND ACTIVE MILITARY

Employers must accommodate disabled veterans in the same manner as they would any other job candidate or employee. There are two main laws, Family and Medical Leave Act (FMLA) and Uniformed Services Employment and Reemployment Rights Act (USERRA), that protect the employment of veterans and active-duty military. Employers may choose, however, to provide additional accommodation to service members. While the employee is away serving, the firm could decide to continue paying for medical coverage and make up the difference in compensation between the salary and military pay. Human resources should create a policy detailing how accommodation requests should be made, how they will be evaluated, and what appeals process exists if the request is denied.

> **Review Video: Diversity and Inclusion**
> Visit mometrix.com/academy and enter code: 990195

Occupational Injury and Illness Prevention

WORKPLACE ILLNESS, INJURY PREVENTION, INVESTIGATION, REPORTING, AND ACCOMMODATION

The **Occupational Safety and Health Act of 1970** mandates that it is the employer's responsibility to provide an environment that is free from known hazards that are causing or may cause serious harm or death to employees. The only workers who are not protected by this act are those who are self-employed, family farms where only family members work, and workplaces that are covered by other federal statutes or state and local government. This act is monitored and enforced by **OSHA**. OSHA ensures employees have a safe workplace free from recognized hazards. It also requires all employers and each employee to comply with occupational safety and health standards, rules, and

regulations. Employers may be found in violation if they are aware or should have been aware of potential hazards that could cause injury or death.

> **Review Video: What is OSHA (Occupational Safety and Health Administration)**
> Visit mometrix.com/academy and enter code: 913559

OCCUPATIONAL INJURIES TO BE REPORTED

OSHA requires that any occupational injury or illness be **recorded** if it results in medical treatment that goes beyond first aid, restricted work activity or job transfer, time away from work, loss of consciousness, or death. An incident that results in an inpatient hospitalization must be reported within 24 hours, and any incident resulting in an employee's death must be reported to the nearest OSHA office within eight hours. For each recordable injury or illness, an **OSHA Form 301 Injury and Illness Incident Report** must be completed within seven calendar days. Employers are obligated to keep a log of all incidents on **OSHA Form 300 Log of Work-Related Injuries and Illnesses**, and a concise report of annual incidents should be reported on **OSHA Form 300A Summary of Work-Related Injuries and Illnesses** at the end of each year. Forms 300 and 300A should be posted no later than February 1 through April 30, and all documentation should be kept for five years so it is available on request for examination. Any procedure or doctor's visit that can be labeled as first aid does not need to be recorded. However, any needle-stick injury, cut from a sharp object contaminated with another person's blood, or incision that requires stitches should be reported.

ILLNESS AND INJURY PREVENTION

Preventing workplace illness and injury includes training employees, following OSHA standards, and being mindful of and preparing for the potential hazards typically seen in the line of duty.

RECORD KEEPING

The Fair Labor Standards Act established regulations requiring employers to record information related to an employee's personal information, pay period, and pay. Personal information required to be recorded are name, address, occupation, and the individual's date of birth if 18 or younger. Pay period information includes the specific day and time the pay period begins, the date payment is issued for the period, the total hours worked by the individual each day, and for the period. The specific pay includes the total regular pay an individual receives per day, the total overtime pay received for the period, the regular wage if overtime is worked, the total pay received for the period, any deductions such as tax withholdings from the individual's pay, and any additions such as bonuses.

Workplace Safety and Security Risks

WORKPLACE VIOLENCE

Due to the growing number of workplace assaults and homicides, it is suggested that human resource managers be prepared and implement policies such as the following:

- **Zero tolerance**—prohibiting any act of violence in the workplace, including verbal threats
- **Prevention**—presenting strategies and training to help managers recognize danger signs
- **Crisis management**—plans for responding to threats or acts of violence
- **Recovery**—providing support and counseling for victims and survivors that may suffer trauma

To reduce the likelihood that a troubled employee might become violent, managers should be encouraged to practice the following:

- Disciplining employees should be done one-on-one as a private matter as opposed to in public.
- Employees should have an opportunity to explain or tell their side of the story.
- Managers should refrain from disciplining employees when the manager is angry. Even if the employee's behavior may warrant immediate action, the employee should be removed from the scene, and disciplinary action should be discussed and decided at a later meeting.
- Try to calm angry workers or have a friend accompany them when leaving.

FRAUD AND THEFT

A serious concern for all companies is illegal or dishonest behavior, such as theft, embezzlement, falsifying records, or misuse of company property. Committing **fraud** often involves at least one of three main forces: situational pressure, opportunity to commit fraud, or personal integrity. When employees are suspected of stealing, companies must decide whether to conduct an investigation or prosecute. Investigations and prosecutions can be costly; however, most cases are investigated, and some will result in termination, whereas others may result in prosecution. Organizations may also adopt **anti-fraud programs** to increase early detection and decrease opportunities. These programs often contain these elements: reporting, oversight, prudence, communication, compliance, enforcement, prevention, and advocating personal integrity. Companies prone to theft and dishonest behavior, such as retail corporations, often have **loss prevention departments** dedicated to protecting assets and cash while minimizing and detecting inventory shrinkage.

CORPORATE ESPIONAGE

When employees give corporate trade secrets to another organization, they are committing **corporate espionage**. They are giving the receiving firm a competitive advantage and may cause the other company to lose customers, sales, human capital, market share, or all of the above. Firms can protect themselves by requiring employees to sign nondisclosure or noncompete agreements. These outline what information is protected and what happens when an employee (or former employee) violates the agreement. Companies should also restrict their most important classified information to a small group of personnel that need it to do their jobs.

SABOTAGE

Sabotage in the workplace is the act of destroying or disrupting business operations. It can be overt through behaviors such as erasing important files, intentionally failing to complete certain key tasks, or spreading rumors. It can also be much more subtle and occur through behaviors such as taking a meeting off topic, practicing perfectionism, or being totally unwilling to bend the rules for overall gain or greater good. To combat deliberate sabotage efforts, firms should have a code of conduct in place that forbids such behavior and spells out what happens when an employee violates the code. To address the less direct forms of sabotage, leaders should be trained to detect that it's happening and firmly take charge to nip those behaviors in the bud.

KIDNAPPING AND RANSOM

When employees are kidnapped and ransomed, it's a terrifying ordeal for them, their families, and the organization. However, the firm can take several steps to both prevent a kidnapping from occurring and handle it effectively should it happen. First and foremost, the company should address the threat of kidnapping in a given area. It should also create a clear plan for how it would negotiate in a hostage situation. If an area is high risk, the firm should consider if it's worth having personnel there. If employees are sent or located in that area, firms should teach them how to

detect threats and be mindful of their surroundings. They should also be trained how to act if they are kidnapped. Best practices include speaking about their personal lives and families so that kidnappers see them as humans and not as a commodity for sale. Those who are kidnapped should avoid speaking about hot button issues like politics or religion. Companies should also inform employees what to do when they're rescued. For example, employees shouldn't run toward the rescue team because they might be mistaken as being a part of the enemy group. As the situation is happening, the company should provide support to the hostage employee's family and keep a low media profile. The media can make things worse depending on what information gets released and is seen by the kidnappers. Finally, companies should consider purchasing kidnap and ransom insurance, which will help cover the cost of the ransom should a kidnapping occur.

MENTAL HEALTH

Although mental health is not covered by Occupational Safety and Health Administration (OSHA), it is integral to a healthy and successful workforce, and employees could receive workers' compensation for physical or mental breakdowns that are caused by the cumulative trauma of a highly stressful occupation. Four of the main challenges to **mental health** are burnout, anxiety, depression, and boredom. Additionally, individuals respond to environmental stressors with three phases: the **alarm reaction** (the adrenaline rush in which endocrine system triggers the body into fight-or-flight mode); the **resistance stage** (in which the body tries to regain balance); and the **exhaustion phase** (at which point the body has endured severe weakening and can no longer adapt). There are a few common **coping strategies**: eliminate the stressor, often through the avoidance of exposure or additional responsibilities; relaxation techniques, such as massage, yoga, breathing exercises, or biofeedback; social support, frequently through a network of family, friends, or community membership; and physical exercise programs that remove tension caused by stress.

Emergency Response, Business Continuity, and Disaster Recovery

PREPARING FOR EMERGENCIES AND NATURAL DISASTERS

Because it is an employer's obligation to provide a safe and healthy work environment, many companies have begun to create **emergency and disaster plans** for handling situations such as fires, explosions, earthquakes, chemical spills, communicable disease outbreaks, and acts of terrorism. These plans should include the following steps:

1. Clarify the **chain of command**, and inform staff who to contact and who has authority.
2. Someone should be responsible for **accounting** for all employees when an emergency strikes.
3. A **command center** should be set up to coordinate communications.
4. Employees should be **trained annually** on what to do if an emergency strikes.
5. Businesses should have **first-aid kits and basic medical supplies** available. This includes water fountains and eye wash stations in areas where spills may occur.
6. An **emergency team of employees** should be named and trained for the following:
   a. Organizing evacuation procedures
   b. Initiating shutdown procedures
   c. Using fire extinguishers
   d. Using oxygen and respirators
   e. Searching for disabled or missing employees
   f. Assessing when it is safe to reenter the building

SAFETY AND HEALTH MANAGEMENT PLANS

According to Occupational Safety and Health Administration (OSHA), there are four characteristics a safety and health management plan should have to be considered effective. First, an effective plan should establish a specific system that an organization can use to identify hazards in the workplace. Second, the plan should establish a training program that teaches employees to avoid hazards and to perform tasks in the safest way possible. Third, an effective safety and health management plan should include specific procedures and programs designed to eliminate hazards that the organization identified or at least minimize the risk that a hazard will injure or kill an employee or cause an employee to become ill. Finally, it should allow employees at all levels of the organization to be involved in the identification, prevention, and elimination of hazards in the workplace.

EMERGENCY ACTION PLANS

There is certain information that should be included in every organization's emergency action plan. All emergency action plans should explain the alarm system that will be used to inform employees and other individuals at the worksite that they need to evacuate. They should also include in-depth exit route plans that describe which routes employees should take to escape the building and in-depth plans that describe what actions employees should take before evacuating: shutting down equipment, closing doors, and so on. All emergency action plans should also include detailed systems for handling different types of emergencies and a system that can be used to verify that all employees have escaped the worksite.

FIRE PREVENTION PLANS

There is a variety of different information that should be included in a fire prevention plan, and the specific information included in a fire prevention plan will vary from organization to organization. However, certain information should be included in every organization's fire prevention plan. All fire prevention plans should provide detailed descriptions of the specific areas where employees can find fire extinguishers and other fire prevention equipment, detailed descriptions of the types of fire hazards present in the workplace, and detailed descriptions of the appropriate procedures that should be followed to avoid these fire hazards. Fire prevention plans should also provide detailed descriptions of any hazardous waste that may be a fire hazard and the appropriate way to dispose of or store hazardous waste to avoid a fire.

EMERGENCY RESPONSE PLANS

All emergency response plans should identify the records and resources essential to the organization, identify the individuals responsible for protecting those records and resources, and describe the procedures that individuals should follow to safeguard the records and resources essential for the organization to continue functioning. Emergency response plans must also establish a system the organization can use to continue communicating with vendors and the public during and after an emergency.

DISASTER RECOVERY PLANS

Certain information should be included in every organization's disaster recovery plan. Equipment and locations that can be utilized temporarily in the event of an emergency should be identified. Also, agencies and personnel that may be able to help the organization continue functioning immediately after an emergency should be identified. It is also wise to establish a set of procedures the organization can use to bring the personnel and equipment together after an emergency. Disaster recovery plans should also identify alternative sources the organization can use to receive supplies or products if the emergency disables the organization's normal supply chain.

BUSINESS CONTINUITY PLANNING AND RECOVERY

Business continuity planning is a process in which an organization attempts to ensure the organization will be able to continue functioning even after an emergency. This type of planning is important because there are a large number of emergencies that an organization can face, and each one may affect the ability of the organization to continue functioning normally. As a result, business continuity planning is a process that organizations use to create a plan or group of plans that will help the organization return to normal after a natural disaster or similar emergency occurs. The process of business continuity planning usually begins with an organization conducting a threat assessment such as a SWOT analysis. Once the organization has identified the threats that exist, the organization can rank those threats based on the risk associated with each threat. Finally, the organization can create a plan or set of plans that establish a system the organization can use to recover from emergencies, which the organization can continually update as threats to the organization change.

> **Review Video: <u>Emergency Response, Business Continuity, and Disaster Planning</u>**
> Visit mometrix.com/academy and enter code: 678024

Internal Investigation, Monitoring, and Surveillance

WORKPLACE INJURY OR ILLNESS INVESTIGATION

When an employee is injured on the job or becomes ill as a result of completing work duties, the employer must investigate the incident to understand why it happened. This investigation should identify ways to prevent similar incidents from occurring in the future. An employer's internal investigation should entail interviewing the sick or injured employee, assessing that employee's immediate work environment, and interviewing other employees who may have witnessed the incident or worked under the same conditions. The OSHA Form 301 Injury and Illness Incident Report should be completed for all recordable incidents. However, employers may want to document the incident further for internal purposes. If that's the case, they should create a standardized form for collecting the details to ensure that each investigation is conducted in a similar fashion and that no important information gets overlooked. Sometimes, OSHA will investigate an employer. These investigations may occur either on- or off-site.

ON-SITE INVESTIGATIONS

In certain situations, OSHA may decide it is necessary to conduct an on-site investigation into the working conditions of a particular worksite. These investigations are usually unannounced, but each investigation will follow a set of specific procedures established by OSHA, which an employer or human resource professional should keep in mind. First, a trained investigator from OSHA known as a compliance safety and health officer (CSHO) will travel to the worksite and inform the employer or a member of the employer's staff that he or she has come to perform an investigation of the worksite. Once the employer has verified that the CSHO's credentials are in order, at an opening conference, the CSHO will inform the organization's management of exactly what is being investigated at the worksite and why the investigation is taking place. The CSHO will then tour the facilities with a member of management and usually with an employee. Once the CSHO has completed his or her tour, the CSHO will then inform the employer of any violations at a closing conference.

The number of investigations OSHA can conduct at any one time is relatively low as the agency has a limited number of CSHOs available at any given time. As a result, OSHA uses a priority system to

identify which worksites should be investigated first based on the level of danger associated with the worksite. This priority system includes five levels, and each priority level represents a certain amount of danger associated with the worksite. The five levels of the priority system from lowest to highest priority are follow-up inspections, planned or programmed high-hazard inspections, inspections resulting from employee complaints, inspections resulting from catastrophes or fatal accidents, and inspections resulting from imminent danger.

Follow-up investigations are any investigation conducted by a CSHO to verify that an employer has taken action to eliminate any health or safety violations the CSHO previously identified. Follow-up investigations are considered to be the fifth priority level, which is the lowest priority assigned by OSHA. A planned or programmed high-hazard inspection is an investigation scheduled for a particular worksite because the worksite is involved in an industry identified as extremely dangerous. These investigations are considered to be the fourth priority level, which is the second-lowest priority assigned by OSHA. Investigations resulting from an employee complaint include any situation in which OSHA has received a specific complaint from an employee about unsafe or unhealthy working conditions and that employee has requested an investigation. These investigations are considered to be the third priority level, which is the mid-level priority.

The OSHA investigation priority system consists of five levels, and the two highest priority levels are the catastrophes and fatal accidents level and the imminent danger level. Investigations resulting from catastrophes and fatal accidents refer to any investigation required because at least three employees have been hospitalized due to an accident at a worksite or at least one employee has died from an accident at a worksite. These investigations are considered to be the second priority level and are therefore given the second-highest priority. Investigations resulting from imminent danger refer to any investigation required because it is likely an individual will die or be seriously injured in the near future due to the working conditions of a particular worksite. Investigations at the imminent danger level are assigned the highest priority by OSHA and are usually investigated first.

> **Review Video: What is OSHA**
> Visit mometrix.com/academy and enter code: 913559

OFF-SITE INVESTIGATIONS

In certain situations, OSHA may decide it is necessary to conduct an off-site investigation into the working conditions of a particular worksite. OSHA may conduct an off-site investigation if the employees at a worksite do not appear to be in imminent danger of harm due to the health and safety violations that may be occurring at a worksite, the worksite is not related to an industry identified as high risk or already scheduled for an investigation, the employer does not have a history of any serious violations, and the employer has complied with any OSHA requests made prior to the complaint or report. If OSHA determines an off-site investigation is necessary, but an on-site investigation is not, it will contact the employer by phone and identify the specific violation(s) that have been reported. Once the employer has been contacted, the company has five days to mail or fax a written description of any health and safety issues identified and a plan for addressing those issues.

VIOLATION TYPES

There are six different types of violations an OSHA investigation can identify: de-minimus, other-than-serious, serious, failure to abate, repeat, and willful. A de-minimus violation is a violation of a standard not currently affecting the health or safety of employees. Other-than-serious is a violation of a standard affecting the health and safety of employees, but there is no imminent danger of harm.

96

A violation identified as serious is a violation of a standard in which there is imminent danger that an employee may be seriously injured or even killed. A violation identified as a failure to abate will be issued if the employer continues to violate a specific standard past the abatement date established by a previous OSHA investigation. A violation will be identified as a repeat violation if the employer continues to violate a standard that is the same or similar to a violation identified by a previous OSHA investigation. Finally, a willful violation will be issued if the employer has intentionally violated or ignored OSHA standards.

PENALTIES

Each of the six types of violations an OSHA investigation has a different penalty range associated with it. In the case of a de-minimus violation, the employer will be informed of the violation, but will not be cited for it. In the case of other-than serious or serious violations, the employer will receive a citation and may have to pay fines up to $7,000 per violation. In the case of a failure-to-abate violation, the employer will receive a citation and may have to pay fines up to $7,000 per day for each day that the violation continues after the abatement date. In the case of a repeat violation, the employer will receive a citation and may have to pay fines up to $70,000 per violation. Finally, in the case of a willful violation, the employer will receive a citation and may have to pay fines of $5,000 - $70,000 and the employer may be subject to additional penalties and jail time if an employee death resulted from the violation.

Data Security and Privacy

DATA INTEGRITY

Data integrity involves maintaining and protecting data content to ensure that it is complete, accurate, and reliable. The design, implementation, and usage throughout the **data life cycle** is critical to any system that stores or processes data. Individual users, management, culture, training, controls, and audits can all affect **data integrity**. Poor configuration and inaccurate data entry can corrupt data. Therefore, thorough testing and safeguarding of data is required to avoid spending many hours debugging and reconciling information. Moreover, policies and training on what to do in the event of a breach can help mitigate risk by increasing staff awareness and ability to fight off breaches.

CONFIDENTIALITY AND DISCLOSURES

Confidentiality disclosures should include definitions and exclusions of confidential information while outlining individual responsibilities. **Confidentiality disclosures** are used to keep private or secure information available only to those who are authorized to access it. It is important to ensure that only the proper individuals have access to the information needed to perform their jobs. Moreover, legislation mandates **due diligence** to protect the confidential information of employees and customers. **Technology breaches** in confidentiality could happen via phone, fax, computer, email, and electronic records. For this reason, some businesses might utilize an encryption software, limit the communications that can be sent via email, and include a statement notifying the reader what to do if it is inadvertently sent to the wrong person.

IMPORTANCE OF IT SECURITY

IT security is becoming a more serious topic and rapidly gaining more attention. It is important for human resource practitioners to be conscientious of controls to mitigate organizational exposure and risk. Some companies may have **IT security policies and acknowledgements** in place to reduce liability. Identify and document compliance and security controls. Multiple layers of corporate IT security might include the encryption of data files, firewalls, access controls or logins,

systems monitoring, detection processes, antivirus software, cyber insurance, and so on. Implementing stronger IT security can provide companies with benefits such as mitigating lost revenue, protecting brand reputation, and supporting mobilization.

Collective Bargaining

NEGOTIATION

Negotiation is a vital technique for every business professional. New or expired contracts and changing behaviors require skillful **negotiations**. Human resource practitioners must know how to handle negotiations to successfully avoid conflicts, improve relations, secure pay rates, and evaluate contracts. It is paramount to note that negotiations are possible only when all parties are open to compromise and finding solutions that are mutually satisfying.

PERSPECTIVE TAKING

Perspective taking involves deeply understanding the position of the other party. If the negotiator understands where the other party is coming from, he or she will be better able to offer a deal that works well for both parties.

PRINCIPLED BARGAINER

The **principled bargainer** views negotiations as fluid, exploratory conversations, guided by principles, to ultimately achieve mutually beneficial solutions. Rather than viewing the other party as an adversary or that a negotiation is something to be won, a principled bargainer sees all parties involved as problem-solvers looking for the most efficient outcome for everyone. This is commonly known as a win-win form of negotiation.

INTEREST-BASED BARGAINING

A principled bargainer will utilize interest-based bargaining to establish a win-win deal for all parties involved. The parties begin the negotiation process by plainly stating their main interests. The process involves coming to an agreement that satisfies those interests while minimizing the pain of any concessions to be made.

AUCTION

An auction can be a great bargaining strategy when a decision needs to be made quickly and will solely be based on price. However, if service and value are important to the parties involved, and time permits, entering into a negotiation process may be a better solution. Negotiations can account for more nuances and can be handled discreetly.

BARGAINING STRUCTURES AND PROCESSES

Although traditional labor agreements are between a single union and a single employer, labor agreements and **collective bargaining** can take many forms. **Single union-single employer bargaining** is by far the most common. **Multi-employer bargaining** or **coalition bargaining** takes place between multiple employers and a single union; if the agreement includes all employers in an industry, it is referred to as industry-wide bargaining. **Coordinated bargaining** involves multiple unions and a single employer. Finally, national or local bargaining consists of agreements negotiated at the national level on economic issues or local on working conditions or other contractual conflicts. The bargaining process contains **four key stages**: opening presentation of demands, analyzing demands, compromises, and informal settlement or ratification.

COLLECTIVE BARGAINING AGREEMENTS

Collective bargaining consists of management and union representatives coming together to reach an agreement that will be acceptable to each respective party. Most labor agreements, or contracts, are negotiated with little fuss or public awareness. Only a few have gained national attention and caused massive economic disruption.

The **Taft-Hartley Act** requires that union and management negotiate on wages, hours, and other terms or conditions of employment. The NLRB and courts have classified **bargaining issues** into three primary groups: illegal items, mandatory items, and voluntary items. Illegal items, such as trying to instate a closed shop, are prohibited by the NLRA. Mandatory items include things like wages, the grievance procedure, and how seniority is handled. Voluntary items, or permissive subjects such as dress code, can be brought up by either the employer or the union representative. Both parties have a right to refuse negotiating on permissive subjects.

Major issues surrounding collective bargaining are who will represent workers, which issues will be negotiated into the contract, what strategies will be used in bargaining, how bargaining impasses will be resolved, and how the contract will be administered. The actual labor agreement can cover many issues or just a few, depending upon the interests of each respective party. However, wording should be carefully considered to avoid any ambiguity or misinterpretation that may cause grievances. Most labor agreements will cover the following:

- Compensation and benefits
- Working conditions
- Seniority and job security
- Individual rights and discipline procedures
- Training and development
- Union security
- Contract duration
- Management freedoms
- How union dues are paid
- Grievance resolution
- Strikes and lockouts

CONTRACT NEGOTIATION

Both the employer and the union representative must negotiate in good faith. This means that they must enter into the negotiation with the goal of reaching consensus. However, that does not mean that either party needs to give in to the other. Bad faith negotiation is prohibited and can be characterized by behaviors such as making radical demands or intentionally delaying the bargaining process.

Negotiation meetings should be held at mutually agreeable times. Human resources needs to be willing to furnish employment-related information to facilitate the discussion. If the two parties cannot agree, they are at what's called a bargaining impasse and may need to use mediation to resolve their differences. Once an agreement is reached, the details must be written down. This document, once voted on by union members, becomes the union contract.

CONTRACT ADMINISTRATION PROCESS

Contract administration is the actual implementation of the labor agreement's provisions. For this process to go smoothly, management and the union steward need to be able to work closely

together and collaborate. This will require both parties to communicate effectively and develop a positive professional working relationship.

Performance Management

Performance management is the human resource function concerned with setting performance standards, evaluating employee effectiveness against those standards, identifying any problem areas, and implementing interventions to correct said problems. Performance management is vital because an organization can't thrive if individuals, teams, and departments aren't effective in their roles.

The performance management process can vary from organization to organization, but most firms follow three basic steps:

- Through activities like goal setting, needs analysis, and the creation of a corporate value statement and code of conduct, company leaders and human resource professionals establish organizational goals. They then identify the knowledge, skills, behaviors, and tasks required to achieve those goals and inform employees how to best work to meet the company's objectives.
- The firm's management then needs to monitor employee performance, document any problems, and help employees correct those problems, if possible.
- At predetermined intervals (typically once a year), managers will conduct in-depth performance appraisals for each employee. The appraisals measure performance during the preceding period (usually a year). Often, the manager and employee will set goals for the employee to work toward in the new appraisal period.

Excellent communication skills are essential for good performance management. They are important competencies used in the entire performance management process, from planning and communicating work expectations to recognizing employees for their successful achievements. To communicate effectively with employees, performance managers must:

- establish strong working relationships with employees.
- promote easy access to information and feedback.
- promote employee involvement in planning and development activities.
- recognize and praise top performers.

It must be remembered that establishing an effective working relationship with each employee takes time and effort. The best managers make certain each employee feels connected and valued. Competent managers individualize their efforts to communicate with employees, recognize employees' strengths, and support their development.

PRINCIPLES OF EFFECTIVE PERFORMANCE APPRAISAL

Performance appraisals serve four main organizational functions:

1. **Guide human resource decisions**—performance data is required for supporting and justifying promotion or termination decisions.
2. **Reward and motivate employees**—pay rate, status, and recognition should be based on performance.
3. **Promote personal development**—performance feedback will help employees identify strengths and improve weaknesses.

4. **Identify training needs**—a well-designed appraisal process establishes necessary skills and abilities for each role and identifies individuals, areas, or departments that could benefit from additional training.

Each employee's **performance** appraisal should assess the following:

1. Progress toward goals set at the last appraisal meeting
2. Completion of normal job duties
3. Organizational behaviors, such as cooperation, innovation, motivation, and attitude
4. Any notable achievements

PERFORMANCE APPRAISAL METHODS

There are many different performance appraisal methods; some involve feedback only from the immediate supervisor, and some involve the feedback of peers, clients, or subordinates. Many organizations begin the process with self-appraisals. **Self-appraisals** are most beneficial when used for personal development and identifying training needs but less beneficial when they are used as a basis for the formal evaluation process. Good supervisors are able to evaluate performance and give meaningful feedback. Hence, it should not be surprising that **supervisor appraisals** are typically required as at least one major component of the overall performance appraisal process. One type of appraisal that considers feedback from multiple sources is a **360-degree appraisal**. These appraisals have rapidly grown in popularity and are expected to share a broader perspective of performance because they include feedback from everyone the employee interacts with—managers, peers, clients, and subordinates.

RANKING TECHNIQUES OF APPRAISAL

Ranking procedures put employees in order from highest to lowest based upon evaluation characteristics, such as performance. There are three main forms of ranking: straight ranking, alternate ranking, and paired comparison. **Straight ranking** involves listing all employees in order with number one being the best, number two being second best, number three being third, and so on. **Alternate ranking** entails choosing the best and the worst from a list of all employees, removing these names from the list, and repeating until there are no names left. **Paired comparison** consists of evaluating only two employees at a time, deciding which is better, and continuing until each employee has been paired against every other employee. Ranking procedures assist with distributing budgeted pay increases that are more clearly tied to performance and eliminate some of the biases found in traditional review criterion. The forced-distribution method, also known as **forced ranking**, uses a bell curve in which the majority of employees will receive an average score and a small group will receive extremely high or extremely low performance scores.

RATING TECHNIQUES OF APPRAISAL

There is a variety of rating appraisal methods, but the two most common are the checklist method and the rating scale method. The checklist method is a series of statements describing a certain level of performance. The performance evaluator can then check a box next to the statement that best describes the individual's performance in each performance area. The rating scale method rates an individual's performance on a point scale, usually a 1–3, 1–4, 1–5, or 1–10 scale, with lower numbers representing poor performance and higher numbers representing superior performance.

BEHAVIORALLY BASED TECHNIQUES OF APPRAISAL

Greater focus on accountability and results has led to new approaches for appraising performance. Three main **behaviorally based appraisal methods** include management by objectives, behavioral anchored rating scale, and behavioral observation scale. **Management by objectives** is

proactive rather than reactive. It focuses on predicting and shaping the future on the company, accomplishing results rather than simply following directions, improving competence and effectiveness, as well as increasing participation and engagement of employees. **Behaviorally anchored rating scales (BARS)** assign numerical values to performance based upon a given range, for example, five-star systems or scales from 1 to 10. The BARS method analyzes the job description for a particular position and identifies the tasks that must be performed for the organization to function effectively. Once the tasks are identified, a determination is made about the specific way the individual should behave to perform each task. For example, if communication is identified as a necessary skill for a management position, an individual in that position must be able to keep others "in the loop." A series of statements that are ranked is then designed that describe how effectively the individual performed. Performance appraisers can then choose the statement that best describes the employee's behavior. The key benefits of behaviorally anchored rating systems are that they create agreement by being less subjective and more based upon observations, whereas characteristics are more carefully considered. **Behavior observation scales** are similar to behaviorally anchored rating scales but with greater focus on frequency of behavior than on quality of performance, for example, a sliding scale of always, sometimes, and never.

NARRATIVE TECHNIQUES OF APPRAISAL

The three most common narrative appraisal techniques are the critical incident method, the essay method, and the field review method. The **critical incident method** documents each performance problem related to an employee occurring during a set period so the evaluator can discuss problems with the employee at the end. The **essay method** requires performance evaluators to write a short essay about each employee describing the employee's performance during the performance period. The **field review method** is a method in which an individual other than the employee's direct supervisor or manager performs the appraisal and writes down a series of assessments and observations about that particular employee's performance.

COMMON PERFORMANCE APPRAISAL PROBLEMS

Performance evaluations are meant to measure performance of job objectives, but they can be tainted by a number of criterion problems. One dilemma is whether to focus evaluations on **outcomes and results** or **behaviors and activities**. Many will advocate that outcomes are more important than behaviors and will base performance on the measure of results. However, focusing only on outcomes can lure individuals to achieve results by unethical or adverse means. Evaluations should also measure performance results without contamination by factors that are beyond an individual's control, such as improper materials, poor equipment, or economic conditions. Furthermore, even performance evaluations that are consistent and reputable may be influenced by biases. The absence of standards to assist with grading performances can lead some evaluators to judge too harshly, some to inflate scores, and some to judge all performers concentrating in the middle. The best method ensures that group results form a **bell curve.**

PERFORMANCE APPRAISAL TRAINING

It is important for an organization to train performance evaluators to use appropriate appraisal methods because a performance appraisal is useful to the organization only if it is fair and accurate. This is because an organization's performance management process relies heavily on the ability of the organization to identify and eliminate performance problems. As a result, a performance appraisal must offer an accurate view of an individual's performance so the organization can accurately identify problem areas or performance issues and then improve these problem areas or handle these issues appropriately. However, there are a number of different factors, such as the evaluator's own biases or the appraisal process that the evaluator uses, that can influence a performance appraisal, so it can often be extremely difficult for a manager or supervisor to conduct

an appraisal that is completely fair and accurate. Therefore, to make sure that each manager or supervisor conducts each appraisal as effectively as possible, the organization must train each manager or supervisor to use the appropriate set of appraisal methods.

Termination

TERMINATIONS

Voluntary terminations may be caused by a variety of reasons, such as new job opportunity, relocation, or personal obligations. **Involuntary terminations** most often occur as a result of employment problems, such as poor performance, excessive absenteeism, insubordination, or theft. Employers should have controls that require all terminations to be **reviewed** in advance to avoid the risk of legal or contract violations. The review should determine whether there are valid, job-related reasons for the termination. If the termination is due to a particular incident, the review should conclude that a proper investigation has been documented. Additional documentation should show that the employee was made aware of performance problems and had an opportunity to correct behaviors. Terminations should also be consistent with prior treatment of other employees. Finally, it is imperative to ensure that the employee is not a victim of retaliation of any civil rights.

EMPLOYMENT-AT-WILL DOCTRINE

An **employment-at-will doctrine** essentially allows both the employer and the employee the mutual right to end the employment relationship at any time. This philosophy of hiring whomever you want for as long as you want was created to protect workers from wrongful terminations. In more recent years, the voluntary relationship has been challenged by state and case law to protect workers, with the exception of implied contracts, retaliatory discharges, and public policy exceptions. **Implied contracts** may be verbal or written promises by an employer to continue an employment relationship. However, some courts have recognized a promissory estoppel exception when an employer makes a promise that he or she reasonably expects the employee to rely upon, the employee does rely upon it, and the employee suffers financial or personal injury as a result.

PHR Practice Test #1

1. A marketing research company is considering budget constraints when implementing a training program. Which of the following roles will the human resources team likely play the biggest part in?

    a. Assist in preparing a cost-analysis review that will consider the expenses and benefits of each testing option

    b. Research the cost of each testing program to eliminate any options that exceed the budget constraints of the company

    c. Review options to determine if the company can utilize part of the testing program and avoid the full cost

    d. Recommend cost-cutting measures for other company activities to ensure that the necessary training can take place

2. Which of the following individuals is MOST appropriate to conduct exit interviews?

    a. direct supervisors

    b. senior executives

    c. a third party

    d. departmental managers

3. What was the primary directive of the Worker Adjustment and Retraining Notification Act?

    a. Employers must submit planned expansions to an employee vote.

    b. Displaced workers must be given assistance in relocating.

    c. The unemployed must have access to training programs.

    d. Employees and unions must be notified in advance about planned plant closings.

4. Which of the following types of health care plans does not require that patients first contact a "gatekeeper" for medical treatment but allows patients to choose from a broad network?

    a. Preferred Provider Organization (PPO)

    b. Point of Service (POS)

    c. Health Maintenance Organization (HMO)

    d. Fee for Service (FFS)

5. Arthur is an employee of a distribution company and is looking to request FMLA-approved leave for personal reasons. Arthur contacts Brad, a human resources professional at the company, to find out if he is eligible for this type of leave. Arthur has worked for the company for 9 months. What is the minimum period of time an employee needs to work for an employer to be eligible for leave according to FMLA guidelines?

    a. 8 months

    b. 10 months

    c. 12 months

    d. 15 months

6. Which of the following is NOT a step in the strategic planning process?
   a. Environmental scanning
   b. Formulating strategy
   c. Creating business plan
   d. Implementing strategy

7. Which of the following areas of risk is LEAST relevant to a human resources professional primary responsibilities:
   a. Workplace privacy
   b. Legal compliance
   c. Safety and health
   d. Business competition

8. Which of the following is not included as a job category under the EEO-1 report?
   a. Sales workers
   b. Service workers
   c. Craft workers
   d. Medical workers

9. The Expectancy Theory (1964) is attributed to which of the following researchers?
   a. Fredrick Herzberg
   b. Clayton Alderfer
   c. Abraham Maslow
   d. Victor Vroom

10. Which of the following steps is not a part of the human resources professional's role in following the guidelines of the Americans with Disabilities Act when an employee requests ADA accommodation?
   a. Request that the employee acquire medical certification of condition
   b. Meet with department supervisor to discuss employee accommodation
   c. Set up and mediate meeting between supervisor and employee
   d. Provide for all employee accommodation requests to ensure continued employment

11. Which of the following is a common problem during the growth phase of the organizational life cycle?
   a. outsourcing
   b. poor communication between management and employees
   c. excessive bureaucracy
   d. slow response to market changes

12. Why might a company's total rewards packages lag the market?
   a. The company is trying to attract top talent.
   b. The company is trying to establish itself in a new area.
   c. Turnover is high at the company.
   d. The company's sales have increased sharply.

13. Which of the following is not a stated category of OSHA violation?

    a. Serious
    b. Repeat
    c. Accidental
    d. Failure to abate

14. Which of the following end results represents a way that a human resources professional can measure how the HR department is bringing value to a company?

    a. A reduced number of lawsuits against a company
    b. Increased expense within the human resources department
    c. An increased number of employee complaints indicating corporate problems
    d. The addition of new employees to the human resources department

15. Arthur is interviewing candidates for a new position within his department. He will be working closely with the person he hires, so he prefers the interview to feel as comfortable as possible so the two can chat about the job and its requirements. His preferred interview method is to ask a few broad questions and to allow the candidate to answer the questions candidly, with his answers guiding the next questions that Arthur asks. In this situation, what type of interview technique is Arthur using?

    a. Behavioral
    b. Patterned
    c. Directive
    d. Nondirective

16. Jocelyn has the responsibility of interviewing the candidates who have applied for an open position as a mechanic in an auto repair shop. As she meets and interviews the various candidates, she is not pleased with the potential employees that she encounters during this interview. One of the candidates, however, is a strongly built young woman with a tough demeanor. Despite this woman's limited resume and experience, Jocelyn decides that this particular candidate is the best employee choice because her appearance fits the image that the auto repair shop will need. In this, Jocelyn is demonstrating which of the following interview biases?

    a. Stereotyping
    b. Similar-to-me
    c. Recency
    d. First impression

17. Which of the following is a passive method of training?

    a. case study
    b. vestibule
    c. presentation
    d. seminar

18. Employers are legally allowed to check and review employee emails, as long as they provide which of the following requirements?

   a. Immediate notification from the legal department of impending review
   b. Evidence that proves wrongdoing on the employee's part
   c. Written policy informing employees of potential for email searches
   d. No notification is required, therefore employers may check and review employee emails at any time

19. After his wife gives birth to their first child, Brian takes four weeks of FMLA leave. These are the only days of work Brian misses during the year. At the end of the year, his boss tells him that he is not eligible for a bonus given to employees who have not missed any days of work. However, his coworker Jill receives the bonus, and she had three days of paid leave after her mother died during the summer. Brian believes this is unfair and that he should receive the bonus too. Does he have a legitimate complaint?

   a. No, FMLA leave is counted differently than other forms of leave.
   b. No, neither Brian nor Jill should receive the bonus.
   c. Yes, FMLA leave should be treated the same as other forms of leave.
   d. Yes, Brain should receive the bonus, but Jill should not.

20. The EEO-1 filing applies to all types of employers except which of the following?

   a. Administrative
   b. Banking
   c. Education
   d. Construction

21. Which of the following does not fall under the Department of Labor's Safe Harbor provision?

   a. Employer commits to appropriate deductions in the future
   b. Employer promises to add correct deduction policy
   c. Employer shows evidence of clear deduction policy
   d. Employer pays employee back for incorrect deductions

22. A new employee is told by her coworkers that one of her duties is to handle customer queries as they arrive. However, her superior informs her that customer queries are to be handled by her department as a whole, and in fact she should defer to her coworkers until she becomes more acclimated. This employee's situation can be defined as

   a. role orientation.
   b. role conflict.
   c. role overload.
   d. role ambiguity.

23. Which of the following best describes adverse impact in the selection of employees for a company?

    a. A selection rate among a protected class of more than 95% the selection rate of the highest group

    b. The negative impact of failing to diversify the selection rate among employees

    c. Any non-compliance with the rules pertaining to the Uniform Guidelines on Employee Selection Process

    d. A selection rate among a protected class of less than 80% of the selection rate of the highest group

24. *Hard bargaining* is another name for which of the following types of collective bargaining?

    a. Principled bargaining

    b. Coordinated bargaining

    c. Integrative bargaining

    d. Positional bargaining

25. The FrogTech Company is growing rapidly, and needs to hire several new engineers. However, the candidates for these jobs are in high demand, so FrogTech has to increase the normal entry-level salary. The human resources department notes that new engineers at FrogTech will now be making almost the same salary as those who have been around for years. This scenario is known as

    a. pay differential.

    b. salary acceleration.

    c. wage garnishment.

    d. wage compression.

26. Which of the following best expresses the definition of benchmark positions?

    a. Common jobs within all organizations

    b. Evaluation of current jobs

    c. Review of market conditions for salaries

    d. Change in significant jobs in a company

27. Which of the following is not a major factor in establishing compensation within an organization?

    a. IRS rules and regulations

    b. Individual employee salary history

    c. Conditions in the labor market

    d. Current economic situation

28. Which of the following is not a step in an analysis of training?

    a. Establish a clear objective for training

    b. Collect data about potential problems and review it

    c. Analyze where the organization is falling short in its objective and its outcome

    d. Develop new and more effective training material

29. Which type of medical insurance plan makes contract arrangements directly with employers?

   a. health maintenance organization
   b. physician hospital organization
   c. preferred provider organization
   d. fee-for-service plan

30. Which of the following is not a part of the due diligence process that a human resources professional must review during a merger?

   a. Affirmative Action plans
   b. Employment contracts
   c. Whistleblower prevention
   d. OSHA compliance

31. Defined contribution plans for organizations include all of the following options except:

   a. 401(k)
   b. Money purchase plans
   c. Profit-sharing plans
   d. Cash-balance plans

32. Standard human resource budget responsibilities for a company might include all of the following EXCEPT:

   a. Performance increases
   b. Payroll taxes
   c. Travel expenses
   d. Repairs and maintenance

33. The Latin phrase *quid pro quo*, used to describe a type of sexual harassment that is forbidden under Title VII of the Civil Rights Act of 1964, means which of the following?

   a. Actions not words
   b. From the stronger
   c. Action follows belief
   d. This for that

34. Any penalties for failing to comply with the Drug-Free Workplace Act must fall in line with standards that were laid out in which piece of legislation?

   a. Davis Beacon Act
   b. Fair Labor Standards Act
   c. Rehabilitation Act
   d. Service Contract Act

35. Which of the following statements about the performance appraisal process is LEAST accurate?

   a. Ranking is the most effective method for appraising large groups of employees.
   b. Annual performance appraisal cycles are becoming less prevalent in favor of review cycles that are more frequent and regular in design
   c. Forced ranking systems assume that most employees are neither exceptionally good nor exceptionally bad.
   d. A behaviorally anchored rating system isolates each job's most important tasks.

36. Caspar is responsible for interviewing the candidates who have passed the first round of the application process for a new position at a large technology firm in Nevada. The first candidate that Caspar speaks to is a young woman with a strong resume and an accessible personality. Caspar is highly impressed and continues to think about the first candidate even while he is interviewing the others. As a result, he rates the other candidates lower than the first one, even though two of the other candidates have more experience than the first one and have even received several awards that she has not received. In conducting the interviews, Caspar has displayed which of the following types of interview bias?

   a. Cultural noise
   b. Halo effect
   c. Contrast
   d. Leniency

37. An unfair labor practice (ULP) is defined as:

   a. Any type of coercion on the part of employers against unions
   b. Discrimination against employees or union representatives during a strike
   c. Activity from an employer or union that hinders employees from exercising rights
   d. Participating in strikes or boycotts that are prohibited by law

38. Which of the following human resources disciplines is most susceptible to poor corporate governance?

   a. Recruiting and retention
   b. Conflict resolution
   c. Performance management
   d. Training and development

39. Which of the following questions is the LEAST effective that a human resources professional should address in a Human Management Capital Plan (HCMP) during strategic planning?

   a. Where have we come from?
   b. Where are we now?
   c. Where do we want to be?
   d. How will we get there?

40. At Danielson Company, the Monday after Labor Day is a paid holiday. Steve, an employee at Danielson Company, works nine-hour days on Tuesday, Wednesday, Thursday, Friday, and Saturday of that week. How many hours of overtime has Steve worked?

   a. None
   b. Five
   c. Nine
   d. Thirteen

41. Richard, who heads up a team within a large corporation's human resources department, is known for his laid-back style of management. For the most part, the team works well together and there are few problems with member interaction on the team. When a problem does arise, Richard's first impulse is to encourage the team members to work out the issue amongst themselves before he intervenes. As a result, Richard's leadership style could be described as which of the following?

   a. Laissez-faire
   b. Coaching
   c. Transactional
   d. Transformation

42. Which of these employees would not be classified as disabled under the Americans with Disabilities Act?

   a. Recovering alcoholic
   b. Heroin addict
   c. Paraplegic
   d. HIV-infected employee

43. Which of the following best summarizes the purpose of talent management for the human resources professional?

   a. Attracting potential new employees and developing the current workforce to optimize business outcomes
   b. Locating new talent that will enable the organization to grow and improve
   c. Training all employees for expected promotions within the organization
   d. Setting apart employees who are currently ready or will be ready for higher positions

44. Employers will typically use which of the following in order to protect confidential company information?

   a. Lie detector test
   b. Nondisclosure agreement
   c. Employee contract
   d. Video surveillance

45. Sandra is the head of a small human resources department. She wants to implement a human resource information system, so she begins by commissioning a needs analysis. What is her next step?

   a. Researching possible systems
   b. Asking for permission to implement the system
   c. Identifying possible conflicts with other organizational systems
   d. Creating a timeline for implementation

46. Which of the following assessments would be MOST appropriate to conduct prior to a conditional offer of employment?

   a. Illicit drug screening
   b. Aptitude test
   c. Background check
   d. Occupational physical

47. In business, what is the primary difference between a goal and a strategy?

    a. The terms are interchangeable.

    b. Strategies are created by executives, while goals are set by middle managers.

    c. Strategies are short term plans while goals stretch for a year or more.

    d. Strategies are the means, while goals are the end.

48. Which of the following legislative acts do NOT provide protection for whistleblowers (employees who choose to speak out against corrupt business practice)?

    a. The Occupational Safety and Health Act

    b. The Foreign Corrupt Practices Act of 1977

    c. The Toxic Substances Control Act

    d. The Sarbanes-Oxley Act

49. During the course of an interview, Adrian notices that the candidate he is interviewing is wearing a religious symbol on a chain around his neck. Adrian wants to ask a question about the employee's religious affiliation. Which of the following questions would be appropriate, according to the equal opportunity laws?

    a. What church do you attend?

    b. Do you belong to any organizations that might be relevant to the position?

    c. I noticed the symbol around your neck – do you attend services regularly?

    d. Have you ever attended a religious service?

50. The National Labor Relations Act (NLRA) establishes the right of employees to engage in "concerted activities for the purpose of collective bargaining or other mutual aid or protection" for which types of employees?

    a. Full-time employees only

    b. Part-time employees only

    c. Union employees only

    d. All employees

51. Employers with a minimum of how many employees are required by federal law to complete OSHA forms?

    a. 6

    b. 11

    c. 32

    d. 100

52. Which of the following would be considered nonmonetary compensation?

    a. flex time

    b. stock options

    c. medical care premiums

    d. paid leave

53. Which of the following federal agencies is responsible for enforcing corporate governance?

    a. SEC

    b. EEOC

    c. OSHA

    d. OFCCP

54. Which of the following pieces of legislation establishes guidelines for retaining and reporting employee identification records for the purpose of child support claims and payment?

    a. Fair Labor Standards Act
    b. Personal Responsibility and Work Opportunity Reconciliation Act
    c. Consumer Credit Protection Act
    d. Small Business Job Protection Act

55. An employer believes that an employee has concealed a USB drive with valuable trade secrets on his person. Is the employer allowed to search the employee's body?

    a. Yes, but the search must be conducted by an employee of the same sex.
    b. Yes, but the search must be conducted by a law enforcement officer.
    c. No, because the employee has a reasonable expectation of privacy.
    d. No, because physical searches by anyone in the workplace are prohibited by law.

56. Which motivational theory resulted in the idea that job enrichment can improve the overall quality of work and the workplace for employees?

    a. Herzberg Motivation/Hygiene Theory
    b. Alderfer ERG Theory
    c. Adams Equity Theory
    d. Skinner Operant Conditioning Theory

57. What is the minimum number of employees that a company must have for Consolidated Omnibus Reconciliation Act (COBRA) guidelines to be in effect?

    a. 10
    b. 20
    c. 30
    d. 40

58. Which of the following is NOT defined as a major life activity by the Americans with Disabilities Act?

    a. personal hygiene
    b. driving
    c. reading
    d. sleeping

59. Ilsa, a manager of a large municipal department, is generally commended for her hands-on approach and effectiveness. However, she has a tendency to lose her temper with employees when she is under stress, and several complaints have been made. Ilsa's boss Kathryn is making an effort to improve Ilsa's behavior, and she has decided to employ Skinner's theory of Operant Conditioning. Which of the following would be an example of negative reinforcement?

    a. For every employee complaint about Ilsa's bad temper, Kathryn will document the incident with an official warning.

    b. To avoid provoking Ilsa into a bad temper due to stress, Kathryn will review her workload to see if more work can be delegated within the department.

    c. For every week that goes by without an employee complaint, Kathryn will reward Ilsa by documenting the behavior with an official commendation.

    d. For every week that goes by without an employee complaint, Ilsa will not have to meet with Kathryn for a behavioral review.

60. Which analytical tool indicates the changes that would produce the greatest improvement?

    a. histogram

    b. Pareto chart

    c. stratification chart

    d. pie chart

61. Second to direct compensation, which of the following rewards is MOST impactful on employee staying plans?

    a. Workers' compensation

    b. Company stock options

    c. Retirement benefits

    d. Wellness programs

62. Which of the following is not considered a type of FMLA leave?

    a. Continuous

    b. Reduced

    c. Permanent

    d. Intermittent

63. Which of the following types of deferred compensation plans offers employees a fixed annual percentage and thus is best in a company that has fairly consistent annual earnings?

    a. Profit-sharing

    b. Money purchase

    c. Cash balance

    d. Target benefit

64. The SMART model outlines the important characteristics of

    a. forecasting studies.

    b. employee training.

    c. effective recruiting.

    d. organizational goals.

65. Which of the following OSHA forms is intended to be a Log of Work-Related Injuries and Illnesses?

    a. OSHA Form 300
    b. OSHA Form 300A
    c. OSHA Form 301
    d. OSHA Form 301A

66. Risk management activities for Civil Rights are covered under which of the following pieces of legislation?

    a. EEOC
    b. SOX
    c. OSHA
    d. SEC

67. OSHA requires that organizations develop three types of plans that will ensure employee protection. Two of these types of plans include an injury and illness prevention plan and an emergency response plan. Which of the following is the third type of plan?

    a. Drug use prevention
    b. Fire prevention
    c. Environmental protection
    d. Clean air

68. The Labor-Management Reporting and Disclosure Act (LMRDA) of 1959 required that *local* unions conduct leadership elections how often?

    a. Every 2 years
    b. Every 3 years
    c. Every 4 years
    d. Every 5 years

69. All of the following would be legally considered unfair labor practices for a union except

    a. Preventing an employee from selecting bargaining representation
    b. Requiring that employees sign a security clause to be part of the union
    c. Requiring an employee to continue in a job that is technologically obsolete
    d. Declining to enter into good faith negotiations with the employer

70. How does the Family and Medical Leave Act define a "key employee"?

    a. Any employee who has subordinates
    b. Any employee whose skills cannot be easily replaced
    c. Any manager or executive
    d. Any employee whose salary is in the top 10% at the company

71. In the event that a potential retaliatory action has occurred from an employer against an employee, what is generally OSHA's first goal?

    a. Have employee reinstated with full benefits and back pay
    b. File criminal charges against employer for illegal retaliation
    c. Attempt reconciliation between employer and employee
    d. Protect employee by requiring continued pay without requiring a return to work

72. Which of the following pieces of legislation made it illegal for a business to discriminate against an employee due to his national origin?

    a. Sarbanes-Oxley Act
    b. Rehabilitation Act
    c. Title VII
    d. HIPAA

73. What is the name for the tendency to assign more responsibility for negative behavior to personality or effort rather than to environment?

    a. nonverbal bias
    b. fundamental attribution error
    c. recency bias
    d. halo effect

74. Risk is defined as Probability x _____:

    a. Prevention
    b. Occurrence
    c. Avoidance
    d. Consequences

75. A human resources department is reviewing its current staffing availability and needs. The company is attempting to reduce unnecessary costs and has asked the human resources department to see if any cuts can be made. After a careful review, the human resources manager realizes that the department can make some positive changes. In particular, two of his employees have been requesting reduced hours, and he realizes that they have similar skills and have essentially been doing the same job. What is one option for the employees in this situation?

    a. On-call
    b. Telecommuting
    c. Internship
    d. Job-sharing

76. During negotiations between an employer and the labor union, a charge of an unfair labor practice on the part of the union has arisen. The union has elections coming up soon, but the NLRA has established an election bar. Under the circumstances, which of the following types of union election bars would result?

    a. Prior-petition
    b. Certification-year
    c. Voluntary-recognition
    d. Blocking-charge

77. In the HAY system, which of the following is not a defined factor for job evaluation?

    a. Knowledge
    b. Accountability
    c. Review
    d. Problem solving

78. Which of the following represents a legitimate reason for company management to conduct a workplace investigation?

    a. An employee is accused of inappropriate behavior toward other employees
    b. The company experiences a rapid reduction in the price of their stock
    c. Management becomes aware of a breach in legal compliance
    d. A supervisor reports a disagreement among co-workers in his or her department

79. FMLA applies to private employers with a minimum of how many employees?

    a. 15
    b. 20
    c. 35
    d. 50

80. The head of the administrative department for a major university has asked Raisa, a human resources professional at the school, for a team-building exercise that will benefit the administrative department. The administrative department is composed of employees who work closely together daily but often experience conflicts that indicate a clash of personalities. The department head hopes to find a team-building exercise that will improve the relationships among staff members in the department. Which of the following should Raisa recommend to the department head?

    a. A team obstacle course
    b. Role-playing situations
    c. Team scavenger hunts
    d. The Meyers-Briggs Type Indicator

81. A small publishing company has decided to advertise for a new open position within the marketing department. Although the new hire will fall under the leadership of the marketing department, the job itself will require ongoing communication with at least two other departments. As a result, the individual that is hired will have to be able to work well with the leadership of the other departments. With this in mind, which of the following types of interview techniques will be best for screening prospective candidates?

    a. Situational
    b. Behavioral
    c. Functional
    d. Panel

82. Philippa, the head of the marketing department of Caledonia Coffee Company, is planning to post a position that will allow current employees of the company to apply before that position opens to the public. Because the posting will be internal (arranged in-house), the process will differ from that of a public posting. Philippa contacts the human resources department to find out which type of application would be best for a single internal position. The best type of application for this situation would be which of the following?

    a. Short-form application
    b. Online application
    c. Long-form application
    d. Job-specific application

83. How is gross profit calculated?

    a. The cost of goods sold is subtracted from total sales revenue.
    b. Operating expenses are subtracted from total profit.
    c. Liabilities are subtracted from the total value of the business.
    d. Distributions to owners are subtracted from net profits.

84. Which of the following is an example of a chemical health hazard?

    a. bacterium
    b. pesticide
    c. fungus
    d. virus

85. Which of the following is an example of bottom-up communication?

    a. brown-bag lunch
    b. poster
    c. newsletter
    d. intranet

86. Which of the following provides the best definition of organization development?

    a. Analyzing the various elements of an organization's makeup and reviewing opportunities for improvement
    b. Discovering methods of strategic intervention to address problems within the organization
    c. Establishing means of employee participation in decisions that are made within organizations
    d. Creating a sense of balance between employers and their employees in a company

87. Which of the following workplace trends is directly leading to the widening of the employee candidate pool?

    a. Increased focus on employee well-being
    b. Increased employee turnover
    c. Increased automation
    d. Increased opportunities for remote work

88. The salesmen at Franklin Company earn bonuses of $500, $750, $1000, $1000, and $1500, respectively. What is the median bonus?

    a. $500
    b. $950
    c. $1000
    d. $4750

89. Which method of reporting does the Department of Labor prefer with regard to time worked by employees who are nonexempt under the Fair Labor Standards Act?

    a. exception reporting
    b. selected reporting
    c. positive time reporting
    d. negative time reporting

90. Which of the following agencies is responsible for enforcing the rights of veterans in the workplace?

    a. EEOC
    b. DOJ
    c. DOL
    d. OFCCP

91. The Greendale Company is thinking about adjusting its executive compensation package. There is some concern, however, that the new program will adversely affect the company's tax burden. The Greendale Company should ask the IRS for a(n)

    a. trade exception.
    b. audit.
    c. private letter ruling.
    d. expansion clause.

92. Which of the following statements about strikes is false?

    a. Unions may not strike in favor of an unfair labor practice.
    b. Work slowdowns are an illegal form of strike.
    c. Employees may strike to support a hot cargo clause.
    d. A strike may be deemed unlawful because of misconduct by strikers.

93. Nine weeks after giving birth, Deirdre comes back to work on a reduced schedule. Instead of her normal 40-hour week, she only works 30 hours. How many weeks of FMLA leave does Deirdre use for each of these thirty-hour weeks?

    a. 1/4
    b. 1/2
    c. 1
    d. FMLA does not apply to partial weeks

94. Which of the following types of analytical tools is used primarily for reviewing a series of random events to locate a potential pattern within them?

    a. Check sheet
    b. Pareto chart
    c. Scatter chart
    d. Histogram

95. Grover's boss tells him that if he will meet with a difficult client, he can have an extra day of paid vacation. However, after Grover meets with the client, his boss fails to provide the incentive. Grover's boss is guilty of

    a. fraudulent misrepresentation.
    b. constructive discharge.
    c. promissory estoppel.
    d. defamation.

96. Why is an understanding of the legal process so valuable for the human resources professional?

    a. Human resources professionals are the ones responsible for contacting members of Congress in the event that legislation should be proposed

    b. The business world is increasingly involved with the legislative process, and the human resources professional is a company's outside contact for legislation

    c. Understanding the legislative process is essential for small businesses pursuing incorporation

    d. Legislation influences the relationship between employers and employees, and the human resources professional is responsible for understanding this relationship

97. Yolanda is a human resources officer at an accounting firm. During tax season, Yolanda contracts with an agency that supplies temporary workers. These workers are paid by the temp agency rather than the accounting firm. What type of contract will Yolanda sign with the temp agency?

    a. temporary contract

    b. resolvable contract

    c. third-party contract

    d. indirect contract

98. How long after filing with the Department of Labor are ERISA records required to be maintained?

    a. 4 years

    b. 5 years

    c. 6 years

    d. 7 years

99. Eamon is a human resources professional for a large firm of attorneys, and he has been assigned the responsibility of developing an instructional method that is most suitable for the support staff at the firm. The support staff has been struggling with problem-solving issues, and Eamon has been instructed to utilize a training method that will allow the staff members to discuss problems and potential resolutions under the supervision of a third party expert. Which of the following instructional methods will be most effective for this situation?

    a. Vestibule

    b. Facilitation

    c. Demonstration

    d. Conference

100. Which of the following is NOT an essential component of an intellectual property agreement?

    a. Identification of confidential information

    b. Prohibition against the hiring of current employees by employees who leave the business

    c. Limitations on use of confidential information

    d. Duration of confidentiality restrictions

101. In which of the following situations would the use of copyrighted material NOT fall under the definition of *fair use*?

   a. Educational purposes within the organization
   b. Limited copies of the material
   c. Use of a single paragraph from a book
   d. Addition of quoted information into the company motto

102. For their first few months, new employees at Flanders Company receive frequent praise and encouragement from their supervisors. After a while, though, supervisors pay less attention to these employees. Performance evaluations indicate that employee productivity declines at this point. The supervisors at Flanders Company are practicing

   a. punishment.
   b. positive reinforcement.
   c. negative reinforcement.
   d. extinction.

103. A labor union must deal with several different employers. The union decides to negotiate with the employers one at a time, hoping to achieve successively better deals. What strategy is this union using?

   a. parallel bargaining
   b. integrative bargaining
   c. positional bargaining
   d. multi-unit bargaining

104. Susannah, who is the head of the human resources department, will be responsible for a training session and must decide on the seating style in the space that she will be using. The training will include a large group and will involve a range of activities, including several lectures, film presentations, and a small amount of group work. Which of the following seating styles will be most appropriate for the training that Susannah will be conducting?

   a. Theater-style
   b. Chevron-style
   c. Banquet-style
   d. Conference-style

105. Which of the following is not an acceptable reason for FMLA leave?

   a. Resting during a difficult pregnancy
   b. Caring for a newborn infant
   c. Caring for an unmarried partner who is ill
   d. Adopting or fostering a child

106. Within the SMART model, the letters stand for Specific, Measurable, Action-Oriented, _____, and Time-based. What does the "R" stand for?

   a. Reasonable
   b. Reversible
   c. Realistic
   d. Representative

107. A realistic job preview (RJP) should be used when

    a. unemployment is high.
    b. recruits have access to plenty of information about the job.
    c. the selection ratio is high.
    d. employee replacement costs are high.

108. Which of the following types of workforce assessments embraces an "earn while you learn" approach to combining classroom environments with on-the-job learning?

    a. Technical apprenticeship
    b. 360-degree assessment
    c. Dual career ladder
    d. Situation judgment test

109. Which of the following is not considered a top-down method of communication delivery?

    a. Posters
    b. Bulletin board postings
    c. Brown bag meetings
    d. Newsletters

110. Which of the following is defined by a union activity in which someone takes a job with a company that the union has targeted for employee unionization, and thus works to encourage employees at the new company to organize a union?

    a. Wildcatting
    b. Salting
    c. Featherbedding
    d. Leafletting

111. Which of the following is the most significant purpose of a total rewards strategy?

    a. To plan for establishing salaries among employees
    b. To represent the employer's brand as effectively as possible
    c. To assist in creating teamwork among employees
    d. To use the firm's budget for rewards in order to retain employees

112. Which of the following statements about the Delphi technique is false?

    a. The participants remain anonymous.
    b. It takes place in a single round.
    c. It is a convenient form of qualitative analysis when participants are distant.
    d. It allows for a broad range of perspectives.

113. What are on the axes of the Blake-Mouton managerial grid?

    a. people and production
    b. profit and production
    c. people and profit
    d. people and presentation

114. Which of the following is closest to the national Lost Work Day Index (LWDI) average for private-sector organizations as calculated by OSHA?

    a. 250
    b. 25
    c. 2.5
    d. 0.25

115. A large university is concerned about the possibility of an act of terrorism on campus, and the supervisor for the school's student affairs program has consulted Angelova, the head of the human resources department, about developing a program for responding to a terrorist attack and assisting students in the aftermath of an attack. Which of the following represents what Angelova could recommend to the student affairs supervisor?

    a. A counseling program that assists students in recovering from the trauma of a terrorist attack
    b. A relocation program that enables students to transfer to other schools in the aftermath of a terrorist attack
    c. A monthly email newsletter that provides recommendations for students should the school experience an act of terrorism
    d. Creation of new department specifically focused on responding to a terrorist attack on campus

Answer Key and Explanations for Test #1

1. A: The human resources professional is sometimes called upon to complete a cost-benefit analysis, and in this case such an analysis would be appropriate. The marketing research company needs to remain within its budget, so it is important to look at each testing option and consider what it will cost the company when compared to what it will potentially yield. Once this comparison is made, a decision can also be made. Answer choice B is an important part of the process of choosing the best testing option, but it is not necessarily a major part that the human resources professional needs to complete. Any options that are already over the budget may be eliminated before they make it to the desk of the human resources professional. Answer choice C provides an option that might not really be an option—utilizing part of a testing program instead of the whole. Since there is little information within the question to justify such a decision, answer choice C has little relevance. Answer choice D may be a value piece of the puzzle to implementing the training program but would not be the primary role for a human resources professional to headline.

2. C: Exit interviews should be conducted by a third party. In many cases, employees will leave an organization because they are not satisfied with it or with the work environment. However, an employee may not feel comfortable sharing these complaints with current members of the organization. Indeed, this reticence may be a result of why they are leaving the organization in the first place. Having exit interviews conducted by a third party ensures that the process will yield more useful information for the organization.

3. D: The Worker Adjustment and Retraining Notification Act stipulates that employers with more than a hundred employees must provide at least sixty days' notice to workers and unions before closing a factory or plant. This legislation is generally referred to as the WARN Act and was intended not only to alert employees, but to enable the federal government to assist in the retraining of the soon-to-be-displaced workers.

4. A: A PPO, or Preferred Provider Organization, plan does not require that patients first contact a "gatekeeper" for medical treatment but allows patients to choose from a broad network. A POS, or Point of Service, plan offers a network (like a PPO) but allows patients to meet with a physician outside this network and request reimbursement later on. An HMO, or Health Maintenance Organization, plan does require a "gatekeeper" but also focuses on lower health care costs for patients and care that aims to prevent higher costs later on. An FFS, or Fee-for-service, plan is generally the most costly for patients but allows them to make their own selection of facilities and physicians.

5. C: According to FMLA guidelines, an employee must work for an employer for a minimum of 12 months (not necessarily consecutively) in order to apply for FMLA-approved leave. Because Arthur has only worked for the company for 9 months, he will not be eligible to apply for FMLA leave. Answer choices A, B, and D are incorrect because each represents the wrong period of time for FMLA leave.

6. C: Creating a business plan, while useful for businesses that are in their early stages, is not an identifiable step within the strategic planning process. On the other hand, completing an environmental scan (answer choice A), formulating a strategy (answer choice B), and implementing that strategy (answer choice D), are all significant steps in the strategic planning process. It is important to bear in mind that strategic planning is related largely to a company's future goals for growth and improvement.

124

7. D: Understanding and responding to the risk of competition a business may face is most often a function of a marketing professional, not human resources. Answer choices A, B, and C are all incorrect because they represent distinct areas of risk that a human resources professional must consider.

8. D: Medical workers are not identified as a separate category under the EEO-1 report. Sales workers, service workers, and craft workers, however, all represent separate EEO-1 categories.

9. D: The Expectancy Theory of 1964, which considers employee motivation in view of the potential for reward, is attributed to Victor Vroom. Fredrick Herzberg is credited with the Motivation/Hygiene Theory of 1959; Clayton Alderfer is responsible for the ERG Theory of 1969; Abraham Maslow is credited with the Hierarchy of Needs Theory of 1954.

10. D: The human resources professional is not required to provide for all employee accommodation requests to ensure continued employment. Human resources professionals are expected to discuss possible employee accommodations with management and to recommend the implementation of certain requests, but there is no requirement to implement all requests. Answer choices A, B, and C are all steps in the human resources professional's role in observing the guidelines of ADA, so they are incorrect.

11. B: Poor communication between management and employees is a common problem during the growth phase of the organizational life cycle. In this phase, the organization often adds new layers of management, and so employees who previously had unfettered access to their superiors may find it difficult to get immediate feedback. This can be alienating for veteran employees. Outsourcing can be found during a variety of phases within the organizational life cycle. Excessive bureaucracy and the resulting inefficiencies are common in mature and declining organizations. Finally, an inability to respond quickly to market changes tends to beset an organization after it has stopped growing and entered its decline phase.

12. B: A company's total rewards packages might lag the market if the company is trying to establish itself in a new area. For instance, if a company simply wants to get a small toehold in a particular market, it may not view hiring top job candidates as a worthwhile enterprise. Of course, if total rewards packages continue to lag the market over a long interval, the company's performance is likely to suffer. However, many fledgling companies have no other choice but to offer lower wages and benefits to new employees at first. Many of these companies do so openly and promise the new employees that their compensation will rise above the market average once the business takes off.

13. C: The stated categories of OSHA violations include willful, serious, other-than-serious, repeat, failure to abate, and de minimus (or minimal violations). Accidental is not one of the categories officially noted by OSHA, so answer choice C is correct. Answer choices A, B, and D all reflect actual categories, so they are incorrect.

14. A: A reduced number of lawsuits against a company definitely indicates that the human resources department is bringing value to a company. Lawsuits often occur when serious policy mistakes are made. If policy mistakes are being reduced or eliminated, the company is moving in a positive direction. Answer choice B is incorrect because an increase in expenses within the human resources department indicates nothing more in the immediate sense than that the human resource department is spending more money. Whether or not that money is being put to good use is not explained sufficiently. Answer choice C makes no sense because an increase in employee complaints cannot indicate if any department – and definitely not the human resources department

125

– is bringing value to the company. Similar to answer choice A, answer choice D does not show anything tangible in terms of value; an increase in employees within human resources only shows that more people are needed and not that better work is being done.

15. D: A nondirective interview style occurs when the interviewer asks broad questions to allow the candidate to answer candidly and comfortably. A behavioral interview would ask the candidate how he behaved in a past situation, with the intent being to use past experience to anticipate future actions. A patterned interview focuses on a group of questions that apply specifically to the job and what will be required in that position. A directive interview is highly focused and organized, with the interviewer asking the same questions of all candidates.

16. A: Jocelyn is allowing a stereotyping bias (how she perceives the female mechanic) to guide her decision about which candidate will be best for the position in the auto repair shop. Answer choice B is incorrect because a similar-to-me bias occurs when the interviewer is influenced by the fact that she and the candidate have similar interests or a similar background. Answer choice C is incorrect because a recency bias occurs when the interviewer compares a candidate to the previously interviewed candidate. Answer choice D is incorrect because a first impression bias happens when an immediate impression of a candidate determines a decision.

17. C: A presentation is a passive method of training. Passive training methods are so designated because the participants are only required to listen, read, or pay attention. In a case study, the participants must strategize a response to a hypothetical situation. In vestibule training, employees participate in a simulation of complex or hazardous tasks. In a seminar, participants engage in a productive conversation with the presenter.

18. C: Employers are legally allowed to check and review employee email as long as they provide a written policy informing employees of the potential for email searches. Without this written policy, workers could legally file complaints about invasion of employee privacy. Answer choice A is incorrect because immediate notification from the legal department of impending review would not be sufficient. Answer choice B is incorrect because if an employer already had proof of a worker's guile it wouldn't be necessary to search his emails. Answer choice D is incorrect because notification is required. Although employers technically own the emails that employees send and receive, they are not advised to search emails without a written search policy.

19. C: Brian has a legitimate complaint because FMLA leave is to be treated the same as other forms of leave with regard to perfect attendance bonuses. Employers have the right to count FMLA leave against perfect attendance awards, but they must treat other forms of leave the same way. Since the employer did not count Jill's leave against her perfect attendance record, he may not count Brian's against him either. Alternatively, the employer could instead disqualify both Brian and Jill from the perfect attendance bonus.

20. C: Private employers within all forms of major educational institutions (primary, secondary, and post-secondary) are excluded from having to complete EEO-1 filings along with state and local governments, and a select few other exemptions. Private employers who fall within the areas of administration, banking, or construction, and have 100 employees or more, must complete the report as well as certain federal contractors with 50 or more employees.

21. B: There are three primary scenarios in which safe harbor may be applied: the employer commits to appropriate deductions in future, the employer shows evidence of clear deduction policy, the employer pays employee back for incorrect deductions. The employer promising to add a correct deduction policy in the future is *not* considered part of safe harbor, however. The obvious

126

problem in this situation is that the correct deduction policy does not already exist and is clearly not being applied within the company. This is unacceptable to the Department of Labor, and no safe harbor provision would exist for such an employer.

22. B: The situation outlined above can be defined as role conflict. Role conflict exists when an employee does not understand exactly what is expected of him. This problem is common when an employee must report to more than one superior. Role orientation is the process of becoming familiar with an employee role. Role overload is a sense of anxiety or panic produced by a perception that one is being asked to do too much. Role ambiguity is a general lack of clarity regarding the parameters of the employee role. Goal ambiguity is particularly common when a new position has been created within the organization, and the requirements of the position have yet to be finalized.

23. D: The phrase adverse impact or unintentional discrimination refers to the selection rate of a protected class being less than 80% of the selection rate of the highest group. In other words, if the selection rate of females is less than 80% of the selection rate of males, there is an adverse impact on females by the hiring process. Answer choice A is the opposite of the correct definition of adverse impact, so it is incorrect. Answer choice B is close to the meaning of adverse impact – in a broad sense – but it is not specific enough to be correct. Answer choice C is also too broad, particularly because there is far more to the Uniform Guidelines on Employee Selection Process than just selection rate.

24. D: Positional bargaining is also known as hard bargaining (and sometimes as distributive bargaining). Integrative bargaining is a form or principled bargaining. Coordinated bargaining is also referred to as multi-unit bargaining.

25. D: The FrogTech Company is experiencing wage compression. Wage compression exists when new employees make either more money than existing employees or more money than existing employees did when they were hired. For obvious reasons, wage compression can create resentment and conflict in the workforce. Some businesses prevent wage compression by periodically adjusting salary increase rates for existing employees.

26. A: Benchmark positions are simply the types of positions that are common within all organizations, such as administrative assistants. Benchmark positions do not, however, relate to an evaluation of current jobs (answer choice B), a review of market conditions for salaries (answer choice C), or a change in significant jobs in a company (answer choice D).

27. B: When establishing employee compensation within an organization, considering summative employee salary history might be a part of the larger process, but individual salary history is not a major factor in the process. Answer choices A, C, and D – IRS rules, conditions in the labor market, and current economic situations – all play a major role in establishing employee compensation.

28. D: The development of new and more effective training material might be an end result of training analysis, but it is not one of the primary steps within the process. Answers A, B, and C all fall within the larger steps of a major instructional design model known as ADDIE: Analyze, Design, Develop, Implement, and Evaluate.

29. B: A physician hospital organization makes contract arrangements directly with employers. In this system, physicians and hospitals act as a single entity. In a health maintenance organization (HMO), patients are managed by a gatekeeper physician, who refers them to other medical professionals when necessary. In a preferred provider organization, patients work with a designated network of medical professionals. Fee-for-service plans allow the patient to shop

around for medical services, the costs of which are initially covered by the patient, who is later reimbursed.

30. C: The due diligence process during a merger should focus primarily on recording the following basics of company employee details: documentation regarding employee names, employment contracts, I-9 forms, benefit contracts, compensation information, company policy and procedures (such as handbooks for employees), compliance documentation for equal opportunity, information about company labor relations (including labor activity), all information about potential legal situations (such as legal violations, sexual harassment claims, and disputes about employee terminations), and legal compliance documentation for COBRA, FMLA, WARN, and OSHA. This means that answer choices A, B, and D all fall within the boundaries of due diligence for a merger, leaving only answer choice C. Preventing whistleblower activity could open the organization up to legal repercussions and can prevent the human resources team from developing an effective workforce strategy through the merger.

31. D: Cash-balance plans fall under the category of deferred contribution but not under the category of defined contribution. Answer choices A, B, and C – 401(k), money purchase plans, and profit-sharing plans – do, however, fall under defined contribution from employers toward employee retirement accounts.

32. D: In terms of standard budget responsibilities, the human resources professional is expected to manage performance increases (answer choice A), payroll taxes (answer choice B), and travel expenses (answer choice C). Repairs and maintenance would rarely be part of the human resources budget, so (answer choice D) is incorrect.

33. D: The Latin phrase quid pro quo translates simply as this for that and under sexual harassment laws it suggests that an employee is expected to provide sexual favors in order to keep their job, or receive a better one. Answer choices A, B, and C, are incorrect because they do not reflect a correct translation of this Latin phrase.

34. C: Any penalties for failing to comply with the Drug-Free Workplace Act (1988) must fall in line with standards that were laid out in the Rehabilitation Act, which was passed in 1973. The Davis Beacon Act of 1931 placed federal regulations on minimum wage. The Fair Labor Standards Act of 1938 also focused on compensation rights for workers. Similarly, the Service Contract Act of 1965 focused on compensation for federal contract workers.

35. A: Ranking is not an effective method for appraising large groups of employees. The ranking method simply entails placing employees in order from most important to least. In a large organization, it will be difficult to make comparisons between jobs. Also, many job groups will be so different that comparisons will be worthless. The other answer choices are true statements. Annual performance reviews are waning in favor of the higher engagement levels required for regular reviews. In a forced ranking system, the appraisers place all employees on a bell curve, and therefore the vast majority end up close to the middle. Behaviorally anchored rating systems (BARS) assess employees based on the behaviors deemed critical to their particular job.

36. C: Caspar's interview bias is one of contrast; he finds himself, however unconsciously, contrasting the other candidates with the first candidate that he interviews. A cultural noise bias (answer choice A) occurs when the candidate responds with pointed answers that are aimed at making the interviewer happy rather than responding in a more natural or general way. A halo bias (answer choice B) occurs when the interviewer considers only one quality of the candidate over his other qualities, such as shyness that might detract from the candidate's true record of achievement.

A leniency bias (answer choice D) means the interviewer is lenient in regard to a candidate's potential weaknesses.

37. C: An unfair labor practice is defined as any activity from an employer or a union that hinders employees from exercising their rights. Answer choices A, B, and D are incorrect. While they describe types of unfair labor practices, they fail to provide a complete definition of ULP. Each is a type of unfair labor practice, but does not encompass the total definition.

38. A: While all areas of human resources responsibilities can be indirectly affected by negligent or unethical decisions, poor corporate governance in an increasingly connected world can directly influence employees staying with an organization or the talent an organization is able to recruit. It is critical for human resources professionals to be involved in governance practices and decisions in order to positively influence the experience of current employees and perspectives of potential recruits.

39. A: A Human Management Capital Plan is forward thinking; the questions asked look at the present and into the future. As a result, a human resources professional who is setting up a HCMP should ask the following questions as demonstrated in answer choices B, C, and D: Where are we now? Where do we want to be? How will we get there? Answer choice A, which asks where have we come from, addresses an issue that does not apply to this portion of strategic planning, so it is correct.

40. B: Steve has worked five hours of overtime. According to the Fair Labor Standards Act, paid holidays do not count as overtime. So, for the purpose of his overtime calculation, Steve has only worked 45 hours this week. Therefore, he has only worked five hours of overtime.

41. A: Richard's laid-back mentality demonstrates a laissez-faire, or "let it be" attitude toward managing his team in the human resources department. A leader who demonstrates the coaching style (answer choice B) has a more hands-on approach to working individually with team members to help them with targeting their skills and giving them the means to function on their own. A transactional leader (answer choice C) sets goals and provides rewards to team members as they reach these goals, while a transformational leader (answer choice D) works on team dynamics for a united approach to reaching goals.

42. B: As long as a person is receiving treatment for alcohol or substance abuse, he is considered disabled. A person who relapses into alcohol or substance abuse is no longer protected by the ADA. A recovering alcoholic would therefore be classified as disabled under the Americans with disabilities act. People with contagious diseases including HIV are classified as disabled under the ADA, and paraplegics are impaired from "major life activities", thus making them disabled, as well.

43. A: The purpose of talent management is twofold: to create a reputation and working situation that draws in new talent and to hold on to the talent by constantly maintaining the most effective work situation for employees. Answer choice A best summarizes this description, so it is correct. Answer choices B and D contain descriptions that are part of talent management, but each fails to encompass the entire purpose of talent management. As a result, answer choices B and D are incorrect. Answer choice C is also incorrect because it steps beyond any purpose of talent management. The goal of this process is not to train all employees for promotion but rather to attract employees with significant talent and to maintain them within the organization.

44. B: Organizations typically use the nondisclosure agreement to protect their confidential company information. The lie detector test is only legal within certain boundaries, so answer choice A is incorrect. An employee contract generally binds an employee to the company for a specified

129

length of time, but it does not necessarily protect confidential company information, so answer choice C is incorrect. Organizations utilize video surveillance and random searches to ensure that employees are performing their tasks appropriately, but these activities alone do not protect confidential company information, so answer choice D is incorrect.

45. A: Sandra's next step is to research possible systems. Since she has obtained a needs analysis, she should have a good idea of the appropriate system for her business. However, her business may not be able to afford the best possible human resources information system. Sandra's next step will be to shop around for the best value. Answer choices B, C, and D represent steps that she will need to take later in the process.

46. B: Any drug screening or medical tests should take place after a conditional offer of employment to remain compliant with various employment laws and Equal Employment Opportunity Commission guidelines. Background checks, while not illegal under federal law to perform prior to a conditional offer of employment, may be illegal under state laws or may be subject to other limitations or restrictions. Aptitude tests can be required prior to a conditional offer of employment to test for the skills and abilities required to perform the job at hand. Any pre-employment testing must be validated as a good predictor of job performance and may not intentionally or unintentionally discriminate against protected classes of applicants.

47. D: In business, the primary difference between a goal and a strategy is that a strategy is a means, while a goal is an end. Business strategies outline where the company seeks to be in the future, how they will get there, and what the steps along the way will look like. Goals are typically part of business strategies and are narrower in scope in defining what will be accomplished by whom and within a certain time frame.

48. B: The Foreign Corrupt Practices Act of 1977 establishes the rules for preventing bribery and penalizing occurrences of it within corporations that exist in several countries. Each of the other answer choices provide some kind of protection for whistleblowers who reveal corrupt business practices.

49. B: Specific questions regarding a candidate's personal life and religious choices are entirely off limits for interviews. The only question from the answer choices that an interviewer may ask a candidate is whether or not the candidate belongs to an organization that may be relevant to the job. Unless the candidate volunteers information, all other questions about the religious symbol that the candidate is wearing are inappropriate during the interview. This is because a question could make a candidate uncomfortable. What is more, should the candidate be asked such a question and then receive the job – or not receive the job – the hiring decision could be viewed as a form of discrimination.

50. D: The rights that are established by the NLRA apply to all employees of an organization and are not limited to specific employees within that organization. As a result, the other answer choices that limit the employee coverage to full-time employees only (answer choice A), part-time employees only (answer choice B), and union employees only (answer choice C), are all incorrect.

51. B: Employers with at least 11 employees are required to complete OSHA forms. A business with only 6 employees does not have to complete the forms (although this might be recommended). Businesses with more than 11 employees are all required by federal law to complete OSHA forms.

52. A: Flex time is considered nonmonetary compensation. Non-monetary compensation is any reward that is not money or that cannot be monetized. The other answer choices represent compensation that is an expense for the business. Flex time systems allow employees to work

130

variable hours of the day, which can be very useful for employees who have numerous responsibilities outside of work.

53. A: The SEC is responsible for enforcing corporate governance. The EEOC and the OFCCP enforce civil rights laws. OSHA is the Occupational Safety and Health Administration within the Department of Labor and enforces occupational safety and health standards within the workplace.

54. B: The Personal Responsibility and Work Opportunity Reconciliation Act, which went into law in 1996, establishes and updates rules for retaining and reporting employee identification records for the purpose of child support claims and payment. Answer choice A is incorrect because the Fair Labor Standards Act has no immediate requirement about record keeping and instead focuses on establishing fair compensation for employees. Answer choice C is incorrect because the workplace application of the Consumer Credit Protection Act relates to wage garnishing. And answer choice D is incorrect because the Small Business Job Protection Act relates to employee deferred compensation plans.

55. B: It is legal for the employee to be searched, but the search should be performed by a law enforcement officer. Body searches are allowed so long as they are conducted for legitimate business reasons. Of course, before requesting a body search the employer should try other means of resolving the situation.

56. A: The Herzberg Motivation/Hygiene Theory, developed by Frederick Herzberg in 1959, was the result of Herzberg's study on what motivated employees and the way that positive motivation could bring quantifiable results to a company. Herzberg concluded that giving employees the opportunity to excel in something will bring overall success to the entire company.

57. B: COBRA regulations state that a company with 20 or more employees must provide a defined amount of health benefits for employees. Answer choices A, C, and D are all incorrect because they fail to recognize the requirements of COBRA regarding minimum number of employees.

58. B: The Americans with Disabilities Act does not count driving as a major life activity. According to the act, major life activities are personal care, manual tasks, seeing, hearing, eating, sleeping, breathing, learning, reading, concentrating, thinking, communicating, and working.

59. D: Negative Reinforcement occurs when a good behavior occurs and a negative result for behavior is removed. The behavioral review would be considered a negative result of poor behavior; when this is removed after a week of no employee complains, Kathryn is applying Negative Reinforcement. Answer choices A reflects Skinner's strategy of Punishment. Answer choice C reflects Skinner's strategy of Positive Reinforcement. Answer choice B reflects a possible combination of Positive Reinforcement and Extinction. It does not, however, represent a single strategy laid out by Skinner.

60. B: A Pareto chart indicates the changes that will produce the greatest improvement. This chart looks like a combination of a bar graph and a line graph. The bars indicate the various causes of a particular problem, while the line indicates the improvement that would result from eliminating each of these causes. This chart is based on the Pareto principle, which is that 80% of the inefficiencies in a process can be removed by changing only 20% of the causes. In other words, a few causes have outsized influence on the process. A histogram, on the other hand, is used to identify patterns in seemingly random events. A stratification chart breaks a complex problem down into its constituent elements. A pie chart is useful for demonstrating the relationship of pieces of a whole for a predetermined period of or point in time.

131

61. C: Workers' compensation is a federally mandated benefit and does not affect an employee's experience compared to what their experience would be elsewhere. Wellness programs can be beneficial for employees but are not as impactful as retirement programs. Company stock options may be a generous perk but are limited in scope and may come as an option within an employer-sponsored retirement option. Retirement programs are one of the most highly regarded benefits options for employees, who are looking for higher rates of employer contributions and other retirement benefit options such as health care and life insurance.

62. C: FMLA leave falls into one of the following three categories: continuous, reduced, or intermittent. FMLA does not provide for permanent leave, in the sense that the employer is not expected to provide coverage if the employee ceases to be part of the company. Permanent leave is ultimately termination and falls under different laws altogether.

63. B: A money purchase plan offers employees a fixed annual percentage and thus is best in a company that has fairly consistent annual earnings. A profit-sharing plan, also known as a discretionary contribution plan, is considered to be best in a company that has highly variable annual profits. A cash balance plan is considered "portable" because employees can remove the money from the plan and convert the payment into other forms. A target benefit plan uses actuarial formulas to determine how much an employee will receive toward retirement.

64. D: The SMART model outlines the important characteristics of corporate goals. This model asserts that goals should be specific, measurable, action-based, realistic, and time-based. In other words, they should be detailed, capable of assessment, based on concrete activities, attainable, and scheduled.

65. A: OSHA Form 300 is intended to be a Log of Work-Related Injuries and Illnesses. OSHA Form 300A is intended to be a Summary of Work-Related Injuries and Illnesses. OSHA Form 301 is intended to be an Injury and Illness Incident Report. OSHA Form 301A does not exist.

66. A: The EEOC, or the Equal Employment Opportunity Commission, is responsible for risk management activities that cover Civil Rights. The SOX (The Sarbanes-Oxley Act) covers a company's obligation to report financial matters. OSHA (the Occupational Safety and Health Act) covers safety and health in the workplace. The SEC (Securities and Exchange Commission) covers workplace security – and primarily financial security.

67. B: The three primary types of plans that OSHA requires organizations to develop include an injury and illness prevention plan, an emergency response plan, and a fire prevention plan. Answer choice A is incorrect because OSHA does not require a drug use prevention plan. Such a plan might fall under illness prevention, but ultimately a drug use prevention plan is voluntary on the part of the organization. Answer choice C is incorrect because OSHA does not require an environmental protection plan. This too might fall under illness prevention, but it is not specified under OSHA's rules. Answer choice D is incorrect because OSHA does not require a clean air plan.

68. B: LMRDA required that local unions conduct leadership elections every three years. Answer choice D reflects the requirement for national unions (discussed in question 151). The other answer choices do not reflect union leadership election requirements.

69. B: Requiring employers to sign a security clause to be part of the union is fairly standard procedure: it protects the union when the time comes for the union to enter into bargaining with the employer. However, preventing an employee from selecting bargaining representation, requiring an employee to continue in a job that is technologically obsolete, and declining to enter into good faith negotiations with the employer may be considered unfair labor practices for unions.

132

70. D: The Family and Medical Leave Act defines a "key employee" as any employee whose salary is in the top 10% at the company. Businesses are not required to promise key employees they will be able to return to their position or an equivalent position after FMLA leave. The intention of this exception in the Family Medical Leave Act is to prevent businesses from suffering significant economic injury. However, the FMLA encourages businesses to find ways to grant leave wherever possible.

71. C: OSHA's first goal is to attempt a reconciliation between the employee and his employer. If there is a possibility of avoiding legal action, it should be taken to avoid weighing down the legal system. (Thus, answer choice B is not correct.) In the process of this reconciliation, OSHA might also work to have the employee reinstated with full benefits and back pay, but this would reflect the individual situation and is part of the larger reconciliation process instead of the primary goal. OSHA could step in to protect the employee by requiring continued pay without requiring a return to work, but again this would reflect an individual situation and would not necessarily be the primary goal.

72. C: Title VII of the Civil Rights Act of 1964 made it illegal for a business to discriminate against an employee due to his national origin. The Sarbanes-Oxley Act was intended to improve accounting practices within public companies. The Rehabilitation Act penalized businesses for discriminating against employees who have a disability. HIPAA, the Health Insurance Portability and Accountability Act of 1996, in part, protects workers against losing their health coverage immediately if they lose their jobs.

73. B: The tendency to overemphasize the impact of personality on behavior is known as the fundamental attribution error. The fundamental attribution error creates problems for organizations when managers punish poor performers rather than try to resolve the issues that are responsible for the poor performance. Nonverbal bias occurs when an individual betrays how they feel about another through their body language. Recency bias is the tendency to weigh more recent events when judging another as opposed to their full body of work across a period of time. The halo effect occurs when the positive experiences or attributes of a person are weighed more heavily than neutral or negative experiences or attributes when considering an individual's full body of work.

74. D: *Risk* is defined as Probability x Consequences. In other words, a business must multiply the odds of something occurring by the results of that occurrence. The occurrence itself is a part of the process that leads to consequences, but it is not a direct element within the standard risk formula. The result of this formula enables a business to employ prevention or avoidance options.

75. D: With both employees having similar skills and looking for reduced hours, job-sharing might be the best option both for them and the company. Having the employees on-call might be useful for reduced hours, but without more information on the type of business it might also be difficult to arrange. (On-call work, for instance, would be of little use in a standard office environment and might do more to disrupt activities.) Telecommuting is useful for cost reduction, but it does not necessarily address the specific needs of this situation. An internship makes little sense as both employees are already full employees instead of students looking to acquire experience.

76. D: As indicated in the answer for question 160, a blocking-charge bar occurs when an unfair labor practice charge remains pending. Since this is the case in the scenario provided, the blocking-charge bar will apply. A prior-petition bar results when the union withdraws an election request petition and then resubmits it. A certification-year bar results when the NLRB has recently recognized and certified a representative for bargaining on behalf of the union. A voluntary-

recognition bar occurs when the employer voluntarily recognizes the union as the primary bargaining unit for employees.

77. C: The HAY system assesses what knowledge is needed to complete the job, what level and scope of accountability is required of the job, and what type of problem solving or critical thinking is required of the job. Review is not considered a part of this system, although it might, by default, fall under one of the other categories.

78. A: If an employee is accused of inappropriate behavior toward other employees, the company management has an obligation to conduct a workplace investigation. Answer choice B is incorrect because a workplace investigation is related to activities and behavior in the workplace; a rapid reduction in the price of the stock would not require a workplace investigation. Answer choice C is incorrect because company management would not require a workplace investigation due to a breach in legal compliance. Answer choice D is incorrect because disagreements among co-workers are par for the course in the workplace. It is the substance of the disagreement that might cause a workplace investigation.

79. D: FMLA applies to private employers with a minimum of 50 employees. The other answer choices – 15, 20, and 35 – are too low for the FMLA minimum.

80. D: In the workplace, the Meyers-Brigg Type Indicator is primarily used as a personality test to enable individuals to understand their personalities better and to assist staff members in appreciating how to interact with their co-workers more effectively. Due to the nature of the administrative department and its situation – employees who work together quite frequently and run into personality conflicts – the Meyers-Brigg test will be Raisa's best recommendation. Answer choices A and C are incorrect because research has suggested a lack of long-term value in team-building activities such as obstacle courses and scavenger hunts. Answer choice B is also incorrect: while role-playing situations might be beneficial to those who work in highly active and often sensitive fields, they will not necessarily be as useful for employees whose jobs are more focused around completing and maintaining paperwork for a university.

81. D: Because the new hire will have to work with the leadership of other departments, a panel-style interview – at which the leadership of other departments is present – would be valuable in this situation. A situational interview style is useful when a candidate needs to be able to explain his decision within a hypothetical situation. That is less relevant under the circumstances described. A behavioral interview would ask the candidate how he behaved in a past situation. Again, that is not immediately relevant in this situation, nor would it be as useful as a panel interview.

82. A: For applications that are completed in-house – that is, for internal applications that current employees complete – a short-form application is usually best. This is because the company will already have most of the employee's information on file and simply needs a formal application for the new job rather than an extensive application detailing information the company probably has. Answer choice B is incorrect because online applications can take many forms, including all of the answer choices represented here. Answer choice C is incorrect because the long-form application is simply unnecessary for internal hiring. Answer choice D is incorrect because the job-specific application (which is used largely for hiring a number of employees for similar positions) will not necessarily be useful for the company looking to hire internally.

83. A: Gross profit is calculated by subtracting the cost of goods sold from total sales revenue. The cost of goods sold is the funds that have been expended on materials and labor to create products.

84. B: A pesticide is an example of a chemical health hazard. The other three answer choices are biological health hazards. OSHA requires businesses to maintain safety data sheets related to every chemical found in the workplace. A safety data sheet outlines the components of the substance, as well as its behavior under various conditions. Most importantly, the safety data sheet indicates whether a chemical is harmful when absorbed, inhaled, or ingested, and how these dangers may be mitigated or avoided.

85. A: A brown-bag lunch is an example of bottom-up communication. Bottom-up communication is directed from employees to managers. It is important for employees to have a chance to share their ideas and problems with more senior officials. A brown-bag lunch is an informal mealtime gathering of executives and lower-level employees. The other answer choices are forms of top-down communication, or communication directed from managers to lower-level employees.

86. A: Organization development is the process by which a human resources professional analyzes the elements of an organization's makeup and considers opportunities for improvement. Answer choices B, C, and D are incorrect because they refer to elements of organization development but do not explain the larger definition of the process as a whole.

87. D: Increased opportunities for remote work allow organizations to recruit beyond the geographical limitations of an in-person office. While remote work can introduce new complexities to management and operations, it can also allow for a more global approach to recruiting and sourcing strategies. Increased focus on employee well-being may be a strategy to improve the employer brand for candidates but does not necessarily affect the size of the candidate pool itself. Increased employee turnover may or may not affect the candidate pool, depending on how the company's turnover rate compares to the rate of its competitors. Increased automation may impact employee tasks and responsibilities but is not directly correlated with the size of a potential candidate pool.

88. C: The median bonus for salesmen at Franklin Company is $1000. The median is that number which evenly divides a set of numbers. In this case, there are five bonuses, and when arranged in order, the value $1000 lies at position 3, in the middle. The mean of a set of numbers is the same as the average. It is calculated by adding the numbers and dividing the sum by the total number of values in the set. So, in this case, the calculation is performed $(500 + 750 + 1000 + 1000 + 1500) \div 5 = 950$. The minimum value of a set is the lowest value, which is $500. Answer D represents the total, or sum, of the group of numbers.

89. C: The Department of Labor prefers that businesses use positive time reporting with regard to the time worked by employees who are nonexempt under the Fair Labor Standards Act. This method is considered more effective because it gives a clear indication of the hours worked, without the need for any calculation. For instance, in the other acceptable method, exception reporting, the business establishes a baseline for time worked and only notes deviations from the baseline. This requires the DOL to consider both the baseline and the exceptions. Positive time reporting is simpler.

90. C: The Department of Labor is responsible for enforcing the rights of veterans in the workplace. The EEOC, DOJ, and OFCCP are all responsible for enforcing other rights within the workplace.

91. C: The Greendale Company should ask the IRS for a private letter ruling. Private letter rulings are a courtesy provided by the Internal Revenue Service. When a company is uncertain about the tax implications of a proposed change, it may submit the details to the IRS and receive an estimate.

In the long run, the effort expended by the IRS on private letter rulings obviates the need for more work cleaning up unanticipated messes.

92. C: Employees may not strike to support a hot cargo clause. A cargo clause is a pledge made by the employer to the union that the employer will not enter into transactions with some other employer. The other answer choices are true statements.

93. A: For every ten-hour week Deirdre works, she uses ¼ of an FMLA leave week. This is calculated by dividing the number of hours off in her reduced schedule by the number of hours in her normal schedule. Because she has three weeks left of FMLA leave, Deirdre may work twelve weeks of this reduced schedule before her leave expires.

94. D: A histogram is useful for reviewing a series of random events to locate a potential pattern within them. A check sheet is equivalent to a checklist of expected results; the human resources professional would then compare results to the check sheet and check off what has occurred. A pareto chart measures two types of data; the information can yield results about the most important factor among many factors. A scatter chart also measures two types of data on an *xy* graph.

95. C: Grover's boss is guilty of promissory estoppel. Promissory estoppel is the failure to deliver a promised reward for services rendered. An employer who is found guilty of this may be forced to deliver the reward or equivalent compensation. Fraudulent misrepresentation is similar, but it is restricted to lies or misleading statements that persuade a candidate to join the company. Constructive discharge occurs when the work environment becomes so unpleasant that the employee is forced to quit. Finally, defamation is a statement that intends to diminish another person's reputation, and which is likely to impede his ability to find other employment.

96. D: Simply put, legislation that will affect a business often will also affect that business's relationship with its employees. Because the human resources professional is, in some ways, the intermediary between the employers and the employees, he or she should be at least somewhat familiar with legislation and the legislative process. Answer choice A is not correct because the human resources professional is not necessarily responsible for contacting a member of Congress about submitting legislation. Similarly, answer choice B is incorrect because the human resources professional is not required to act as the company's outside contact. Answer choice C is largely irrelevant to the larger question and, if true, would only refer to human resources professionals at small companies that are hoping to expand.

97. C: Yolanda will sign a third-party contract with the temp agency. A third-party contract requires actions to be taken by a party other than the two signing the deal. In this case, the temporary workers are addressed in the contract even though they do not sign it.

98. C: Once a company has filed ERISA records with the Department of Labor, that company is required to maintain those records for a minimum of six years. Answer choices A, B, and D are incorrect because they do not reflect accurate federal guidelines for ERISA record keeping.

99. B: Facilitation is an instructional method that enables employees to work together on problem-solving techniques while under the guidance of a facilitator (a third-party expert in helping different groups interact effectively). Answer choice A is incorrect because the vestibule instructional method is a type of simulation, in which the employees receive hands-on experience on the equipment they will be using. Answer choice C, demonstration, is largely just a presentation of information in a lecture-style setting, so that would be inappropriate for this situation. Similarly,

a conference style of instructional method is primarily focused on presenting information without employee interaction, so answer choice D is also incorrect.

100. B: An intellectual property agreement does not need to include a prohibition against the hiring of current employees by employees who leave the business. Many intellectual property agreements do contain such language, however, commonly known as a nonsolicitation clause. The other answer choices represent the essential components of an intellectual property agreement.

101. D: Fair use includes the following scenarios: use of material for educational purposes, limited copying of material (i.e., 10 or fewer copies for a limited number of individuals), and use of a single paragraph from a book (i.e., small percentage of total). Using quoted information—that is, information from another source—within a company motto is definitely *not* considered fair use; as the company motto represents the company and, in this sense, applies to its larger goal of making a profit, the use of the quoted material would be considered a copyright violation.

102. D: The supervisors at Flanders Company are practicing extinction, though they are most likely unaware of doing so. Extinction occurs when the positive reinforcement that followed a behavior ceases, and the behavior gradually ceases as well. Punishment is a negative consequence to a behavior. The absence of positive reinforcement is not considered punishment. Positive reinforcement is a reward, while negative reinforcement is the removal of a punishment. Positive and negative reinforcement are both used to encourage certain behaviors.

103. A: This labor union is using a parallel bargaining strategy. Parallel bargaining is often used when the union believes that one particular employer will agree to an especially favorable deal. By negotiating this deal first, the union can set a standard that other employers will reluctantly meet. In the integrative bargaining approach, the union and employers lay all the facts on the table and compromise. In positional bargaining, the union and the employer are adversaries, each side using its leverage to get as much as possible. In multi-unit bargaining, a single employer must deal with multiple unions representing different job groups.

104. B: As the question states, the training will encompass several features – lectures, film presentations, and group work. Among the available styles of seating, the chevron-style – with the chairs angled in a V-shape toward the stage or front of the meeting space – will offer the most versatility for trainees. Answer choice A is incorrect because the theater-style seating would be useful for lectures and film presentations but would offer no good way for trainees to break into groups. Answer choice C is incorrect because the banquet-style seating would be excellent for group work but would be impractical for lectures and film presentations. Similarly, answer choice D is incorrect because the conference-style seating would place participants around one large table, which would not necessarily be useful for any of the three activities that will occur in the training.

105. C: FMLA rules allow an employee to take off time to care for a family member within one of the following categories: spouse, child, or parent. In some cases, an extended family member may apply, if the individual can prove a close relationship with that family member. ("Distant uncle rarely seen" does not apply.) Additionally, a romantic partner does not apply; FMLA rules make it clear that, regardless of sex, the partner must be recognized as a married spouse in the state in which they entered the marriage. FMLA rules do apply, however, to an individual who needs to rest during a difficult pregnancy, care for a newborn infant, or adopt or foster a child.

106. C: In the SMART model, the letter "R" stands for Realistic. The other options (Reasonable, Reversible, and Representative) do not fit into the SMART model, which is designed to assist a company in defining its long-term goals for development.

107. D: A realistic job preview should be used when employee replacement costs are high. If it is expensive to hire and train new employees, it is important to maximize the number of new employees who stay with the organization. A realistic job preview winnows out recruits who are less likely to thrive. The other answer choices are scenarios in which a realistic job preview would not be appropriate. When unemployment is high, recruits will be less likely to decline an unsuitable job, because they will doubt their ability to find another. When recruits have access to plenty of information about the job, a realistic job preview is unnecessary. When the selection ratio is high (there are few applicants relative to the number of jobs available), an organization may not be able to afford scaring away potential employees.

108. A: Technical training apprenticeships, often found within various skilled trades industries, employ an "earn while you learn" approach to skills training and testing. Apprenticeships are typically programs where full-time workers spend their off time on evenings or weekends in a classroom environment to learn about and test competency at the skills, knowledge, and abilities required for the industry and position they work in. A 360-degree assessment is a type of workforce test that addresses all angles of performance review to include the employee themselves, customers, peers, supervisors, subordinates, and others. A dual career ladder is less an assessment and more an alternate career path for employees who are skilled at what they do but are not suitable for, or do not want to pursue, management positions. A situation judgment test assesses the skills of leaders in the workforce in scenario-based tests to see how they would respond in various situations.

109. C: A brown-bag meeting is considered more of a bottom-up form of communication: at a brown bag meeting, employees are invited to take part in the discussion and share their ideas. Top-down communication would focus more on the management informing employees of decisions. As a result, the other answer choices reflect more of top-down communication: posters, bulletin board postings, and newsletters.

110. B: Salting occurs when someone takes a job with a company that the union has targeted for employee unionization, and thus works to encourage employees at the new company to organize a union. This would be viewed as a form of instigation and is thus not a fair labor practice. Wildcatting, per se, does not exist, although there is a *wildcat strike*, which occurs in spite of a contractual prohibition against strikes. Featherbedding refers to the activity of keeping an employee in a position despite that position being considered obsolete due to changes in technology. And leafleting is a union activity that involves passing out leaflets about the union's position and thus drumming up support.

111. D: A total rewards strategy is the comprehensive, long term plan for direct and indirect compensation that will ultimately drive high-talent employee recruitment and retention. Answer choice A is incorrect. While a total rewards program might cover salaries, the total rewards strategy encompasses far more than basic salary. Answer choice B is incorrect because the total rewards strategy is only one piece of an employer brand. Answer choice C is incorrect because while certain compensation practices can be designed with the intent to improve teamwork amongst coworkers, that will only apply in specific situations.

112. B: The Delphi technique requires several rounds of questioning before a consensus is reached. In this method of decision-making, a panel of anonymous experts is given a short questionnaire. Their written responses are subjected to another series of questions. This process continues until a consensus is reached. The Delphi technique is good for getting a wide range of honest perspectives, and is convenient when the participants are geographically distant from one another.

113. A: People and production are on the axes of the Blake-Mouton managerial grid. The Blake-Mouton managerial grid is a tool for assessing leadership. It simplifies this complex subject by reducing leadership to its focus on people and its focus on production. In some cases, attention to one of these factors will necessitate inattention to the other. This model suggests, however, that the best leaders are those who maximize their concern for both people and production.

114. C: The national lost work day index (LWDI) average for private-sector organizations is approximately 2.5. This means that there are about 2.5 lost work days per day for every hundred employees. This figure is calculated by the Occupational Safety and Health Administration. LWDI is calculated by dividing the number of workdays missed because of personal injury for each hundred employees, dividing by the total number of employees, and then multiplying by a hundred.

115. A: As a human resources professional, Angelova's best recommendation would be a counseling program that assists students in recovering from the trauma of a terrorist attack. Answer choice B is incorrect because the human resources professional would not do well to recommend a relocation program for students away from the university. Answer choice C is incorrect because a monthly email newsletter providing recommendations for students would hardly suffice to help students in the aftermath of a terrorist attack. Answer choice D is incorrect because the human resources professional is not generally authorized to advise the creation of a new department.

PHR Practice Test #2

1. Which of the following correlation coefficients would indicate the strongest relationship between two variables?

    a. +0.7
    b. 0
    c. -0.1
    d. -0.9

2. The Foreign Corrupt Practices Act (FCPA) was designed to do which of the following?

    a. Prevent illegal trafficking of merchandise
    b. Curtail extensive imports to bolster domestic manufacturing
    c. Set high standards for American businesses that have locations abroad
    d. Prevent American businesses from bribing foreign governments

3. Vince is a middle manager at Foster Company. He earns a base salary of $85,000, and the midpoint of the salary range for middle managers is $110,000. What is Vince's compa-ratio?

    a. 29%
    b. 77%
    c. 85%
    d. 129%

4. Which compensation system is typical of unionized workplaces?

    a. seniority-based
    b. membership-based
    c. performance-based
    d. incentive-based

5. OSHA forms require privacy standards to protect employee records. Apart from the employee's specific request, in which of the following cases would it be legally advisable to label the employee's file with a case number instead of the employee's name on OSHA Form 300?

    a. An employee develops hepatitis in the workplace
    b. An employee develops the flu after receiving a flu vaccine in the workplace
    c. An employee develops food poisoning in the workplace
    d. An employee receives a head injury in the workplace

6. OSHA 300 represents which of the following?

    a. Summary of Workplace Problems
    b. Injury and Illness Incident Report
    c. Log of Work-Related Injuries and Illnesses
    d. Employee Privacy Case List

7. The Stanley Corporation wants to avoid lawsuits, so the human resources department occasionally reviews the hiring process to ensure compliance with all equal opportunity regulations. This is an example of

   a. risk avoidance.
   b. risk elimination.
   c. risk mitigation.
   d. risk transfer.

8. Which of the following human resources responsibilities can be the most impactful approach to creating a sense of accountability for ethical behavior?

   a. Employee communication
   b. Total rewards design
   c. Coaching and mentoring programs
   d. Performance management

9. How long after signing does an Executive Order become law?

   a. 15 days
   b. 30 days
   c. 45 days
   d. 60 days

10. When considering the purchase of an HRIS that includes ATS capabilities, which of the following metrics would be the MOST important as it relates to increasing recruiting volume?

   a. Candidate demographics ratios
   b. Employee participation rate
   c. Application conversion rate
   d. Return on investment ratio

11. Louisa is in the process of interviewing the prospective employees for an open position in the accounting department of a small publishing company. She has already interviewed several strong candidates, but she is looking forward to interviewing one of the candidates whose resume has struck her as showing significant potential. When this employee enters the room, however, it is obvious that he has not fully conquered his pre-interview nerves, and he stumbles through the first few questions. By the end of the interview, however, the candidate is doing well, responding articulately and living up to the potential indicated in his resume. Louisa, though, is unable to overcome her disappointment with the candidate's earlier nervousness and fails to see his improvement during the interview. Louisa is displaying which of the following types of interview bias?

   a. Knowledge-of-predictor
   b. Stereotyping
   c. Recency
   d. Nonverbal bias
   e. First impression

12. Which of the following types of collective bargaining positions results when the different sides agree to compromise on certain issues by taking the big picture into account?

   a. Positional bargaining
   b. Integrative bargaining
   c. Interest-based bargaining
   d. Distributive bargaining

13. When designing a total rewards plan, which of the following actions would be MOST effective at designing a benefits strategy to improve employee retention?

   a. Research market surveys to determine the current industry standards
   b. Coordinate with the accounting department to determine the maximum possible budget for benefits
   c. Perform a job analysis to determine benefits stratification across the workforce hierarchy
   d. Survey employees to better understand their needs and desires

14. The Drug-Free Workplace Act of 1988 applies to which of the following types of organizations?

   a. Large corporations
   b. Federal contractors
   c. Government agencies
   d. Local businesses governed under municipal laws

15. Which of these businesses is most likely to have an outbreak of tuberculosis?

   a. assisted-living facility
   b. gym
   c. restaurant
   d. gas station

16. Which piece of legislation declared that back pay awards cannot be a part of compensatory damages but instead must be paid in addition to applicable compensatory damages?

   a. Civil Rights Act of 1964
   b. Civil Rights Act of 1991
   c. Equal Employment Opportunity Act of 1974
   d. Americans with Disabilities Act of 1990

17. In Alderfer's theory of motivation, what do the letters ERG stand for?

   a. energy, relatedness, and growth
   b. existence, responsibility, and growth
   c. energy, responsibility, and growth
   d. existence, relatedness, and growth

18. The final step in a job pricing exercise is

   a. a salary range recommendation.
   b. a wage target.
   c. hiring the least costly candidate.
   d. weighing candidate qualifications against available funds.

19. As he arrives at work, Sven accidentally bumps into a tree when driving in the company parking lot. He experiences some neck pain later in the day. Is this a work-related injury?

a. No, injuries sustained in vehicle accidents on company property before or after work are not considered work-related.
b. No, because Sven had not yet clocked in.
c. Yes, because the accident took place on company property.
d. Yes, because the symptoms emerged at work.

20. The Hierarchy of Needs Theory (1954) is attributed to which of the following researchers?

a. Fredrick Herzberg
b. Clayton Alderfer
c. Abraham Maslow
d. Victor Vroom

21. Which of the following is a primary reason for the failure of total quality management programs?

a. Micromanaging by employees at all levels of the organizational hierarchy
b. Overemphasis on core objectives
c. Failure to use ISO 9000 standards
d. Inability to identify the advantages of change

22. Which of the following is NOT considered a *voluntary* benefit that employers may provide for employees?

a. Short-term disability insurance
b. Vision insurance
c. Medicare
d. Life insurance

23. A Scanlon Plan is an example of a(n)

a. individual incentive.
b. sales bonus.
c. group incentive.
d. Employee Stock Ownership Plan.

24. Lewis is in charge of collecting feedback from employees about a new program that his company has implemented. The company has a number of locations, spread out across four different countries. Which of the following methods of data collection would be most effective for Lewis to employ?

a. Focus group
b. Interviews
c. Questionnaire
d. Observation

25. Which of the following is not considered a statutory deduction?

a. Union dues
b. Social Security
c. State income tax
d. Federal income tax

26. **Which piece of legislation made it illegal to discriminate on the basis of health?**
    a. Retirement Equity Act of 1984
    b. Health Insurance Portability and Accountability Act of 1996
    c. Civil Rights Act of 1991
    d. Pregnancy Discrimination Act of 1978

27. **Which approach to budgeting requires that every expense be justified?**
    a. historical budgeting
    b. flexible budgeting
    c. zero-based budgeting
    d. bottom-up budgeting

28. **In Vroom's expectancy theory, what is the name for the reasoned decision to work?**
    a. valence
    b. instrumentality
    c. proclivity
    d. expectancy

29. **Felix is interviewing a candidate for a position in an oil and gas company with locations around the world. As they talk, the candidate mentions his wife. What is an appropriate question that Felix may ask the candidate about his family?**
    a. Are you willing to relocate?
    b. Do you and your wife plan to have children?
    c. Do any other family members live with you?
    d. Does your wife also work?

30. **Employment contracts seeking to protect company intellectual property would most likely include which of the following attachments?**
    a. Conditions of employment
    b. Nondisclosure agreement
    c. Employee handbook
    d. At-will employment statement

31. **Which of the following pieces of legislation was intended to improve accounting practices within public companies?**
    a. Sarbanes-Oxley Act
    b. Rehabilitation Act
    c. Title VII
    d. HIPAA

32. **ERISA mandates that employees who use grade vesting must be fully vested in a qualified plan**
    a. immediately.
    b. within four years.
    c. within seven years.
    d. before being laid off.

33. When a Compliance Safety and Health Officer (CSHO) holds an inspection of a business, all of the following must occur during the inspection except:

   a. Opening conference
   b. Presentation of credentials
   c. Resolution of problem
   d. Tour of facilities

34. A small restaurant is looking for a new short order cook. Because the job requires that the individual be able to work quickly and efficiently, the restaurant presents candidates with a pre-employment test that will measure how well each completes a variety of food preparation tasks. Which of the following types of tests would be most appropriate?

   a. Cognitive Ability Test
   b. Psychomotor Assessment Test
   c. Physical Assessment Test
   d. Aptitude Test

35. Which of the following does not represent a step in Enterprise Risk Management (ERM)?

   a. Identify risks
   b. Identify those responsible for risks
   c. Identify mitigation options for risks
   d. Make decisions about dealing with risks

36. Which type of voluntary benefit program utilizes a typical pension plan in which the employer adds an established benefit to the plan when the employee retires?

   a. Benefit accrual plan
   b. Defined contribution
   c. Nonqualified plan
   d. Defined benefit

37. Which of the following is the LEAST effective tool to use in total quality management?

   a. Pareto chart
   b. pie chart
   c. scattergram
   d. histogram

38. Which motivational theory focuses on the ability to alter behavior through intervention options, such as positive or negative reinforcement?

   a. Alderfer ERG Theory
   b. Skinner Operant Conditioning Theory
   c. Maslow Hierarchy Theory
   d. Vroom Expectancy Theory

39. *Pattern bargaining*, *whipsawing*, and *leapfrogging* are all alternate names for which of the following collective bargaining strategies?

   a. Single-union bargaining
   b. Multi-employer bargaining
   c. Parallel bargaining
   d. Multi-unit bargaining

40. A data management company is looking to hire several new candidates who will be responsible for researching current data and cleaning up outdated files within the database. The database clean-up will cover four separate departments within the company, so the new employees will be required to work with the heads of each of the department. Lydia, who is the human resources professional for the company, has been asked about which type of interview would be most effective for this position. Considering the job situation, what type of interview should Lydia recommend?

    a. Panel
    b. Behavioral
    c. Patterned
    d. Stress

41. *Risk transfer* can typically be affected by doing which of the following?

    a. Reviewing employment policies frequently to avoid the chances of an employee lawsuit
    b. Purchasing employment practices liability insurance to protect a business
    c. Taking advance action to consider potentials for risk and prevent problems from occurring
    d. Being familiar with chances of risk and creating a financial buffer against future costs

42. The Health Insurance Portability and Accountability Act (HIPAA) was added to ERISA to do which of the following?

    a. Establish new guidelines for employee health insurance programs within organizations
    b. Ensure that all employers are responsible for covering minimum health conditions among employees
    c. Link ERISA to COBRA to protect any employees that are covered under COBRA guidelines
    d. Forbid any discrimination based on pre-existing health problems or conditions

43. Within the Hersey-Blanchard (1977), there are four leadership styles: Selling, Telling, Delegating, and which of the following?

    a. Participating
    b. Directing
    c. Motivating
    d. Guiding

44. The Henderson Company needs to hire a large number of unskilled employees to perform data entry. Which type of application would be most appropriate?

    a. long-form employment application
    b. short-form employment application
    c. weighted employment application
    d. job-specific employment application

45. Which of the following statements about unions is true?

    a. Unions may require employers to terminate anti-union employees.
    b. Unions may not be held liable for coercive acts by union members.
    c. Unions may not participate in secondary boycotts.
    d. Unions may picket even where another union is the legal bargaining representative.

46. During which phase of the strategic planning process would a SWOT analysis be most useful?

    a. evaluation

    b. environmental scan

    c. construction

    d. adjustment

47. What is the largest possible damage award under the Civil Rights Act of 1991?

    a. $50,000

    b. $100,000

    c. $200,000

    d. $300,000

48. Which type of strike is launched despite a no-strike clause in the employee contract?

    a. sit-down strike

    b. secondary strike

    c. hot cargo strike

    d. wildcat strike

49. What are the four styles of leadership identified by the Hersey-Blanchard theory?

    a. telling, selling, participating, delegating

    b. showing, growing, sowing, bestowing

    c. managing, administrating, inspiring, following

    d. giving, taking, making, doing

50. The Needlestick Safety and Prevention Act of 2000 requires organizations to do which of the following?

    a. Quarterly audits to check for sharp objects that could cause workplace injuries

    b. Removal of specified sharp objects from workplace due to potential for injury

    c. Listing of sharp objects recognized for having caused workplace injuries in the past

    d. Report workplace injuries from sharp objects and consider replacement object to prevent future injuries

51. Which of the following is NOT an eligibility requirement for Trade Adjustment Assistance?

    a. The employer's sales must have declined.

    b. Applicable only to manufacturing sector workers.

    c. The employer's production must have increased.

    d. Increased imports must have caused job loss.

52. Tara's boss asks her to pick up an important client from the airport. The client's flight is delayed, so Tara goes to a nearby restaurant and eats dinner. Should Tara be compensated for this time?

    a. Yes, because she has been engaged to wait.

    b. Yes, because she is waiting to be engaged.

    c. No, because she has been engaged to wait.

    d. No, because she is waiting to be engaged.

53. Phyllis wants to hire several college students as seasonal employees in her shop. She refers these students to a temp agency, who hires them and sends them to work for Phyllis. This is called

    a. payrolling.
    b. on-call employment.
    c. in-house employment.
    d. temp-to-perm employment.

54. What is the fiduciary role of the human resources professional regarding ERISA?

    a. Setting up pension accounts for employees
    b. Handling and managing pension funds
    c. Ensuring that the HIPAA guidelines of ERISA are observed
    d. Creating the rules that govern individual retirement account for employees

55. Which of the following best describes what an employer can do when employees begin to unionize?

    a. Employers may contact union leaders and forbid unionization.
    b. Employers may block employees who begin the process of unionization
    c. Employers may threaten to replace workers who choose to unionize
    d. Employers may explain problems with unionization to employees

56. Which of the following is defined as an attempt to improve overall business operations so that customers benefit from the process?

    a. Workforce expansion
    b. Divestiture
    c. Reengineering
    d. Offshoring

57. Within how many months of an incident must a labor charge be filed with the NLRB?

    a. 3
    b. 4
    c. 5
    d. 6

58. How far in advance of a planned union picketing must a representation petition be completed?

    a. 15 days
    b. 30 days
    c. 45 days
    d. 60 days

59. What is the youngest age at which most children may legally work, under certain conditions, as stipulated by FLSA?

    a. 13
    b. 14
    c. 15
    d. 16

60. Three barriers resulted in the need for the 1991 Glass Ceiling Act. These barriers were internal structural barriers, societal barriers, and which of the following types of barriers?

a. Governmental
b. Recruitment
c. Educational
d. Corporate

61. The components of an effective substance abuse program include all of the following except:

a. A written statement regarding the company's no-tolerance policy about substance abuse
b. Upper-level management support for all substance abuse programs and policies
c. Targeted drug testing for employees who have substance abuse problems
d. Management training programs for implementing substance abuse policy

62. Based on federal recommendations, for how long should OSHA forms be retained by an employer?

a. 2 years
b. 3 years
c. 5 years
d. 7 years

63. During a lawful economic strike, employers have the right to do which of the following?

a. Confront employees and require that they return to work at the risk of being fired
b. Hire new employees to replace striking employees
c. Encourage the union to disband or a suggest the formation of a new union
d. Dissolve the union and require new representation

64. In terms of "foreseeable leave" for FMLA rights, how long in advance must an employee notify his employer?

a. 15 days
b. 30 days
c. 45 days
d. 60 days

65. Gabriela is a human resources professional who has been given the responsibility of filling a position within the HR department. She is ready to begin making the details of the position available to interested candidates and pursuing potential employees who meet the requirements of the job as best as possible. The process of pursuing potential employees is known as which of the following?

a. Hiring
b. Recruiting
c. Tracking
d. Selection

66. Which of the following recruiting methods is MOST efficient at creating an interactive talent pool?

    a. Job fairs
    b. Staffing agencies
    c. Social media
    d. Internships

67. An automotive plant with 170 employees will be closing within the next six months, and the majority of the workers will be laid off. Based on the requirements of the WARN Act of 1988, how long in advance of the closing is the plant expected to inform the workers of the impending lay-offs?

    a. 30 days
    b. 60 days
    c. 90 days
    d. 120 days

68. A corporate university is an

    a. academic institution run for profit.
    b. independent academic institution that produces recruits for a corporation.
    c. extensive training program administered by a corporation to existing employees.
    d. alternative to community college.

69. Which of the following types of deferred compensation plans is considered "portable" because employees can remove the money from the plan and convert the payment into other forms?

    a. Profit-sharing
    b. Money purchase
    c. Cash balance
    d. Target benefit

70. Which of the following is a strategic function of the human resources department?

    a. Creating retention plans
    b. Recruiting new employees
    c. Ensuring compliance with federal regulations
    d. Keeping employee data confidential

71. What is one common problem with cost-per-hire metrics?

    a. They make no distinctions between job groups.
    b. They are overly dependent on external economic factors.
    c. They overemphasize advertising.
    d. They omit costs that are not related to specific candidates.

72. Fran is interviewing candidates for an accounting position. Glenda seems like a very qualified candidate, but Fran finds her voice very annoying. Despite Glenda's solid record, Fran hires another candidate. Fran's decision demonstrates the

    a. central tendency.
    b. horn effect.
    c. stereotyping bias.
    d. cultural noise bias.

73. Which of the following types of employee rating systems usually results in rating employees along a bell curve?

 a. Paired comparison
 b. Forced distribution
 c. Ranking
 d. Nominal scale

74. Which of the following is not a recognized type of picketing?

 a. Organizational
 b. Informational
 c. Petitional
 d. Recognitional

75. Which of the following is the best definition of an employer's brand?

 a. The public relations strategy for a company's success
 b. The human resources policy of marketing the company to prospective employees
 c. A clear portrayal of the company's identity
 d. The total rewards philosophy for a company

76. For how long after Department of Labor filing must ERISA records be maintained by a business?

 a. 3 years
 b. 4 years
 c. 5 years
 d. 6 years

77. The point factor method is used to

 a. ensure compliance with OSHA regulations.
 b. identify the most important positions in an organization.
 c. create fair performance incentives.
 d. incentivize waste elimination.

78. Which of the following OSHA forms is intended to be a Summary of Work-Related Injuries and Illnesses?

 a. OSHA Form 300
 b. OSHA Form 300A
 c. OSHA Form 301
 d. OSHA Form 301A

79. In which type of dispute resolution do both parties agree to accept whatever decision is reached by the third party judge?

 a. binding arbitration
 b. compulsory arbitration
 c. constructive confrontation
 d. ad hoc arbitration

80. How old must one be to take a non-farm job that has been designated hazardous by the Secretary of Labor?

    a. 16
    b. 18
    c. 21
    d. There is no age restriction on hazardous employment.

81. Which metric compares the number of new employees to the total number of employees?

    a. replacement rate
    b. turnover rate
    c. accession rate
    d. succession rate

82. How many weeks of unpaid leave is an employer required to give a new mother under the Family Medical Leave Act of 1993?

    a. 3
    b. 12
    c. 16
    d. 52

83. Which of the following steps should come FIRST when developing an organizational emergency response plan?

    a. Gather employee input
    b. Develop emergency testing drills
    c. Risk identification
    d. Hire emergency planning consultants

84. Byron wants to analyze the relationship between the size of the holiday advertising budget and sales. Which analytical strategy will he use?

    a. trend analysis
    b. ratio
    c. simple linear regression
    d. multiple linear regression

85. Administrative laws, such as agency rules and regulations, take effect how many days after being published in the *Federal Register*?

    a. 15 days
    b. 30 days
    c. 45 days
    d. 60 days

86. The Williamson Company is using the paired comparison method to appraise performance. There are seven people in the sales job group. With how many people will each member of this group be compared?

    a. One
    b. Two
    c. Six
    d. Seven

87. A new employee enters the training room and notices that the seats have been arranged in a banquet style. What can the new employee expect to do during the training session?

    a. Work in a small group

    b. Watch a video

    c. Take notes

    d. Fill out a questionnaire

88. Helena is the human resources professional for a large legal firm. The upper management is interested in polling employees about ideas for improvements, but the firm has a solid hierarchy in place. As a result, many of the lower-level employees have confided in Helena that they do not feel comfortable speaking up. Which of the following ideas might Helena recommend to allow employees to voice their opinions without fear of upsetting higher-ranking employees?

    a. Brown bag lunch

    b. Focus group

    c. Email

    d. Suggestion box

89. Which of the following best defines featherbedding?

    a. When an employer ceases to do business with another employer

    b. When an obsolete job is retained to ensure an employee is not terminated

    c. When a union coerces an employee to participate in union activities

    d. When a union overcharges employees the union fees

90. Which of the following pre-selection assessments would be most appropriate to utilize when selecting candidates for a team that will be managing a new computer system?

    a. Personality test

    b. Cross-cultural assessment tool

    c. Cognitive ability test

    d. Aptitude test

91. Which of the following is not considered a bottom-up method of communication delivery?

    a. Open-door policy

    b. Company-wide letters

    c. Webcasts

    d. Staff meetings

92. In which of the following businesses is the research and development department likely to be distinct from the marketing department?

    a. fertilizer manufacturer

    b. toy manufacturer

    c. publisher

    d. clothing manufacturer

93. **Which of the following is not one of the seven recognized racial categories for EEO-1?**
    a. Native Hawaiian
    b. Alaska Native
    c. Asian
    d. European

94. **In the sales department of Fitch Company, employees know that the size of their annual bonus is tied to their performance. The company has published a chart indicating the relationship between sales and compensation. The employees of Fitch Company have**
    a. an entitlement philosophy.
    b. line of sight.
    c. intrinsic rewards.
    d. fiduciary responsibility.

95. **The orientation program at Company X is considered very intense. New employees are given a crash course in organizational philosophy, and are discouraged from voicing their opinions or concerns. Which type of people processing strategy is Company X using?**
    a. investiture
    b. contest
    c. collective
    d. divestiture

96. **The Uniform Guidelines on Employee Selection Procedures declare that**
    a. employers may never use selection tools that adversely impact protected classes.
    b. employers may use whichever selection tool they prefer.
    c. employers must use the selection tool that has the least adverse impact on protected classes.
    d. a selection tool has an adverse impact when the hiring rate for protected classes is less than half the rate for the class hired most often.

97. **Which of the following scenarios represents a legitimate exemption status for an employer?**
    a. The high school football coach of a large high school is exempt from overtime requirements due to taking students to out-of-town games
    b. A large farm that employs teenagers during the summer months is exempt from child labor requirements
    c. The firefighters in a twelve-person department of a medium-sized town are exempt from minimum wage requirements
    d. The police officers in the four-person police department of a small town is exempt from overtime requirements

98. **Which of the following HRIS functions is the MOST impactful when reducing the transactional responsibilities for a human resources team?**
    a. Employee self-service
    b. Data reporting and analytics
    c. Performance management
    d. Training platform

99. During the holiday season, Marsha works 30 hours of overtime. Her employer elects to give her compensatory time off instead of direct pay. How many hours of comp time has Marsha earned?

   a. 15 hours
   b. 20 hours
   c. 30 hours
   d. 45 hours

100. Which component of an affirmative action plan provides demographic information for the labor market related to each job group?

   a. job group analysis
   b. determination of availability
   c. comparison of incumbency to availability
   d. organizational profile

101. The Archibald Corporation has offices in thirteen countries besides the United States. In these foreign offices, the management positions are held by locals and the corporate positions are held by Americans. Which of the following is the most likely possible drawback of this arrangement?

   a. Organizational culture is too homogenous
   b. Resentment by the foreign community
   c. Lack of communication among the foreign offices
   d. Exaggerated hiring costs

102. Which of the following is NOT part of Kirkpatrick's training evaluation framework?

   a. reaction
   b. results
   c. context
   d. learning

103. As of July 24, 2009, the federal minimum wage was established at $7.25 per hour. Grace Clothing, a successful line of retail clothing stores located in California, will be hiring 10 new workers at minimum wage with the option for commission. California has a statewide minimum wage of $15.00 per hour, so the company owners have contacted human resources manager Edwina regarding the disparity in minimum wage pay at the state and federal level. Which statement below best describes the policy Edwina would cite to help Grace Clothing resolve the difference?

   a. Grace Clothing is required to pay employees the lowest minimum wage of any state in the country, which is $5.15
   b. When a federal minimum wage is lower than a state minimum wage, companies may use the federal minimum wage as their standard
   c. When a state minimum wage is higher than the federal minimum wage, the company is required to pay the state minimum over the federal minimum
   d. The size of Grace Clothing makes it exempt from minimum wage requirements, so the company has no obligation to follow either federal or state minimum wage

104. When one company acquires another, what is the first step for the acquiring company's human resources department?

    a. Survey of the workforce for both organizations

    b. Elimination of redundant positions

    c. Review of collective bargaining agreements

    d. Assurance of OSHA compliance

105. Abbey, the head of the human resources department for a book distribution service, accidentally discovers that an employee has a genetic disease that could potentially affect the employee's ability to continue in the job. According to the Genetic Information Nondiscrimination Act of 2008, all employee genetic information is private, and companies are not allowed to make decisions based on employee conditions. Now that Abbey has discovered this information, what is her responsibility?

    a. Abbey is required to report the information to her superiors, but they will not be allowed to alter the employee's work situation

    b. Abbey must inform the Department of Labor about her inadvertent acquisition of the knowledge

    c. Abbey must let the employee know what she has discovered and counsel the employee to consider requesting a change in the employee's job situation

    d. Abbey must not divulge any of the information or change the employee's working situation, though she has not violated any law

106. Which of the following human resources audits would be most effective for assessing the performance and efficiency of payroll procedures?

    a. Compliance audit

    b. Handbook audit

    c. Functional audit

    d. Strategic audit

107. The Labor-Management Reporting and Disclosure Act (LMRDA) of 1959 required that *national* unions conduct leadership elections how often?

    a. Every 2 years

    b. Every 3 years

    c. Every 4 years

    d. Every 5 years

108. The Motivation/Hygiene Theory (1959) is attributed to which of the following researchers?

    a. Fredrick Herzberg

    b. Clayton Alderfer

    c. Abraham Maslow

    d. Victor Vroom

109. The role of the human resources professional regarding FMLA rules includes all of the following except:

    a. Being familiar with FMLA requirements and changes

    b. Educating those in management about FMLA rules

    c. Developing an FMLA documentation policy for the company

    d. Working to avoid simultaneous FMLA leave among employees

110. What is the purpose of the Training Adjustment Assistance (TAA) program?

   a. To create funding for employees who have been terminated for any reason
   b. To help employees who lose their jobs due to a rise in the number of imports
   c. To establish health benefits for employees after they have been laid off
   d. To improve the quality of employee working conditions

111. The Fair Labor Standards Act (FLSA) has two significant amendments that have been added since the legislation was first passed in 1938. One of these amendments forbids any type of discrimination based on the employee's gender. Which of the following reflects this amendment?

   a. Portal to Portal Act
   b. Equal Pay Act
   c. Davis Beacon Act
   d. National Labor Relations Act

112. To be eligible to collect unemployment, an employee must meet all or some of the following criteria EXCEPT:

   a. Being part of a short-term, department-wide layoff
   b. Actively seeking employment with a new company
   c. Previously employed with company for the appropriate "base period"
   d. After voluntary termination to start a new business

113. According to the Pregnancy Discrimination Act of 1978, employers should treat pregnancy like a

   a. work-related illness.
   b. work-related injury.
   c. short-term disability.
   d. long-term disability.

114. Why does the Uniform Guidelines on Employee Selection Process (UGESP) require reliability and validity in testing?

   a. To ensure the same results from all tests
   b. To avoid discrimination against protected classes
   c. To quantify the success rate for the company doing the testing
   d. To create a better standard for testing

115. When developing an inappropriate-absence policy for an organization, a human resource professional should include all of the following except:

   a. Statement about how many sick days each employee receives
   b. Indication of how sick days are counted within the calendar
   c. Information about how each absence is counted in days
   d. Requirement for a doctor's note for each sick day absence

Answer Key and Explanations for Test #2

1. D: Of the given correlation coefficients, -0.9 would indicate the strongest relationship between the two variables. Correlation coefficients exist on a range from -1 to +1. The strength of the correlation is indicated by the distance from zero, or absolute value, of the coefficient. In other words, whether a correlation coefficient is positive or negative does not influence its strength.

2. D: The Foreign Corrupt Practices Act (FCPA) was created specifically to prevent American businesses from bribing foreign governments. This act has nothing to do with the illegal trafficking of merchandise (answer choice A) or changing the level of imports (answer choice B). And while the larger role of the act is to maintain fair standards, answer choice C is incorrect because it is not clear about the nature of these fair standards.

3. B: Vince's compa-ratio is 77%. Compa-ratio is calculated by dividing the individual salary by the midpoint of the base salary for the job group, and then multiplying the quotient by 100. It is a handy way of comparing one person's salary with the salaries of other people who fill the same position.

4. A: A seniority-based compensation system is typical of unionized workplaces. One reason for this is that the compensation system of a unionized business is based on negotiation between the employer and the union, rather than on internal measures of performance. One complaint about unions is that by encouraging a seniority system of compensation, they encourage complacency.

5. A: Given the sensitive nature of the disease, the contraction of hepatitis, even in the workplace, would be grounds for the employer to use a case number instead of the employee's name. Unless an employee specifically requests a case number, there is no need to assign one to a case file in any of the following situations: an employee contracts the flu after receiving a flu vaccine in the workplace, an employee develops food poisoning in the workplace, or an employee receives a head injury in the workplace.

6. C: OSHA 300 is officially the Log of Work-Related Injuries and Illnesses. Answer choice A is incorrect because it more closely reflects OSHA 300A, which is a separate log. Answer choice B is incorrect because the Injury and Illness Incident Report is officially OSHA 301. Answer choices D is incorrect because it reflects an element of OSHA 300 but does not encompass the correct title of the log.

7. C: This is an example of risk mitigation. The Stanley Corporation minimizes the potential for lawsuits by monitoring its own compliance. Some risks cannot be entirely avoided; there is no perfect strategy for avoiding litigation. This risk cannot be eliminated. Risk transfer is similar to risk mitigation, but it involves increasing expense in one area to minimize a risk elsewhere. For instance, a company might increase insurance payments to account for a particular risk.

8. D: Human resources professionals can leverage all of these options when creating an ethical work environment; however, an "ethical work environment" can mean a great number of things and present in a variety of ways. Building accountability within business ethics can be directly derived from regular performance management practices. Employee communication is useful for building a culture of honesty and transparency. Total rewards design can encourage ethical behaviors before correction needs to occur. Coaching and mentoring programs can help align employee development within the values of an organization's mission and vision.

9. B: Unless otherwise stipulated, an Executive Order becomes law after 30 days. The other answer choices are either too low (15 days) or too high (45 days and 60 days).

10. C: An Applicant Tracking System (ATS) can be a standalone software or can be packaged within an overarching Human Resources Information System (HRIS). The application conversion rate is the percentage of candidates who complete a job application after the first click on the "apply" button or link. Factors that can affect the application flow include the number of clicks from start to finish, the presentation of the ATS program compared to the company's website, and other barriers such as forcing applicants to create system logins or re-input their resume data after uploading the original document; improved application flow leads to an increased number of applications and increased pool of candidates to consider when recruiting. Candidate demographics ratios can be important for a company focusing on employee diversity but may not affect the overall volume of candidates. Employee participation rate focuses on candidates after they've completed the hiring process and are using other elements of the HRIS. The return on investment ratio focuses on the financial impact of the system and can include a number of outcomes within the measurement—not just recruiting.

11. E: Louisa's response to the candidate is influenced by her first impression of the candidate's behavior. A knowledge-of-predictor bias (answer choice A) means the interviewer responds to the candidate based on knowledge about the candidate's scores on evaluative tests that were given. A stereotyping bias (answer choice B) occurs when an interviewer bases a personal opinion about a candidate on a stereotype of the candidate rather than evaluating the candidate as objectively as possible. A recency bias (answer choice C) means the interviewer compares a candidate to the most recent candidate that was interviewed. A nonverbal bias occurs when the interviewer is over-influenced by body language instead of by the candidate's responses.

12. B: Integrative bargaining results when the different sides agree to compromise on certain issues by taking the big picture into account. Positional bargaining results when each side establishes a clear position and aims to achieve the goal or goals of that position. Interest-based bargaining results when both sides acknowledge that they have a strong motivation in the continuity of business activities, and thus proceed in negotiations with this acknowledgement. Distributive bargaining is another name for positional bargaining.

13. D: In the wake of the Great Resignation, historic levels of job turnover have been spurred by employee desire for better compensation, improved work/life balance, and improved benefits. The most effective way to determine what total rewards will inspire employees to stay is to ask employees what they want out of their rewards in order to stay. Market research and coordinating across organizational functions are useful steps in the process but do not necessarily lead to rewards specific to the needs and desires of the workforce. Job analysis can be a useful tool during organizational design and restructure but does not directly link employee retention and total rewards.

14. B: The Drug-Free Workplace Act of 1988 applies specifically to federal contractors (specifically, those with federal contracts worth at least $100,000). Answer choices A, C, D, and E are incorrect because they inaccurately reflect the types of organizations to which the Drug-Free Workplace Act of 1988 refers. Specifically, answer choice A is incorrect because it is far too vague. A federal contractor might be a large corporation, but not all large corporations are going to be federal contractors. Answer choice C is incorrect because federal contractors might be funded through government agencies but are entirely different organizations. Answer choice D is incorrect because it simply makes no sense: all local businesses will, in some way, be governed under municipal laws.

159

15. A: An assisted-living facility would be the most likely of these businesses to have an outbreak of tuberculosis. Tuberculosis is an airborne disease, and spreads quickly in places where people work closely together. An assisted-living facility, where people share the same space and breathe the same air every day, is an excellent breeding ground for TB.

16. B: The Civil Rights Act of 1991 declared that back pay awards cannot be a part of compensatory damages and introduced emotional stress damages as a potential outcome. This act also made it illegal for businesses to claim that discriminatory practices were somehow necessary to their operations. This act also directly prohibited all racial harassment, whereas earlier legislation had limited its scope to hiring practices.

17. D: In Alderfer's theory of motivation, the letters ERG stand for existence, relatedness, and growth. Like Maslow, Alderfer asserted that basic needs must be met before a person can attend to more sophisticated desires. Whereas Maslow defined the hierarchy of needs, in ascending levels of importance, as physiological, safety, love, status, and esteem, Alderfer reduced it to three. The first, existence, refers to all the activities aimed at maintaining life. The second, relatedness, refers to the need for connection with other people. The third, growth, is the innate human desire for personal evolution.

18. A: The final step in a job pricing exercise is a salary range recommendation. Job pricing is an exercise for determining the appropriate salary for a new or modified position. It begins by fully defining the job description. The next step is to obtain a relevant salary survey and analyze the compensation for similar positions. The final step is to recommend a range of salaries, from which executives can choose. Job pricing typically happens during the planning stages of compensation design, not when candidates are actively being considered.

19. A: This is not considered a work-related injury because vehicle accidents that occur on company property are not considered work-related under the Occupational Health and Safety Act. If Sven had sustained this injury while driving somewhere in a company vehicle or in the pursuit of company business, the accident would be considered work-related.

20. C: The Hierarchy of Needs Theory of 1954, which discusses the relationship between an employee and his job and which is also the starting point for many of the other theorists, is attributed to Abraham Maslow. Fredrick Herzberg is credited with the Motivation/Hygiene Theory of 1959; Clayton Alderfer is responsible for the ERG Theory of 1969; Victor Vroom is credited with the Expectancy Theory of 1964.

21. D: Inability to identify the advantages of change is a primary reason for the failure of total quality management programs. If managers are unable to convey the intended benefits of a new program, employees are less likely to comply with the new standards and regulations. Micromanagement by employees at all levels is a common characteristic of total quality management programs during the implementation phase. These programs are comprehensive, and require the participation of employees at all levels. Total quality management experts would deny that it is possible to overemphasize core objectives, since TQM depends on isolation of key production components and constant attention to improvement. Finally, failure to use ISO 9000 standards does not cause TQM efforts to fail, since there are a number of other standard systems available. Indeed, many industries have special standards that are more appropriate.

22. C: Medicare is not a voluntary benefit; in other words, employers must provide it. Short-term disability insurance, vision insurance, and life insurance are all considered voluntary benefits that the employer may choose, or not choose, to offer.

23. C: A Scanlon Plan is an example of a group incentive. When a business implements a Scanlon Plan, employees are given a share of whatever savings they can create for the company. In order for a Scanlon Plan to work, employees must have access to the company's financial data. This is considered a group incentive because it depends on the performance of the company as a whole and because the reward is given to each employee in the same measure.

24. C: The widespread nature of the company locations means that a questionnaire is going to be the most effective way to acquire feedback; the questionnaire can be sent out, and employees can then complete it and return it by a certain time. A focus group is impractical, as it might be difficult to get enough people together for the discussion. Interviews and observation can prove to be cumbersome, both to employees and management, because they might require extensive travel and/or arranging of schedules.

25. A: Social Security, state income tax, and federal income tax are considered statutory deductions because they are mandated by government agencies. Union dues are not considered statutory deductions, although they may be provided for in some states.

26. B: The Health Insurance Portability and Accountability Act of 1996 made it illegal to discriminate on the basis of health. This act is an amendment to the Employee Retirement Income Security Act of 1972. It also made it harder for insurers to deny coverage based on pre-existing conditions.

27. C: In zero-based budgeting, every expense must be justified. Zero-based budgeting programs attempt to streamline the business by judging the necessity of every item. Historical budgeting, on the other hand, assumes that the expenses from previous years will be carried over. Obviously, zero-based budgeting is a more time-consuming process, though it can produce substantial savings. Zero-based and historical budgeting programs may be executed in a top-down or bottom-up fashion, depending on whether top managers or all relevant managers are included. Flexible budgeting is subject to change based on the business' needs as opposed to a traditionally static budget.

28. A: In Victor Vroom's expectancy theory, the reasoned decision to work is called valence. According to this theory, people make a rational calculation of the reward they anticipate receiving in exchange for doing some amount of work. If this reward is deemed sufficient, the person will do the work. Expectancy is the initial assessment of whether the work can be done. Instrumentality is the assessment of the reward.

29. A: If the candidate mentions family, an appropriate question, particularly for a company that has locations around the world, would be to ask if the candidate is willing to relocate. The other questions are inappropriate (Do you and your wife plan to have children? Do any other family members live with you? Does your wife also work?); the only way to acquire this information would be if the candidate decides to volunteer it.

30. B: A nondisclosure agreement seeks to protect a company's intellectual property by limiting how an employee may use certain information outside the scope of their position. Conditions of employment are more likely to cover more generalized information such as job status, location, and pay rate. An at-will employment statement acknowledges the lack of a time commitment or promised length of employment within the employment agreement. An employee handbook may mention the protection of intellectual property but is more general in nature and covers all employees instead of the specific responsibilities of one.

31. A: The Sarbanes-Oxley Act was intended to improve accounting practices within public companies. The Rehabilitation Act penalized businesses for discriminating against employees who have a disability. Title VII of the Civil Rights Act of 1964 made it illegal for a business to discriminate against an employee due to his national origin. HIPAA, the Health Insurance Portability and Accountability Act of 1996, in part, protects workers against losing their health coverage immediately if they lose their jobs.

32. C: ERISA (the Employee Retirement Income Security Act of 1974) mandates that employees who use graded vesting must be fully vested in a qualified plan within seven years. The original version of this act had looser vesting requirements. ERISA also asserts that employees who use cliff vesting must be fully vested in a qualified plan within five years.

33. C: During a CSHO inspection, the following should occur: the CSHO should present his credentials, the CSHO should hold an opening conference, the CSHO should tour the facilities, and the CSHO should hold a closing conference. It cannot be expected that the problem, if one is determined to be present, will be resolved during the inspection. A resolution is usually a follow-up result of the inspection.

34. B: The Psychomotor Assessment Test is useful for measuring a candidate's motor skills in completing certain tasks. A short order cook would need to be able to prepare food quickly and efficiently, so such a test would be appropriate in this case. A Cognitive Ability Test focuses more on a candidate's problem-solving and analytical skills. A Physical Assessment Test measures whether or not a candidate is physically able to handle certain tasks. (For example, working for a delivery company might require the physical ability to lift and carry heavy objects; a Physical Assessment Test would be appropriate in such a situation.) An Aptitude Test measures basic skills such as typing, reading, or calculating simple math problems.

35. B: The steps for Enterprise Risk Management are focused primarily on identifying risk and pursuing means of managing and reducing risk. As a result, this includes identifying risks, identifying mitigation options for risks, and making decisions about dealing with risks (answer choices A, C, and D.) The steps of Enterprise Risk Management do not, however, include identifying the employees who are responsible for the risk. This might be part of the larger process of understanding risk, but it does not fall under the primary steps of Enterprise Risk Management. Answer choice B is, therefore, correct.

36. D: A typical pension plan is a type of defined benefit retirement plan that may be used by an organization. A typical pension is referred to as a defined benefit because the employer payouts for the plan are guaranteed once certain conditions are met as opposed to a defined contribution plan (answer choice B) where it is only the contributions that are guaranteed – not the end result. Answer choice A is incorrect because the benefit accrual plan is not a type of voluntary benefit plan. Answer choice C is incorrect because the nonqualified plan provides benefits to specified employees (for example, executives) and shareholders.

37. B: Pie charts are not commonly used in total quality management. Total quality management is a comprehensive approach to reducing errors and streamlining every aspect of an organization's operations. The other answer choices are charts frequently used to identify waste and make TQM plans. A Pareto chart combines line and bar graphs to identify the problems that are causing the most waste. A scatter plot represents the relationship between two variables. A histogram looks like a bar graph; it is used to identify variations in a set of experimental data.

38. B: B.F. Skinner is famous as a behaviorist, concluding that all human actions can be conditioned through behavior modification, or different types of behavioral reinforcement.

39. C: Pattern bargaining, whipsawing, and leapfrogging are all alternate names for parallel bargaining. Single-unit bargaining has no alternate names. Multi-employer bargaining also has no recognized alternate names. Multi-unit bargaining is also known as coordinated bargaining.

40. A: Because the new employees will be working with the heads of several departments, the panel interview style is most effective when the job incumbent will be working with a variety of teams and/or managers. It enables each of the department heads to be there during the interview process. A behavioral interview might be useful in some cases, but there is nothing specific about this case that would require candidates to indicate how their prior behavior would affect the current position. A patterned interview might be useful, but it will not necessarily be the most useful type of interview for this situation. A stress interview is unnecessary for this type of position (database management).

41. B: Employment practices liability insurance is available to provide businesses with a form of *risk transfer*; with the insurance, the business can transfer at least part of the cost of risk to another source. Reviewing employment policies to avoid the chances of an employee lawsuit is considered *risk mitigation*. Taking advance action to consider potentials for risk and prevent problems from occurring is part of *risk avoidance*. Being familiar with chances of risk and creating a financial buffer against future costs is considered *risk acceptance*.

42. D: The Health Insurance Portability and Accountability Act was added to ERISA for the express purpose of forbidding any type of health benefit discrimination toward employees based on pre-existing health problems or health conditions. Answer choice A is incorrect for several reasons. On the one hand, it is simply too vague to explain the purpose of HIPAA. What is more, HIPAA does not simply establish new guidelines for employee health insurance programs, so it is incorrect. Answer choices B and C are incorrect because both refer to COBRA (answer choice B references COBRA inferentially), and HIPAA is not immediately connected to COBRA or to providing minimum health benefits for employees.

43. A: The fourth leadership style as presented in the Hersey-Blanchard theory is Participating. Directing and Guiding fall under the leadership style Telling; Motivating falls under the leadership style Selling.

44. B: A short-form employment application would be the most appropriate in this situation. The Henderson Company is hiring for an unskilled position, so it should not have extensive requirements for candidates. Using a short-form employment application will minimize the amount of reading for the human resources department. Longer applications should only be used when necessary.

45. C: Unions may not participate in secondary boycotts. A secondary boycott occurs when the union tries to make the employer stop doing business with a third party. The other answer choices are false statements.

46. B: A SWOT analysis would be most useful during the environmental scanning phase of the strategic planning process. During this phase, the strategy team tries to get the most accurate picture of the current state of the organization. A SWOT (strengths, weaknesses, opportunities, and threats) analysis is a common template for organizational self-assessment. It is a useful format because it requires planners to consider both internal (strengths and weaknesses) and external (opportunities and threats) factors.

47. D: Under the Civil Rights Act of 1991, the largest possible damage award is $300,000. Only businesses with more than 500 employees may be assessed this amount. Businesses with from 15 to 100 employees may be liable for damage awards of up to $50,000. Businesses with 101 to 200 employees may be liable for damage awards of up to $100,000. Businesses with 201 to 500 employees may be liable for damage awards of up to $200,000.

48. D: A wildcat strike is launched despite a no-strike clause in the employee contract. Obviously, these strikes create intense conflict between employer and union. Sit-down strikes, which are prohibited by law, occur inside the work facility. Secondary boycotts are attempts by the union to keep an external company from doing business with the employer. In most cases, secondary strikes are illegal. A hot cargo strike, more commonly known as a hot cargo picket, aims to keep the employer from doing business with some other employer opposed by the union. Hot cargo pickets are prohibited by law as well.

49. A: The four styles of leadership identified by the Hersey-Blanchard theory are telling, selling, participating, and delegating. This model was developed by Paul Hersey and Kenneth Blanchard in the late 1970s. The appropriate style of leadership in a particular situation depends on the sophistication and experience of the subordinates. The range, from least sophisticated audience to most, is telling, selling, participating, and delegating. Telling is explicit instruction, while selling is more general encouragement and inspiration. Participating is working alongside employees, and delegating is setting goals and assigning responsibility to others.

50. D: The purpose of the Needlestick Safety and Prevention Act is to require the employers report workplace injuries as a result of sharp objects and consider replacing objects to prevent further injuries. Answer choice A is incorrect because the purpose of the act is not to require that companies perform quarterly audits. Answer choice B is incorrect because the Needlestick Safety and Prevention Act does not require that organizations remove specified sharp objects but instead recommends the replacement of dangerous sharp objects. Answer choice C is incorrect because the act does not create a list of sharp objects that are recognized for having caused workplace injuries but instead leaves the decision about these objects up to the organization.

51. C: Increased production by the employer is not an eligibility requirement for Trade Adjustment Assistance. This program was established in 2002 to help those adversely affected by the rise in imported goods. If three or more workers from the same business meet the eligibility requirements, they may receive retraining and employment advice at federal centers.

52. A: Tara should be compensated for this time, because she has been engaged to wait. She is not responsible for the flight delay, and so long as her employer wants her to keep waiting for the delayed flight, she should continue to be compensated.

53. A: Arranging for temporary employees to be hired by an agency and then sent to work at one's business is known as payrolling. This is a way to avoid the administrative costs of hiring and filling out paperwork for new employees. The temp agency usually requests payment for rendering this service. On-call employment refers to regular employees who are scheduled to come in as the business needs for peak hours or special events. In-house employment is traditional full or part time employment by the company itself. Temp-to-perm employment refers to employees who are hired on a temporary basis with the intent to hire the individual to a permanent position after that period of time; this would not be appropriate for this question as the positions are considered seasonal and not permanent.

54. B: The fiduciary role of the human resources professional regarding ERISA is primarily one of handling and managing the pension funds that the organization provides for retirement accounts. Answer choice A is incorrect because the fiduciary role does not include setting up pension accounts for employees. (This might be another part of the human resources professional's job, but this is not the immediate fiduciary role with respect to ERISA.) Answer choice C is incorrect because the fiduciary role has nothing to do with ensuring that HIPAA guidelines are observed. Answer choice D is incorrect because the human resources professional is not responsible for creating retirement account rules.

55. D: When an employer discovers that employees are beginning to unionize, the employer is not allowed to prevent unionization. The employer can, however, provide information to employees about the problems involved with unionization. Answer choice A is incorrect because the employer may not contact union leaders and forbid unionization. Answer choice B is incorrect because employers are not allowed to block employees who begin to unionize. Answer choice C is incorrect because employers may not threaten to replace workers who choose to unionize (although employers may replace workers during a lawful economic strike).

56. C: Reengineering is defined as an attempt to improve overall business operations so that customers benefit from the process. Workforce expansion, as the name indicates, is an increase in employees for a business to reach certain goals. Divestiture is a business decision to eliminate a department by laying off employees or moving them to another department. Offshoring, or outsourcing, refers to a business's decision to move certain activities to another location (usually international) to reduce costs.

57. D: A labor charge must be filed with the NLRB within 6 months of an incident. The charge may, of course, be filed within 3, 4, or 5 months, but these options do not reflect the full legal provision.

58. B: A representation petition must be completed at least 30 days in advance of a planned union picketing. Failing to submit the petition within this time frame can result in the petition being unrecognized and thus being deemed an unfair labor practice. Among the answer choices, 15 days is obviously too short of a notice, and both 45 days and 60 days exceed the legal expectation. The union may, of course, notify that far in advance, but it is not necessary.

59. B: Children as young as 14 may work, according to FLSA, but there are conditions that apply to hiring children this age. Children of 13 may not be legally hired by most businesses. Children of 15 and 16 are beyond the minimum age.

60. A: Governmental barriers were identified as part of the need for the Glass Ceiling Act of 1991. Recruitment and corporate barriers fall under the category of internal structural barriers; educational barriers fall under the category of societal barriers.

61. C: Effective substance abuse programs require that drug testing be completely fair, and targeted drug testing for employees who betray substance abuse problems would not necessarily fall under the description of "fair." Answer choices A, B, and D are incorrect because all represent components of an effective substance abuse program within an organization. Additionally, answer choices A, B, and D can each be practiced and applied consistently with all employees to set clear and fair expectations for the entire workforce and not just a targeted population.

62. C: Federal recommendations state that employers should retain OSHA forms for a minimum of 5 years. Retaining forms for 2 or 3 years is too brief. Forms may certainly be retained for 7 years, but this exceeds the minimum federal recommendations.

63. B: During a lawful economic strike, employers do have the right to hire employees to replace the striking employees. Answer choices A, C, and D are incorrect because they each represent types of unfair labor practices. Employers may not fire employees who refuse to cease striking instead of returning to work. They also may not encourage the union to disband and/or suggest the formation of a new union. Nor may the employer disband the union and require new representation, or restrict union bargaining if this negatively impacts company's finances.

64. B: If the leave is considered foreseeable, the employee is expected to notify his employer at least 30 days in advance. Foreseeable leave can be considered a medical procedure, birth, adoption or other similar life event planned in advance. An advance notice of 15 days is too short, while an advance notice of 45 or 60 days is not required (though certainly not inappropriate, if the employee expects the leave to be necessary that far in advance).

65. B: The process described in question 62 is that of recruiting, or making the details of the position available to interested candidates and pursuing potential employees who will fill the requirements of the job as best as possible. Answer choice A is incorrect because the process of hiring follows the process of recruiting. Answer choice C is incorrect because tracking is also a separate process from recruiting. Answer choice D is incorrect because selection is the next step beyond recruiting but does not belong within the recruitment process.

66. C: Creating an interactive talent pool over social media is highly efficient due to the wide reach that social media can offer. Additionally, recruiting over social media offers diverse options for interactive types of content, immediate feedback, and conversational tools that help create conversations. Job fairs and internships can be effective at creating interactive talent pools but require additional resources to reach a comparable number of people. Staffing agencies can be efficient at creating placements but lack the interactive element of vetting and building relationships with a talent pool prior to hiring.

67. B: The WARN Act of 1988 requires that the plant inform employees at least 60 days in advance of the impending lay-offs. The other options – 30 days, 90 days, or 120 days – are either too short or are unnecessarily early. (The plant might not know 120 days in advance, so it would be difficult to inform employees this long before the event.)

68. C: A corporate university is an extensive training program administered by a corporation to existing employees. Rather than rely on local colleges to keep their employees up to date, many organizations have created in-house training programs. Corporate universities often have detailed curricula and "professors" whose only job is to maintain the skills and competence of existing employees. Those who complete a program at a corporate university may be eligible for a raise or promotion. Corporate universities are able to be much more specific and targeted in their instruction.

69. C: A cash balance plan is considered "portable" because employees can remove the money from the plan and convert the payment into other forms. A profit-sharing plan, also known as a discretionary contribution plan, is considered to be best in a company that has highly variable annual profits. A money purchase plan offers employees a fixed annual percentage and thus is best in a company that has fairly consistent annual earnings. A target benefit plan uses actuarial formulas to determine how much an employee will receive toward retirement.

70. A: Creating retention plans is a strategic function of the human resources department. This activity is considered strategic because it is concerned with maintaining an optimal workforce over the long term. Recruiting new employees is more of an operational function, in that it is a practical

application of the organization's strategic planning. Insuring compliance with federal regulations and maintaining the confidentiality of employee data are considered administrative functions, because they are part of the normal course of business for a human resources department.

71. D: One common problem with cost-per-hire metrics is that they omit costs that are not related to specific candidates. The cost-per-hire measure is determined by dividing total costs by number of hires. It is important that the costs and hires be taken from the same time interval. To be comprehensive, a cost-per-hire measure should include the salaries of those employed to make hires, the cost of advertising, and any other administrative costs incurred during the hiring process.

72. B: Fran's decision demonstrates the horn effect. This phenomenon, also known as the harshness bias, is the tendency to allow one irritating aspect of the interviewee's performance to dominate perception. An interviewer should be aware of this potential pitfall, and should consider whether the characteristic he finds distracting will likely be so to other people, or whether it bears significantly on job performance. In this case, Glenda's voice will probably not have much effect on her performance as an accountant. The central tendency, meanwhile, is a bias towards rating all candidates roughly equal. Stereotyping bias is a tendency to attribute certain characteristics to an interviewee because of his gender, ethnicity, religion, etc. The cultural noise bias is created when an interviewee answers questions not honestly, but in the way he believes the interviewer wants them to be answered.

73. B: A forced distribution usually results in rating employees along a bell curve. In a paired comparison, each employee's performance viewed in the context of another employee's performance. A ranking system is usually better for a smaller group of employees but can be difficult to organize with a larger group. A nominal scale is not recognized as a type of employee rating system.

74. C: A "petitional" form of picketing does not exist. The recognized forms of picketing are as follows: organizational, informational, and recognitional. Organizational picketing seeks to persuade the employer to recognition of the picketing union as the collective bargaining union, usually amongst other unions. Informational picketing seeks to inform the public of a matter of concern. Recognitional picketing seeks union recognition from the employer.

75. C: An employer brand is simply a clear indication of a company's identity; it is essentially the unique characteristic(s) that define a company. An employer brand might be related to a public relations strategy (answer choice A), but it is not contained entirely within the public relations strategy. Similarly, the human resources policy of marketing (answer choice B) might reflect the employer brand, but this is not a clear definition of it. The total rewards philosophy is a separate part of a company's identity, so answer choice D is incorrect.

76. D: ERISA records must be maintained for six years beyond the filing date with the Department of Labor. All other answer choices (three/four/five years) are too low; ERISA records must be maintained for the minimum of six years.

77. B: The point factor method is used to identify the most important positions in an organization. In this method, organizational leaders assign a certain number of points to each organization depending on various factors, such as, the responsibility, the education required, and the working conditions. The total number of points assigned to each job group indicates its significance to the organization. The point factor method can also be a type of job evaluation method but that does not apply within the context of this question.

78. B: OSHA Form 300A is intended to be a Summary of Work-Related Injuries and Illnesses. OSHA Form 300 is intended to be a Log of Work-Related Injuries and Illnesses. OSHA Form 301 is intended to be an Injury and Illness Incident Report. OSHA Form 301A does not exist.

79. A: In binding arbitration, both parties agree to accept whatever decision is reached by the third party judge. Compulsory arbitration, meanwhile, exists when the terms of a contract dictate that any future disputes will be settled through arbitration. Constructive confrontation is a system for handling disputes within an organization, usually by dividing them into their central and peripheral elements. Ad hoc arbitration is a one-time dispute resolution aimed at handling one particular problem.

80. B: A person must be at least 18 years old to take a job that has been designated hazardous by the Secretary of Labor. The Fair Labor Standards Act instituted a number of policies to prevent the exploitation of children. The only hazardous jobs children younger than 18 may be allowed to perform are related to farming.

81. C: The accession rate compares the number of new employees to the total number of employees. This metric indicates whether an organization is experiencing too much or too little turnover. Human resources departments use the accession rate to identify focus areas for their recruiting and retention efforts.

82. B: The Family Medical Leave Act of 1993 requires employers to give new mothers at least twelve weeks of unpaid leave. New mothers and fathers can take this leave once in a twelve-month period. Employees are required to give thirty days' notice before taking FMLA leave. Also, in order to take this leave, an employee must have been working for the company for at least a year, or 1250 hours.

83. C: Emergencies can come in all shapes and sizes, and the emergency response plan will need to vary accordingly. The process of risk identification, often occurring within a larger enterprise risk management (ERM) effort, seeks to not just identify all possible risks but weigh the probability of their occurrence, as well as their overall impact if they were to occur. Any employee input and practical drills will be affected by what type of emergency is being planned for, such as weather (tornado warning), structural (kitchen fire), health (customer heart attack), environmental (active shooter), etc. Risk consultants may be involved in the later stages of risk identification as well as response planning, but an organization will need to do at least a basic risk identification process in order to research and hire the most appropriate and equipped consultant.

84. C: Byron will use a simple linear regression. A simple linear regression is good for examining the relationship between two variables. In this case, Byron wants to look at the relationship between the advertising budget and sales. A trend analysis, on the other hand, focuses on a single variable. A ratio considers the relationship between two variables, but it is more aimed at establishing a traditional benchmark then in learning more about the relationship. Finally, a multiple linear regression analyzes the relationships among more than two variables.

85. B: The *Federal Register* is referred to as the Daily Journal of the United States Government where proposed rules, significant documents, notices, and other public information is posted by federal agencies and bodies. Administrative laws take effect 30 days after being published in the *Federal Register*. The option for 15 days is far too short, and the options for 45 days and 60 days reflect a time frame in which the law would already have taken effect.

86. C: Since the Williamson Company is using the paired comparison method, each member of the sales job group will be compared with six other people. The paired comparison method requires

every member of the job group to be compared to every other member. This means that each member of the Williamson Company's sales group will be compared to the other six members. The paired comparison method is a good way to rank employees systematically.

87. A: The new employee can expect to work in a small group during the training session. In banquet-style seating, participants are placed in small groups around several tables. They will be able to turn and face a single presenter if necessary, but they will probably be spending most of their time interacting with their tablemates.

88. D: A suggestion box offers employees a measure of anonymity in proffering ideas to the company's upper management. Brown bag lunches and focus groups require employees to participate actively, and as the scenario indicates many employees would be uncomfortable with this. Email might be private, but it certainly is not anonymous, so it would not represent the best recommendation for Helena to make.

89. B: Featherbedding occurs when a union requires that an otherwise obsolete job remains intact at an organization in order to avoid terminating an employee. Answer choice A is incorrect because it describes a hot cargo agreement. Answer choice C is incorrect because it simply describes a type of union coercion. Answer choice D is incorrect because it describes another type of union coercion or restraint of employees.

90. D: Aptitude tests assess a candidate's abilities, skills, or ability to learn new tasks. In a situation where an employee is being hired to manage a new computer system, an aptitude test may help identify the candidate who will be best suited to learning the new system while also learning about a new team and new organization. Cross-cultural assessment tools test a candidate's familiarity with and agility among different demographics of people or places and may be useful for a position being hired within a global company/environment. Cognitive ability tests assess a candidate's raw intelligence and may be useful for a position that requires certain skills, knowledge, or reasoning abilities. Personality tests measure more personal characteristics such as attitudes, emotional responses, and motivations; it is important to note that the use of a personality test in pre-employment screening may be perceived as an invasion of privacy or discriminatory in nature if it does not apply to the job responsibilities.

91. B: Bottom-up methods of communication include an open-door policy, webcasts, and staff meetings; in each case, the employees are considered an active part of the discussion and even decision making. Individual letters represent a top-down method of communication, because top-down communication focuses more on the management informing employees of decisions.

92. A: In a fertilizer manufacturer, the research and development department is likely to be distinct from the marketing department. As a general rule, the more technologically sophisticated and complex the product, the greater distinction between the R&D and marketing departments. The development of useful and safe fertilizers requires a great deal of experimentation and technical knowledge. Therefore, it is more likely that a fertilizer manufacturer would have a special department for creating and refining products. For a toy manufacturer, publisher, or clothing manufacturer, product development is largely stimulated by the demands of the consumer, so it makes more sense for the marketing department to be loosely involved in research and development.

93. D: The categories for EEO-1 do not include an option for European. The EEO-1 includes the following options for racial categories: 1) Hispanic or Latino, 2) White, 3) Black or African

American, 4) Native Hawaiian or Pacific Islander, 5) Asian, 6) Native American, and 7) Two or More Races.

94. B: The employees of Fitch Company have line of sight. Line of sight exists when employees feel that their performance will determine their compensation in the future. Companies in which employees have line of sight tend to have higher levels of performance. A company with an entitlement philosophy rewards employees for seniority. Intrinsic rewards are the pleasures and satisfactions of a job well done. Businesses should seek to maximize the opportunities for creating intrinsic rewards for their employees. A fiduciary responsibility is the duty to handle someone else's affairs, typically with regard to financial matters, with appropriate care.

95. D: Company X is using a divestiture people processing strategy. This type of strategy aims to reduce the influence of personal characteristics on the organization. Military institutions typically employ a divestiture people processing strategy, with the aim of making individual soldiers subservient to the imperatives of the group. Investiture people processing strategies, on the other hand, give new employees a chance to express themselves and apply their personal idiosyncrasies to the organization. Contest people processing strategies do not sort new employees by interest or ability; instead, they put every new employee through the same program, and make decisions about placement once orientation is complete. Finally, collective people processing strategies emphasize cooperation between new employees.

96. C: The Uniform Guidelines on Employee Selection Procedures declare that employers must use the selection tool that has the least adverse impact on protected classes. Of course, this provision is only applicable when the employer has access to more than one selection tool. When there is no other option, employers may use selection tools that adversely impact protected classes. According to the UGESP, an adverse impact exists when the selection rate for a protected class is 4/5 or less of the normal selection rate.

97. D: Exemptions are specific, and in this case only answer choice D reflects a legitimate exemption status: due to the nature of the job, and the fact that the police department only has four members, these officers would be exempt from overtime requirements. The high school coach would not necessarily be exempt from overtime requirements, just because he has to take students to games. The large farm that employs teenagers during the summer would definitely *not* be exempt from child labor requirements. And the firefighters might be exempt from overtime requirements – under certain circumstances (which do not appear to be present in this situation) – but they are certainly not exempt from minimum wage requirements.

98. A: An Employee Self-Service (ESS) function with HRIS allows employees to perform transactional tasks for themselves instead of going through their manager or human resources representative. These tasks can include requesting time away from work, selecting benefits, updating personal data, filing expense reports, and more. The other functions listed can also help reduce the transactional responsibilities for a human resources team but still require intervention in the design, collection, and use of the other functions. Additionally, functions like training, performance management, and data analytics can play critical roles in the transformational side of human resources responsibilities.

99. D: Marsha has earned 45 hours of compensatory time off. Compensatory time off is calculated as 1.5 times the amount of overtime. Since Marsha worked 30 hours of overtime, her compensatory time off can be calculated by multiplying 30 by 1.5.

100. B: In an affirmative action plan, the determination of availability provides demographic information for the labor market related to each job group. Specifically, this part of the affirmative action plan indicates how many women and minorities are available to fill positions in each job group. A determination of availability should include internal and external candidates. A job group analysis indicates how the business categorizes various positions. The comparison of incumbency to availability calculates the company's success at employing minorities compared with the job market as a whole. Finally, the organizational profile is a simple list of the positions within the business.

101. C: One possible drawback of this arrangement is a lack of communication among the foreign offices. The Archibald Corporation is using what is known as the polycentric approach to international staffing. The advantages to this system are that it is cheaper to employ foreign nationals than to use expatriates and that it gives the foreign community a sense of investment in the business. However, if a corporation has multiple overseas offices, linguistic and cultural barriers may impede communication among them.

102. C: Context is not part of Kirkpatrick's training evaluation framework. Even though it was created in 1967, Kirkpatrick's description of training evaluation is still widely used. It outlines four criteria: reaction, learning, job behavior, and results. Reaction is the trainee's immediate response to the program. Learning is the information and skills that were obtained during the program. It is important that trainees acquire the skills they are supposed to acquire during training. Job behavior is the extent to which what has been learned during training is applied to real work. Finally, results are the overall impact of the training program on company performance.

103. C: Minimum wage law is as follows: the federal minimum wage is primary if the state minimum wage is lower than the federal minimum wage. If the state minimum wage is higher than the federal level, however, the company is required to pay the state minimum wage. In other words, companies are expected to pay whatever happens to be higher. There are, of course, a number of variables that can affect minimum wage and what a company is expected to pay, but in question 10 one should assume that Grace Clothing in California is required to pay whatever happens to be the higher minimum wage. This means that answer choices A and B are immediately incorrect. In the case of answer choice D, the question does not provide any information about the size of the company, so the answer choice becomes irrelevant to the discussion. (Again, it must be assumed based on the question that Grace Clothing is required to pay minimum wage; the real question is which minimum wage?). The minimum wage is the minimum a company is expected to pay employees. Any commissions represent an addition to payment, but because commissions cannot be guaranteed they cannot compensate for lower minimum wage.

104. A: When one company acquires another, the first step for the acquiring company's human resources department is a survey of the workforce in both organizations. The goal is to identify redundant or conflicting positions. It may be that some of the employees in the acquired organization will need to be let go. Human resources departments will need to review the acquired organization's collective bargaining agreements and ensure compliance with OSHA regulations, but these activities should be performed subsequent to the workforce survey.

105. D: The Genetic Information Nondiscrimination Act of 2008 does not make employers responsible for information acquired by accident. However, employers have no legal right to make decisions or change an employee's work situation based on that information, so Abbey's only option is to keep the information to herself and take no action. Answer choice A is incorrect because the law does not require Abbey to report the employee's personal information to her superiors, nor should she take such a step. Answer choice B is incorrect because the Department of Labor does not

need to be updated on this type of individual employee information (and reporting it could make Abbey legally responsible for divulging an employee's personal details). Answer choice C is incorrect because Abbey has no legal responsibility to discuss the situation with the employee, nor should she counsel the employee about changing the work situation.

106. C: A functional audit (also known as a function-specific audit) hones in on specific human resources functions such as payroll, performance management, or recruiting to assess processes and outcomes. A compliance audit assesses business practices and policies within federal, state, and local government regulations. A handbook audit assesses the accuracy, relevance, and awareness of an organization's employee handbook. A strategic audit assesses the alignment of human resources practices and systems with the overarching organizational strategy.

107. D: LMRDA required that national unions conduct leadership elections every five years. As noted in the answer for question 150, the option for three years reflects the requirement for local unions. The other answer choices do not reflect union leadership election requirements.

108. A: The Motivation/Hygiene Theory of 1959, which focuses on raising the value of a job in the eyes of the employee, is attributed to Fredrick Herzberg. Clayton Alderfer is responsible for the ERG Theory of 1969; Victor Vroom is credited with the Expectancy Theory of 1964; Abraham Maslow is credited with the Hierarchy of Needs Theory of 1954.

109. D: The human resources professional is not expected to avoid simultaneous leave within the company. This may be inevitable, and the company cannot block employees from taking approved FMLA leave. The human resources professional is, however, expected to be familiar with FMLA requirements and changes, to educate management about FMLA rules, and to develop an FMLA documentation policy for the company.

110. B: The Training Adjustment Assistance (TAA) program was designed specifically to provide assistance to employees who have lost their jobs due to a rise in the number of imports. In other words, when import levels shift and companies in the US begin importing items that were previously manufactured here, the manufacturing companies might close, leaving employees without jobs. Answer choice A is incorrect because the TAA was designed for a far narrower reason than just employees losing their jobs for any reason. Answer choice C is incorrect because the TAA is related to providing training for laid-off workers to receive new jobs instead of providing them with health benefits. Answer choice D is incorrect because the TAA program is designed for workers who have already lost their jobs rather than for those who currently have jobs.

111. B: The Equal Pay Act, created in 1963, forbids any type of discrimination based on the employee's gender. The Portal to Portal Act of 1947, determined that employers cannot be required to compensate employees who commute long distances to work. The Davis Beacon Act was created in 1931, and the National Labor Relations Act was created in 1935; both fall before the legislation of the Fair Labor Standards Act of 1938, so both are irrelevant.

112. D: Employees are not eligible to apply for unemployment insurance if they voluntarily resign their positions (assuming the resignation was not due to discrimination or other harassment in the workplace). The specific requirements vary from state to state, but typically, to be eligible to file for unemployment, an individual must be actively seeking a new job so they can eventually come off unemployment and must also have satisfied their respective state's "base period" for how long they worked with their previous employer prior to their termination. Eligibility for unemployment also depends on the conditions of the individual's termination; short-term layoffs for business reasons qualify as an eligible termination event.

113. C: According to the Pregnancy Discrimination Act of 1978, employers should treat pregnancy like a short-term disability. The Pregnancy Discrimination Act is an amendment to Title VII. Pregnant women are entitled to all of the benefits and accommodations due to the disabled.

114. B: The required qualities of reliability and validity are established for the express purpose of avoiding discrimination against protected classes. Answer choice A is incorrect because it makes no sense to ensure the same results from all tests – the tests would have no value at that point. Answer choice C is incorrect because the testing of candidates for a new position is about assessing the qualifications of the candidates and not quantifying the success rate of the company. Answer choice D is incorrect because it is too vague. Such guidelines would always be intended to create better standards for testing, but this is not specific enough to be a correct answer.

115. D: An employee-absenteeism policy might include information about *when* a doctor's note is required, but it does not necessarily need to require a doctor's note in all situations. This might prove to be onerous to employees who are genuinely ill at home for a day but are not ill enough to visit a doctor. Additionally, a requirement for a note for *each* sick day absence would be an inappropriate policy, as the employee might be out for 4-5 days but is not likely to see the doctor each of those days. A good policy should, however, include the following: a statement about how many sick days each employee receives, an indication of how sick days are counted within the calendar, and information about how each absence is counted in days.

PHR Practice Test #3

1. Which of the following OSHA forms is intended to be an Injury and Illness Incident Report?

    a. OSHA Form 300
    b. OSHA Form 300A
    c. OSHA Form 301
    d. OSHA Form 301A

2. Fernando shows up for work on Monday morning, but the office has been overstaffed, so his boss sends him home almost immediately. The compensation owed to Fernando is called

    a. on-call pay.
    b. call-back pay.
    c. reporting pay.
    d. shift pay.

3. When Jared takes over a supervisory position in the marketing department, he tries to set a good example for his subordinates. He recognizes that there are already strong creative partnerships within the department, so he tries to foster even more cooperation. What style of leadership is Jared practicing?

    a. authoritarian leadership
    b. coaching
    c. democratic leadership
    d. transformational leadership

4. Which of the following retention strategies would be MOST effective for a human resources professional to leverage in an effort to reduce the turnover rates of valuable seasoned employees?

    a. Internal mobility
    b. Job description review
    c. Streamlined onboarding
    d. Remote work

5. Following a particularly harsh hurricane season, a large company is assembling a team to create business continuity plans in the event that their organization would need to respond to and survive future severe storms. Which of the following tasks would MOST likely be led by the human resources team?

    a. Coordinate with suppliers and community partners to ensure resource access
    b. Flex employee schedules for personal and organizational preparations
    c. Secure employee computer systems data and access
    d. Establish and update employee emergency contacts and family information

6. What are the four Ps of marketing?

    a. product, price, payment, persistence
    b. preview, position, price, persuasion
    c. product, price, place, promotion
    d. promotion, place, position, (market) penetration

174

7. All of the following would be legally considered unfair labor practices for an employer except

   a. Entering into positional bargaining with the employee union
   b. Entering into a hot cargo agreement with the employee union
   c. Taking disciplinary action against those who participate in unions
   d. Declining to enter into a bargain with the employee union

8. Which of the following is not considered one of the criteria under which the NLRB recognizes a successor employer, or a new employer who has taken over a company?

   a. Indicating a significant continuity in standard business activities
   b. Establishing a clear agreement with the previous employer
   c. Demonstrating a clear parallel in the products and procedures of the company
   d. Assimilating all employees under the previous employer into the company

9. In the view of the Office of Federal Contract Compliance Programs, what is the best source for data related to employee race and ethnicity?

   a. self-reporting
   b. census forms
   c. birth certificates
   d. employer judgment

10. For human resources departments, what is the first step in enterprise risk management?

   a. audit
   b. insurance
   c. forecasting
   d. employee interviews

11. The ADDIE model outlines the components of

   a. leadership.
   b. employee recruiting.
   c. manufacturing.
   d. instructional design.

12. Which of the following is defined as the knowledge employees have about how their work behavior affects their compensation?

   a. Entitlement philosophy
   b. Line of sight
   c. Total rewards strategy
   d. Organizational culture

13. The human resources department wants to see if experienced employees are more productive. The department takes a measure of each employee's productivity, and then plots it on a graph, on which the other axis is employee experience. Which correlation coefficient would be the strongest suggestion that productivity increases with experience?

   a. +0.8
   b. +0.2
   c. 0
   d. -0.9

14. How are vacation pay policies established for organizations?

    a. Vacation pay policies are created under the guidelines of the FMLA
    b. Vacation pay policies are established by each company
    c. Vacation pay policies fall under the rules of ERISA
    d. Vacation pay policies fall under the jurisdiction of state-established guidelines

15. Which of the following is defined as a business decision to eliminate a department by laying off employees or moving them to another department?

    a. Workforce expansion
    b. Divestiture
    c. Reengineering
    d. Offshoring

16. A human resources officer at a rapidly growing company is interviewing candidates for a position that has just been created. Management is not yet sure what the precise duties of the new employee will be, but it is very important for the new employee to fit into the organizational culture. What type of interview should the human resources officer conduct?

    a. directive interview
    b. panel interview
    c. stress interview
    d. nondirective interview

17. Sally is a mid-level manager at an accounting firm and has stumbled across questionable documents when working on a project for her supervisor. Sally does not particularly like her manager due to his authoritarian style of leadership, so instead of confronting him over the documents, she brings up her observations with the division's human resources representative. Which of the following responses would be the most effective first step for the representative to take?

    a. Review the company handbook to determine if the supervisor broke policy or procedure
    b. Conduct a fact-finding investigation to determine the full scope of the situation
    c. Advise Sally to take the documents to her supervisor to determine their origin
    d. Reach out to the CEO to alert him of the possible ethics breach

18. Ron and Marcy apply for the same job at the Brown Company. During Ron's interview, the interviewer outlines the major responsibilities of the available position, and asks Ron a series of questions about his ability to fulfill them. Marcy's interview covers much of the same ground, but the interviewer asks different questions related to Marcy's unique educational background. Ron and Marcy have participated in

    a. structured interviews.
    b. stress interviews.
    c. patterned interviews.
    d. behavioral interviews.

19. A SWOT analysis has four parts: Strengths, Weaknesses, Opportunities, and which of the following?

    a. Tools
    b. Threats
    c. Targets
    d. Techniques

20. The Green Company is putting together a group incentive. To begin with, management assesses the baseline productivity levels of the organization. Incentives are given when the group exceeds baseline productivity. What type of program has the Green Company established?

    a. gainsharing
    b. Scanlon Plan
    c. improshare
    d. profit sharing

21. The National Labor Relations Act (NLRA) does not apply to which types of workers?

    a. Administrative
    b. Corporate
    c. Financial
    d. Agricultural

22. Which of the following of collective bargaining results when both sides acknowledge that they have a strong motivation in the continuity of business activities, and thus proceed in negotiations with this acknowledgement?

    a. Positional bargaining
    b. Integrative bargaining
    c. Interest-based bargaining
    d. Distributive bargaining

23. The WARN Act was designed to do which of the following?

    a. Prevent massive lay-offs that disrupt the economy
    b. Provide new positions for employees that have been laid off
    c. Establish rights for employees who have been laid off
    d. Mandate full severance pay for those who have been laid off

24. Eric is in charge of interviewing candidates for an open position in a hotel chain. As he considers each candidate, he finds himself quick to write off one young man in particular. This candidate has a strong resume and excellent credentials, but Eric decides that he just does not like this person and is disinclined to consider him as a contender for the position. In doing so, Eric is demonstrating which of the following interview biases?

    a. First impression
    b. Cultural noise
    c. Gut feeling
    d. Leniency

25. If the leave is foreseeable but the employee fails to provide his employer with appropriate advance notice, for how long after the start of the leave may the employer delay the employee's FMLA coverage?

    a. 15 days
    b. 30 days
    c. 45 days
    d. 60 days

26. While interviewing a candidate, Geraldine notices that the individual's answers seem to be oddly phrased, and Geraldine ultimately notices that the candidate is trying to give her the answers that she wants, rather than offering candid answers. In this case, what type of interview bias is occurring?

    a. Halo effect
    b. Cultural noise
    c. Central tendency
    d. Horn effect

27. Which of the following staffing alternative solutions would be most appropriate for a company struggling to find full-time employees for a position that requires 40 hours per week but does not necessarily depend on continuity in the position?

    a. Job rotation
    b. Independent contractors
    c. Job sharing
    d. Temp-to-hire program

28. The Latin phrase *respondeat superior* translates to which of the following?

    a. Friend of the court
    b. Let the master answer
    c. With connected strength
    d. Thrown to the lions

29. Which of the following types of bargaining strategies between an employer and union employees is considered to be illegal?

    a. Double breasting
    b. Lockout
    c. Distributive bargaining
    d. Sit-down strike

30. Which of the following is a voluntary deduction from gross earnings?

    a. Social Security
    b. state income tax
    c. Medicare
    d. 401(k) contribution

31. In B.F. Skinner's theory of Operant Conditioning (1957), he provided a list of four strategies for behavioral intervention: Positive Reinforcement, Negative Reinforcement, Punishment, and which of the following?

    a. Termination
    b. Encouragement
    c. Extinction
    d. Actualization

32. The Age Discrimination in Employment Act requires that any employee records related to charges of discrimination must be retained

    a. until the charges are resolved.
    b. for one year.
    c. for two years or until the charges are resolved, whichever comes first.
    d. for seven years.

33. The extent to which the results of research can accurately identify a difference between trained and untrained employees is called

    a. statistical confidence.
    b. marginal difference.
    c. selectivity.
    d. statistical power.

34. An employee's performance on an assembly line is likely to follow a

    a. negatively accelerating learning curve.
    b. proportionally accelerating learning curve.
    c. positively accelerating learning curve.
    d. statically accelerating learning curve.

35. Which of the following tools can a human resources professional leverage to most effectively determine what skills an organization needs compared to the skills an organization has?

    a. Labor market forecast
    b. Organizational strategy
    c. Gap analysis
    d. Performance management results

36. Barbara contracts the flu from her daughter. While she is at work, her stomach becomes upset and she vomits. She has to go home for the day. Is this a work-related illness?

    a. No, because vomiting is not considered a significant symptom.
    b. No, because the influenza exposure occurred away from work.
    c. Yes, because the symptoms were exhibited at work.
    d. Yes, because any incidents of vomiting must be reported.

37. Which of the following is a rating method of performance appraisal?

    a. checklist
    b. field appraisal
    c. essay
    d. critical incident review

38. Which of the following institutions did not receive Title VII coverage pursuant to the Equal Employment Opportunity Act of 1972?

    a. Religious institutions
    b. Universities
    c. State government agencies
    d. Federal legislative bodies

39. As part of his new job in the finance department, Julian is taught to use a new accounting program. However, he finds that he does not often need to use this program in his work. So, although he quickly attains decent competence with the program, he does not make much progress thereafter. Which style of learning curve illustrates this situation?

    a. plateau learning curve
    b. positively accelerating learning curve
    c. negatively accelerating learning curve
    d. S-shaped learning curve

40. A human resources professional is putting together a training session, during which employees will be expected to complete a number of small group activities. What type of seating would be most effective for this training session?

    a. Classroom
    b. Chevron
    c. Banquet
    d. Theater

41. After an initial business assessment, an organization has determined that it needs to invest in a new HRIS. Which of the following steps should the organization's HR and business team take FIRST?

    a. Set an implementation timeline
    b. Determine the budget
    c. Request HRIS vendor quotes
    d. Perform an organizational needs assessment

42. Which of the following is considered indirect compensation?

    a. variable compensation
    b. performance bonus
    c. leave of absence
    d. base pay

43. Which of the following statements about union decertification is true?

    a. Decertification does not prevent employees from joining a different union later.
    b. Decertification is an employer-led process.
    c. Employers may lobby employees during the decertification process.
    d. At least half of the employees must petition the NLRB before a decertification vote is held.

44. Which of the following examples is MOST likely to be deemed a constructive discharge?

    a. An employee is terminated after a series of poor performance reviews.
    b. An employee resigns after harassment in the workplace.
    c. An employee is terminated as part of a short-term layoff.
    d. An employee resigns in order to pursue a different career path.

45. To save costs, a call center located in Ohio has decided to outsource one of its largest departments to a country overseas. The manager of this department, Gina, has the task of informing her employees about this event. She consults the human resources professional, Silvia, about the best approach to take. What advice should Silvia give to Gina?

    a. Recommend that Gina provide all employees with a hand-written note explaining the situation

    b. Recommend that Gina assist employees in finding new positions once their jobs end

    c. Recommend that Gina be honest and share with her employees as many facts as possible

    d. Recommend that Gina petition the call center to retain the department by proving the employees' value

46. Which type of voluntary benefits plan offers specified tax benefits for employers as well as employees and does not provide extra benefits for shareholders or executives?

    a. Nonqualified plan

    b. Defined contribution

    c. Qualified plan

    d. Cash balance

47. What is the established radius for which FMLA applies to employees working for private employers?

    a. 30 miles

    b. 50 miles

    c. 75 miles

    d. 85 miles

48. Which of the following types of employee rating systems is usually better for a smaller group of employees but can be difficult to organize with a larger group?

    a. Behaviorally anchored rating scales

    b. Forced distribution

    c. Ranking

    d. Competency-based

49. Classic change process theory fails to account for which of the following organizational factors:

    a. Resource management

    b. Legal precedents

    c. Customer feedback

    d. Dynamic environments

50. A small landscaping company argues that complying with ADA regulations would constitute an undue hardship. Which of the following company characteristics would NOT be considered by the government when evaluating this claim?

    a. Size of the company

    b. Location of the company

    c. Cost of making reasonable accommodations

    d. Financial status of the company

51. Which of the following statements about payroll systems is false?

 a. Payroll systems must monitor tax payments.
 b. Large companies often develop their own payroll software.
 c. Payroll systems must maintain employee confidentiality.
 d. Payroll systems are always the responsibility of the human resources department.

52. Which of the following is defined as an occasion when an employer offers an employee some form of reward for completing an action, and then fails to follow through with that reward?

 a. Professional libel
 b. Promissory estoppel
 c. Constructive discharge
 d. Duty of good faith

53. Which of the following might be an example of *Transactional Leadership*?

 a. A manager sets monthly goals for his department and offers motivational rewards to employees if they accomplish these goals.
 b. A manager takes the time to sit down with each employee and assist him in utilizing individual skills within the department.
 c. A manager has a series of tasks that need to be completed and assigns each employee a task, based on the employee's particular skill sets.
 d. A manager allows employees to determine where they fit best within the department and encourages them to work at their own pace.

54. If Congress passes a bill while in session, regardless if it is signed by the President, that bill becomes law within how many days?

 a. 10 days
 b. 12 days
 c. 15 days
 d. 20 days

55. When offering a job candidate a position, which of the following steps would come FIRST?

 a. Pre-employment drug testing
 b. Notifying non-selected candidates
 c. Contingent job offer
 d. Written employment contract

56. When faced with an ethical challenge, which of the following approaches to a solution considers which path will help advance society and create the most good for the future of the community?

 a. Fairness approach
 b. Utilitarian approach
 c. Virtue approach
 d. Common good approach

57. In an environmental, social, and governance (ESG) approach to business, organizational policies, procedures, and decisions prioritize _____ value over _____ value:

    a. investor, customer
    b. employee, executive officer
    c. human resources, accounting
    d. stakeholder, shareholder

58. The ERG Theory (1969) is attributed to which of the following researchers?

    a. Fredrick Herzberg
    b. Clayton Alderfer
    c. Abraham Maslow
    d. Victor Vroom

59. Which of the following is the acronym used to describe an exception to any of the anti-discrimination laws for employment?

    a. EEOC
    b. AAP
    c. KPM
    d. BFOQ

60. How do corporations fund business operations?

    a. Bank loans
    b. Investments by partners
    c. Government subsidies
    d. Sale of stock

61. Which of the following elements is not a part of the ADDIE model of instructional design?

    a. Administration
    b. Design
    c. Development
    d. Implementation

62. Which of the following acts requires workplaces to maintain an environment that is "free from recognized hazards that are causing or are likely to cause death or serious physical harm"?

    a. Occupational Safety and Health Act
    b. Americans with Disabilities Act
    c. Drug-Free Workplace Act
    d. Sarbanes-Oxley Act

63. Which type of testing is not part of the medical examination conditions of ADA and may be required of any candidate?

    a. Polygraph test
    b. Drug screening test
    c. Driving test
    d. Aptitude test

64. Which of the following is a provision of the Fair Labor Standards Act of 1938?

a. All previous compensation laws are obsolete.
b. Overtime pay must be 1.5 times the normal hourly wage.
c. The maximum work week is 45 hours.
d. Children may work unlimited hours, provided working conditions are safe.

65. Which word best characterizes employee movement in the team-based model of career development?

a. lateral
b. upward
c. static
d. frequent

66. All of the following are acceptable salary deductions for exempt employees except:

a. Unpaid leave under FMLA
b. Suspensions for two days due to inappropriate workplace behavior
c. During the first week of employment when employee works a full week
d. To offset an employee's military pay

67. Which of the following refers to the measurement of the relationship between the characteristics of each employee and their actual performance in the position? For example: the job description of a dancer for a dance company requires members to perform in the company so an audition is held; the _____ of the audition measures whether or not those at the audition have acceptable dance training.

a. Construct validity
b. Criterion validity
c. Concurrent validity
d. Content validity

68. Hubert contracts food poisoning from a tuna fish sandwich he made at home. He eats the sandwich in the break room and becomes sick in the employee bathroom. Is this a work-related illness?

a. Yes, because the food was consumed at the workplace.
b. Yes, because he became sick at the workplace.
c. No, because food poisoning is not a significant illness.
d. No, because the food was prepared at home for personal consumption.

69. If OSHA fails to issue the final order, what is the next step that the employee may take?

a. Contact his congressional representative to discuss the matter
b. File a law suit in a U.S. district court
c. Request a restraining order against the employer
d. Submit an official request that the company improve its whistleblower policy

70. What are the typical hours of the swing shift?

a. 10 p.m. to 6 a.m.
b. 12 a.m. to 8 a.m.
c. 4 p.m. to 12 a.m.
d. 5 p.m. to 1 a.m.

71. A labor union has recently been created at a company that manufactures heavy industrial equipment. Before negotiations can begin, the company chooses freely to acknowledge the union as the primary bargaining union for employees. In the meantime, the labor union has upcoming union elections to consider. Due to the company's decision, which of the following types of union election bars would result?

    a. Prior-petition
    b. Certification-year
    c. Voluntary-recognition
    d. Blocking-charge

72. Harold, the head of the human resources department for a large industrial machine manufacturing company, has discovered an issue that requires ERM, or Enterprise Risk Management. Upon reviewing important employee documentation, he has found out that that required forms are not being completed, placing the human resources department at risk for non-compliance with federal guidelines. Using the guidelines of ERM, what should Harold consider doing to prevent further non-compliance?

    a. Terminate the employee responsible for failing to ensure correct documentation
    b. Create a new department within the human resources department that keeps an eye on completing the documentation
    c. Contact the federal agency responsible for documentation and request a reprieve
    d. Establish quarterly reviews of the documentation to ensure that it is completed as required

73. A company is looking to design more flexibility into its compensation practices in order to empower managers to more accurately reward their employees for high performance. Which of the following compensation practices is most likely to achieve this goal?

    a. Pay grades
    b. Market pricing
    c. Broadbanding
    d. Pay policy line

74. The Youngblood Company is too small to have its own health insurance plan, so it joins several other businesses in a combined plan. This is known as a(n)

    a. administrative services only plan.
    b. third party administrator plan.
    c. partially self-funded plan.
    d. health purchasing alliance.

75. When employees leave work early or purposefully work at a slow pace, they are engaging in

    a. property deviance.
    b. production deviance.
    c. political deviance.
    d. personal aggression.

76. In a collective bargaining agreement, which clause requires all new employees to join the union within a defined interval?

a. maintenance of membership clause
b. closed shop clause
c. union shop clause
d. contract administration clause

77. Which of the following would be considered primary research?

a. interviews performed by the researcher
b. journal articles
c. books
d. trend analyses

78. Michal is interested in applying for a promotion within the publishing company where she works. What type of application would be most appropriate for the human resources professional to provide in this situation?

a. Job-specific application
b. Short-form application
c. Long-form application
d. Weighted application

79. In terms of required document retention, which of the following is not covered by Title VII of the Civil Rights Act of 1964?

a. Apprentice selection records
b. Employee resumes
c. Tax deductions
d. Affirmative action plan

80. Before a newly forming labor union may submit a demand for recognition to the employer, what step must occur?

a. Petition the NLRB for voluntary recognition
b. Establish a bargaining position for the union
c. Acquire signed authorization cards from employees
d. Meet with the employer to discuss alternatives

81. The EEO-1 report must be completed on or before which date each year?

a. January 31
b. April 1
c. June 15
d. September 30

82. How many managers does each employee report to in a matrix organization?

a. 0
b. 1
c. 2
d. 4

83. According to the Labor-Management Relations Act (LMRA) of 1947, if the President steps in during a labor strike, how long of a "cooling-off" period may he require, should the strike be deemed to have national consequences?

   a. 30 days
   b. 50 days
   c. 80 days
   d. 100 days

84. What is the human resources professional's primary role in assisting a department with conducting an effective interview?

   a. To offer any requested advice on preparing for and setting up interviews
   b. To choose the members of the prospective interview board
   c. To create the official list of questions that will be asked during the interview
   d. To conduct all interviews for prospective employees of the company

85. In which business structure do partners exist mainly as investors, without much influence on daily operations?

   a. limited liability partnership
   b. sole proprietorship
   c. general partnership
   d. joint venture

86. Which of the following pieces of legislation does not, at this time, apply to private employers?

   a. Fair Credit Reporting Act of 1970
   b. Immigration and Nationality Act of 1952
   c. Civil Rights Act of 1991
   d. Privacy Act of 1974

87. During succession planning, a human resources professional may categorize employees as all of the following except:

   a. Employees who are ready for a new position in the company
   b. No employee is necessary because the position is now obsolete
   c. Employees who show indications that he or she is ready for a promotion
   d. Employees who fulfill all of the requirements of the position

88. Which of the following communication skills is MOST impactful when having challenging conversations?

   a. Active listening
   b. Well-researched responses
   c. Assertive opening statements
   d. Confident body language

89. Polygraph testing for employment falls under which of the following federal departments?

   a. Department of Labor
   b. Federal Trade Commission
   c. USCIS
   d. Department of Justice

90. Not all employees will agree on all topics of conversation when communicating with one another in the workplace; topics such as politics, current events, technology, and the economy can all elicit emotional responses that affect workforce collaboration and output. Which of the following would be the MOST effective approach to addressing divisive topics of employee conversation in the workplace?

    a. Update company policy to restrict topics of conversation to be only work-related
    b. Emphasize an open door policy for employees to know where they can go if faced with challenging conversations
    c. Closely monitor employees' social media accounts to identify confrontational personalities
    d. Take a hands-off approach to respect employees' right to free speech

91. How much COBRA coverage is allowed if an employee is terminated due to "gross misconduct"?

    a. 0 months
    b. 18 months
    c. 29 months
    d. 36 months

92. Derek is delivering a presentation to a group of trainees. During the presentation, the trainees will need to take comprehensive notes. How should Derek arrange the seats in the training room?

    a. conference style
    b. U-shaped style
    c. classroom style
    d. chevron style

93. Which of the following would reduce information overload during orientation?

    a. Focusing on the positive aspects of the organization
    b. Handing out documents supplementary to lecture material
    c. Conducting the program in one installment rather than in a series of meetings
    d. Preventing open-ended discussion after presentations

94. What is the distinguishing characteristic of a seamless organization?

    a. Low turnover
    b. Multiple chief executives
    c. Lack of hierarchy
    d. Employees report to two managers

95. How long must an executive order be published in the Federal Register before it becomes law?

    a. 30 days
    b. 60 days
    c. 6 months
    d. 1 year

96. The EEO-1 filing is required of private employers with a minimum of how many employees?

   a. 50
   b. 75
   c. 100
   d. 200

97. The second of these important amendments to FLSA determined that employers cannot be required to compensate employees who commute long distances to work. Which of the following reflects this amendment?

   a. Portal to Portal Act
   b. Equal Pay Act
   c. Davis Beacon Act
   d. National Labor Relations Act

98. Which of the following is NOT an injury or illness prevention plan required by OSHA?

   a. emergency action plan
   b. safety and health management plan
   c. sanitation plan
   d. fire prevention plan

99. Dalton, a human resources professional for an engineering firm, is completing a series of annual reports. During his analysis of employee status, he divides the average number of employees for the year (150) by the number of employees who left the firm during the year (8). He arrives at a rate of 18.75. What is this type of result called?

   a. Accession rate
   b. Replacement cost
   c. Turnover analysis
   d. Quality of hire

100. Which of the following represents an occasion when picketing would be illegal?

   a. When an election for union representation has occurred within a 12-month period
   b. When employees try to provide potential customers with information about business practices
   c. When a union tries to encourage non-union employees to join the union
   d. When a union attempts to encourage the employer to recognize union representation

101. Which of the following statements about drug testing programs is true?

   a. Scheduled drug testing programs are the most effective.
   b. Testing for illicit drugs is considered a medical exam and is regulated by the ADA as such.
   c. Businesses can decide to test certain job groups only.
   d. Candidates may be drug tested before an offer of employment has been made.

102. The National Institute of Occupational Safety and Health (NIOSH) describes a certain workplace condition as "harmful physical and emotional responses that occur when the requirements of the job do not match the capabilities, resources, or needs of the worker." Which of the following workplace conditions does this define?

a. Stress
b. Depression
c. Disorganization
d. Insecurity

103. Which of the following strategies would be MOST effective when communicating with the workforce about impending changes to the organization?

a. Compartmentalization of information to ensure the right people get the right information
b. Transparency in decision-making to promote trust building among the workforce
c. Reassurance of job status to ease any workforce anxiety or stress
d. Restriction of information release to protect from workforce pushback until the change takes place

104. Which of the following is a consequence of the Sarbanes-Oxley Act?

a. Employees may trade stock during pension fund blackout periods.
b. Companies are allowed to conduct their own stock appraisal.
c. CEOs may be punished for fraudulent financial reports.
d. Audit partners must alternate every two years.

105. When performing a job evaluation, which three factors does the HAY system use to classify jobs?

a. knowledge, experience, and seniority
b. knowledge, skill, and ability
c. knowledge, accountability, and problem solving
d. knowledge, skill, and responsibility

106. A private company is a contractor for a federal defense agency. Many of the contractor's employees will be in positions of extreme sensitivity, and the contractor would like to give polygraph tests to employees. What is the federal policy regarding polygraph tests in this situation?

a. The polygraph test may be administered only to those who will be working in defense-related jobs
b. Federal law makes polygraphs illegal for anyone or any institution but the government to administer
c. The employer may utilize anyone in the company to administer the polygraph
d. Because the contractor has other contracts not related to its work with the defense agency, polygraphs are not allowed

107. Which of the following employees would be most likely to receive on-call pay?

a. Dermatologist who owns their own practice
b. High school janitor with the keys to the school's generator
c. Receptionist for a child care facility
d. Police officer in a large precinct

108. How many complaints about an employer's potential violation of FLSA rules can cause the government to step in and perform an audit of the business?

    a. 1
    b. 2
    c. 3
    d. 5

109. Which of the following organizations must complete an annual EEO survey?

    a. A bank with one hundred employees
    b. A university with two hundred employees
    c. A local government with fifty employees
    d. A federal subcontractor with ten employees

110. Which of the following agencies is responsible for enforcing privacy laws?

    a. Department of Justice (DOJ)
    b. Equal Employment Opportunity Commission (EEOC)
    c. Federal Trade Commission (FTC)
    d. Department of Labor (DOL)

111. According to Maslow's hierarchy, which needs must be met first?

    a. social needs
    b. safety needs
    c. self-actualization needs
    d. physiological needs

112. Which of the following best explains workers' compensation laws regarding an employer's responsibility?

    a. Employers are responsible for any work-related injuries or health problems
    b. Employers are responsible for any health problems that an employee develops while working for the employer
    c. Employers do not have to assume responsibility for employee problems unless the employee proves definitively that the problem is job related
    d. Employers may utilize federal aid for most work-related injuries and problems that employers develop on the job

113. The LMRA is also referred to by which of the following names?

    a. Norris-LaGuardia Act
    b. Taft-Hartley Act
    c. Wagner Act
    d. Landrum-Griffith Act

114. Within how many days of employment must a business complete the I-9 form for new employees?

    a. 1 day
    b. 3 days
    c. 5 days
    d. 7 days

115. Which of the following is defined as pay legally required whether or not an employer has immediate work available for an employee?

    a. Geographic pay

    b. On-call pay

    c. Reporting pay

    d. Call-back pay

Answer Key and Explanations for Test #3

1. C: OSHA Form 301 is intended to be an Injury and Illness Incident Report. OSHA Form 300 is intended to be a Log of Work-Related Injuries and Illnesses. OSHA Form 300A is intended to be a Summary of Work-Related Injuries and Illnesses. OSHA Form 301A does not exist.

2. C: Fernando is owed reporting pay. He has been asked to come in at a certain time, so he should not be penalized or uncompensated simply because the boss has made an error. Typically, reporting pay is less than a full day's wage. On-call pay is given to employees who may be called in to deal with an emergency at any time. Not all employees who are on call are paid for it. Employees who are forced to return to work either before or after their allotted time may be eligible for call-back pay. Shift pay, finally, is the compensation associated with the employee's normal work schedule.

3. D: Jared is practicing transformational leadership. A transformational leader capitalizes on the good relationships in the group, and acts more as a model than a guide. Transformational leaders create an environment in which employees can improve themselves. Authoritarian leadership practices a rigid top-down approach to management. Coaching helps to develop the employee in both professional and personal goals. Democratic leadership seeks to make the voice of the team heard and equally impactful in the final decisions.

4. A: Streamlined onboarding is a valuable retention tool for newly hired employees who are just being introduced to the organization. Remote work may be a valuable perk or working condition for some employees, but it is not a one-size-fits-all strategy nor is it feasible for all positions or organizations. Job description reviews can be useful during job analysis processes, but if an employee has taken on responsibilities and grown in their role to the point of a job description review, leveraging internal mobility is a more impactful way to recognize the value the employee brings to the organization. Recognition for value added and a job well done in the form of a promotion or other career enhancement encourages employees to stay and continue to grow within the organization.

5. D: Human resources professionals will have their hands in many tasks during both short- and long-term emergency preparations. Keeping up-to-date emergency contact data for every employee is an essential task for human resources professionals in the event that the emergency weather event is severe and displaces or harms company employees. While direct managers may have access to this data as well, the human resources team is responsible for company-wide accountability in the event that the storm causes extreme damage or communications disruption. Coordinating with suppliers for resource access will more likely be led by operations teams. Human resources may advise in flexing employee schedules leading up to the storm, but it is the operations managers who will lead this action due to their institutional knowledge of the day-to-day operations. Human resources may advise in securing employee data and the systems that support that data, but it will be the IT department that leads the digital preparations due to their expertise.

6. C: The four Ps of marketing are product, price, place, and promotion. Product refers to the characteristics, appearance, and specifications of the item or service being sold. Price refers to the art of maximizing profits by establishing the right cost for the product. Placement refers to the venues in which the product or service will be sold. Finally, promotion refers to the set of advertising and public relations activities designed to stimulate sale of the product.

7. A: Positional bargaining is one among many bargaining options for employers, and entering into positional bargaining is not considered to be an unfair labor practice. However, entering into a hot cargo agreement with the union, taking disciplinary actions against those who participate in unions, and declining to enter into a bargain with the employee union may be considered unfair labor practices for employers.

8. D: Among the criteria under which the NLRB recognizes a successor employer, or a new employer who has taken over a company, are the following: indicating a significant continuity in standard business activities, establishing a clear agreement with the previous employer, and demonstrating a clear parallel in the products and procedures of the company. The NLRB also recognizes as a successor employer one who assimilates a reasonable number of employees from under the previous employer, but the successor employer is not necessarily expected to assimilate *all* employees.

9. A: The Office of Federal Contract Compliance Programs prefers that data related to employee race and ethnicity be generated by self-reporting. In other words, it is best if employees indicate their own race or ethnicity, as often happens during the hiring process. Self-reported data is more accurate, and is less likely to be influenced by a desire to demonstrate diversity.

10. A: For human resources departments, the first step in enterprise risk management is an audit. Enterprise risk management is a systematic assessment of the potential dangers to an organization, as well as the creation of a strategy to mitigate these dangers. A human resources audit looks for areas in which the business is at risk, whether because of suboptimal working conditions or noncompliance with regulations. Employee interviews may be a part of the audit. The purchase of insurance may be one consequence of an audit. Forecasting may only occur after the completion of an audit.

11. D: The ADDIE model outlines the components of instructional design. The acronym stands for Analysis, Design, Development, Implementation, and Evaluation. These are the steps in the creation, execution, and evaluation of an effective training program. They are very similar to the steps in other quality management programs. Because evaluation is the final step, the ADDIE model indicates that improvement should be ongoing.

12. B: Line of sight is defined as the knowledge employees have about how their work behavior affects their compensation. An entitlement philosophy provides greater compensation for employees with more seniority. A total rewards strategy reviews a business's resources for bringing in, and retaining, certain employees. Organizational culture is the larger category of which line of sight and entitlement philosophy are a part; organizational culture is simply the overall "culture" of a business and its relationship between management and employees.

13. A: A correlation coefficient of +0.8 would be the strongest suggestion that productivity increases with experience. Only a positive correlation coefficient indicates that productivity and experience are positively correlated. A negative correlation coefficient would indicate that productivity declines with experience. For this reason, the answer is +0.8, even though -0.9 (answer choice D) represents the strongest correlation.

14. B: Each company is responsible for establishing the vacation pay policies that will apply to their employees. The FMLA does not specify vacation pay policies, so answer choice A is incorrect. ERISA is the Employee Retirement Income Security Act of 1974, so it does not relate to vacation pay policies; therefore, answer choice C is incorrect. States do not establish vacation pay guidelines

(apart from basic compensation requirements established at the federal level), so answer choice D is incorrect.

15. B: Divestiture is defined as a business decision to eliminate a department by laying off employees or moving them to another department. Reengineering is an attempt to improve overall business operations so that customers benefit from the process. Workforce expansion, as the name indicates, is an increase in employees for a business to reach certain goals. Offshoring, or outsourcing, refers to a business's decision to move certain activities to another location (usually international) to reduce costs.

16. D: In this situation, the human resources officer should conduct a nondirective interview. Nondirective interviews follow no particular plan: they are more like casual conversations between the interviewer and the candidate. Because the available position remains undefined, it would not be fruitful to ask specific questions or to identify particular knowledge and skills. A non-directive interview would be a better way to determine whether candidates have the right attitude and temperament for the organization. Directive interviews follow a predetermined list of questions. A panel interview features multiple interviewers, typically from different departments. A stress interview requires the candidate to react to a demanding situation.

17. B: While some version of each of these options may occur during the human resources representative's response to the situation, the critical first step to any unclear situation is to collect pertinent information and facts that illustrate what is actually happening. Reviewing the company handbook is dependent on a clear picture of what actions the supervisor took that may or may not have broken company policy. If Sally did not feel comfortable going to her supervisor right away, there may be more at play than just the questionable documents; by fact-finding first, the representative can determine what communication, if any, may need to happen between Sally and her supervisor. Reaching out to the CEO may or may not be appropriate based on the size of the organization; alerting the correct organizational leader(s) may be an important step, depending on the results of the initial fact-finding investigation.

18. C: Ron and Marcy have participated in patterned interviews. This type of interview covers a predetermined set of subjects, but does not adhere to a script. In other words, the interviewer will know in advance what topics are to be discussed, but will not have a list of questions to be asked verbatim. Patterned interviews allow the interviewer to follow up on interesting and provocative comments, but the resulting interviews may be difficult to compare. A structured interview follows a predetermined list of questions. In a stress interview, the prospective employee is subjected to a very difficult or challenging situation. A behavioral interview digs into a candidate's past experiences that relate to the specific job being interviewed for.

19. B: The fourth element in SWOT is Threats. A SWOT as an environmental scanning tool that assesses the internal and external conditions as well as their helpful and harmful aspects. A helpful internal trait or condition is considered a Strength, a harmful internal trait or condition is considered a Weakness, a helpful external trait or condition is considered an Opportunity and a harmful external trait or condition is considered a threat.

20. C: The Green Company has established an improshare program. In this type of group incentive program, employees are rewarded for performing above a pre-established baseline standard. If the employees consistently exceed the baseline, it may be raised in the future. A gainsharing program is a more general attempt to improve the performance of the entire organization. A Scanlon plan gives employees a share of the cost savings achieved through increased productivity. A profit-sharing plan gives employees a percentage of the organization's profits.

21. D: The NLRA specifically does not apply to agricultural workers (among other types of workers – domestic workers, contract employees, federal and state workers, etc.). There is nothing within the NLRA to prevent it from applying to administrative, corporate, or financial employees. Within each of these categories, it might be possible to find a type of worker that fits the NLRA caveat, such as a contract employee or a federal worker, but there is nothing about these other four categories that fails to fall under NLRA.

22. C: Interest-based bargaining results when both sides acknowledge that they have a strong motivation in the continuity of business activities, and thus proceed in negotiations with this acknowledgement. Positional bargaining results when each side establishes a clear position and aims to achieve the goal or goals of that position. Integrative bargaining results when the different sides agree to compromise on certain issues by taking the big picture into account. Distributive bargaining is another name for positional bargaining.

23. C: The WARN Act is the Worker Adjustment and Retraining Notification Act, which was designed to established certain rights for workers who have been laid off. Answer choice A is incorrect because the act was certainly not designed to prevent massive lay-offs but rather to give workers "adjustment and retraining" in the event of massive lay-offs. Answer choice B is incorrect because the act cannot necessarily provide new positions for workers who have been laid off. And answer choice D is incorrect because the act doesn't mandate severance pay for those who have been laid off.

24. C: By allowing his intuition to guide his preference, Eric is relying on the bias of his gut feeling. Answer choice A is incorrect because a first impression bias means the interviewer allows an immediate impression of a candidate to determine a decision. Answer choice B is incorrect because a cultural noise bias means the candidate responds with pointed answers that are aimed at making the interviewer happy rather than responding in a more natural or general way. Answer choice D is incorrect because a leniency bias occurs when the interviewer is lenient in regard to a candidate and fails to take potential weaknesses into account.

25. B: If the leave is foreseeable but the employee fails to provide his employer with appropriate advance notice, the employer may delay FMLA coverage for 30 days from the date of notification. The employer may, of course, delay coverage for less than 30 days—so 15 days is an option—but the employer has a full 30 days. The employer may not, however, delay coverage beyond this, so 45 days or 60 days is far too long.

26. B: Cultural noise is a type of bias in which the candidate begins responding as he believes the interviewer would prefer. For instance, for a job that requires extensive travel, a candidate might attempt to sway the odds in his favor by claiming to enjoy travel, even if he has no travel experience in other jobs (and/or might not really care to travel but hopes to get the job). The halo effect results from an interviewer focusing on a single good quality to define the candidate. The horn effect is the opposite of this; it occurs when the interviewer focuses on a single negative quality, over all other qualities, to rate the candidate. The central tendency occurs if an interviewer is unable to make a clear decision about a preferred candidate and averages their results.

27. C: Job sharing is an alternative job practice where two part-time employees are hired to cover the hours of one full-time position. Job sharing can range in structural flexibility to accommodate employee and business needs such as morning/afternoon shifts, three-day/two-day shifts, or alternating schedules to match the needs of the parties involved. Job rotation can be utilized as employee experience enhancement to help cross-train staff in different departments or functions and can also serve as a staffing alternative to help fill a temporary skill gap until a new employee can be hired to fill the role. Independent contractors do not function as W2 employees but can be used as a staffing alternative in cases where highly specialized work is required beyond the scope of the current job force. Temp-to-hire programs utilize temporary employees if the job need is short-term but there may be full or permanent positions available at the end of that period of time.

28. B: The Latin phrase *respondeat superior* translates to mean "let the master answer" and suggests that companies have a measure of responsibility for employee actions, if employee actions result from job responsibilities. A human resources professional may see this used if a manager is accused of discriminatory practices and the employer as a whole is held liable for the manager's actions. The phrase "friend of the court" comes from the Latin *amicus curiae*. The phrase "with connected strength" comes from the Latin *coniunctis viribus*. The phrase "thrown to the lions" comes from the Latin *damnatio ad bestias*.

29. D: While some types of strikes are fully legal, a sit-down strike is considered illegal. Double breasting is a reference to different types of businesses-- one being union and the other being non-union--and it has no immediate connection to bargaining strategies, so answer choice A is incorrect. A lockout is the result of an employer stopping work indefinitely, but it is not a bargaining strategy, so answer choice B is incorrect. Distributive bargaining is simply a strategy an employer or union could take when compromising on bargaining issues, so answer choice C is incorrect.

30. D: A 401(k) contribution is a voluntary deduction from gross earnings. That is, employees are not required to have this money taken out of their paycheck. The other answer choices are statutory deductions, meaning they are required by law.

31. C: The fourth of B.F. Skinner's strategies is Extinction. The other answer choices – Termination, Encouragement, and Actualization – are not specific strategies laid out by Skinner but rather might fall under the four he did describe. Positive reinforcement is a strategy in which desired behavior is rewarded positively. Negative is a strategy in which desired behavior is rewarded by removing a negative state or condition. Punishment is similar to the two reinforcement strategies but is designed in a way to eliminate and undesired behavior. Extinction is a measure of how long a behavior will persist without reinforcement.

32. A: The Age Discrimination in Employment Act requires that any employee records related to charges of discrimination must be retained until the charges are resolved. Once the charges are resolved, records may be expunged. The Age Discrimination in Employment Act was passed with the intention of helping older people find jobs. It required businesses to declare any reasons for failing to hire older workers at an appropriate rate.

33. D: Statistical power is the extent to which research results accurately identify differences between trained and untrained employees. Of course, researchers want to design a method that will have the maximum statistical power. If the statistical power of the research is low, it is likely that a difference between the trained and untrained employees will pass unnoticed. It can be difficult to obtain powerful statistical results from research into employee training in large part because the methods of assessing performance are so subjective.

34. A: An employee's performance on an assembly line is likely to follow a negatively accelerating learning curve. This type of learning curve is typical of rote tasks, which can be learned and indeed mastered in a short time, but which do not permit much improvement after the initial learning. A positively accelerating learning curve, on the other hand, is marked by a slow start followed by a gradually increasing speed of learning. A positively accelerating learning curve is typical of complex tasks, which are difficult at first but which may be improved upon over a long interval.

35. C: A skills gap analysis aims to define the gap between the skills an organization has and the skills it needs. Each of the other answer options may make up steps of the gap analysis process but do not cover the full spectrum of data required. Performance management results can help illustrate the current skills of the workforce. Organizational strategy can give insight into where the organization is going and what skills it may need. Labor market forecasts can help map what external labor will be needed to close the gap or what skills shortages may be present both internally and externally.

36. B: This is not a work-related illness because the influenza exposure occurred away from work. Of course, it is not always possible to ascertain when exposure occurred, but the mere fact that symptoms began at work is not enough to make this illness work-related.

37. A: A checklist is a rating method of performance appraisal. In a checklist system, the various elements of the job description are listed, and the employee receives a check mark for each element he performs with competence. This is considered a rating system because the number of checks can be converted into a score, which makes it possible to compare employees. In a field appraisal, someone besides the employee's supervisor observes and reports on the employee's performance. In an essay appraisal, the evaluator writes a short prose passage about the employee's performance. In a critical incident review, the supervisor discusses the especially positive and negative aspects of the employee's performance.

38. A: The Equal Employment Opportunity Act of 1972 did not extend Title VII coverage to the employees of religious institutions. These organizations were exempted from the original version of Title VII (in the Civil Rights Act of 1964), and this exemption was maintained in 1972. Religious institutions are allowed to give preferential treatment to job candidates and employees who are adherents of that religion. Universities, state government agencies, and federal legislative bodies all became subject to Title VII with the passage of the Equal Employment Opportunity Act.

39. A: This situation could be illustrated by a plateau learning curve. In this model, the learner makes rapid progress at first, but learning then slows almost to a halt. A plateau learning curve might occur when a task is easy to become competent at but difficult to master, or when a skill is easy to acquire but rarely practiced.

40. C: Banquet-style seating, in which groups of employees will be arranged at tables, is best for a training session with small group activities. Classroom-style seating is best if the employees will simply be facing the front of a room and listening to a speaker. Chevron-style seating is best for a combination of activities that include video presentations and group interaction. Theater-style seating accommodates the largest number of people and also works well for various presentations.

41. D: The critical first step when purchasing a new HRIS is determining what the organization needs from a system as well as what it may want from a system. A comprehensive needs assessment sets the foundation for then determining a system budget and project timelines. Once needs, budget, and timelines are defined, then an organization can seek vendor quotes within each of these parameters.

42. C: A leave of absence is considered indirect compensation. Compensation is indirect when it cannot easily be assigned a monetary value. Since an employee is not paid during a leave of absence, granting one is not a direct expense for the company. Of course, the employee's absence may result in diminished productivity and therefore less revenue for the company, but it is difficult to quantify this loss.

43. A: Decertification does not prevent employees from joining a union later – either the same union or a different union. Decertification is not always indicative of problems with the union but can only be initiated and led by employees. In some cases, a union will decertify because it has outgrown its usefulness, or because the workers wish to file suit against ownership without the interference of the union. Employers are not allowed to lobby employees during the decertification process, and only 30% of the employees need to petition the NLRB for there to be a decertification vote.

44. B: Constructive discharge is determined in situations where an employee resigns due to working conditions that would cause most "reasonable" people to resign. These working conditions can range from discrimination in the workplace to a hostile work environment to other intolerable working conditions. Constructive discharge can lead to legal ramifications such as the awarding of unemployment to the employee or other discrimination or harassment charges against the employer. Constructive discharge does not apply in cases where there is standing documentation of poor performance that leads to the employee's termination, where the termination is part of business decisions that do not have to do with the individual employee, such as layoffs, or where the employee resigns to pursue external opportunities, as opposed to in response to internal working conditions.

45. C: When addressing complex and emotional situations, the most effective approach is one that is honest, transparent, and active. Advising Gina to write hand written notes each employee is inefficient and takes can take away from transparency if not all employees receive the same message. Assisting employees in their job search may be appropriate as a secondary course of action but is not Gina's primary concern or responsibility. Advocating to retain the department likely falls outside of Gina's scope of the business and may take away from the communication needed first and foremost with the employees.

46. C: Question 84 describes the qualified plan, which provides IRS-approved tax advantages but without any extra benefits for shareholders and executives. Answer choice A is incorrect because the nonqualified plan provides benefits to specified employees (i.e., executives) and shareholders. Answer choice B is incorrect because the defined contribution plan utilizes a standard pension plan but without the added benefits defined in advance. Answer choice D is incorrect because the cash balance plan is a combination of the defined benefit and defined contribution plan but does not fall under the immediate grouping of voluntary benefits programs.

47. C: According to FMLA rules, the established radius for employees in private businesses (as opposed to state or federal agencies) is 75 miles. The radius of 30 or 50 miles is too small. The radius of 85 miles exceeds the FMLA standard.

48. C: A ranking system is usually better for a smaller group of employees but can be difficult to organize with a larger group when multiple departments, positions, and supervisors come into play. Behaviorally anchored rating scales and competency-based ratings set clear parameters for assessing performance based on an employee's behaviors or the job's required competencies and can be applied uniformly across individuals within a position. Forced distribution ranking is more effective for larger groups of data and is, therefore, the incorrect answer here.

49. D: Kurt Lewin's classic three-stage change process theory describes change in three easy-to-understand steps: unfreeze the status quo, implement the change, and then refreeze the new status quo. This theory fails to take into account that change is not easy and in a dynamic work environment, the idea of a "status quo" is little more than an illusion. Depending on the organization and the change at hand, resource management, legal precedents, and customer

feedback may all be factors but are only one element of many that may make up the dynamic environment that influences change processes and outcomes.

50. B: The government would not consider the location of the company when evaluating a claim that complying with ADA regulations would constitute an undue hardship. The government does issue some exceptions to the ADA in cases where compliance would significantly impair a business' viability. However, the precise location of the business should not have any effect.

51. D: Payroll systems are not always the responsibility of the human resources department. In some organizations, payroll is handled by the finance department. The other answer choices are true statements.

52. B: A promissory estoppel is defined as an occasion when an employer offers an employee some form of reward for completing an action, and then fails to follow through with that reward. Libel is a form a written defamation. Constructive discharge is defined as an employee's decision to quit when an employer creates hostile working conditions. Duty of good faith is simply a tradition of common law by which those who work together are expected to behave in all fairness and honesty toward one another.

53. A: Transactional leadership occurs when a leader offers some form of a transaction as the result of meeting a goal; in other words, the manager is utilizing transactional leadership by offering a reward if employees complete certain monthly goals. Answer choice B reflects a coaching style of leadership. Answer choice C reflects more of a directive style of leadership. Answer choice D reflects a *laissez-faire* style of leadership.

54. A: If Congress passes a bill while in session, regardless if it is signed by the President, that bill becomes law within 10 days. The other answer choices—12 days, 15 days, and 20 days—are all too high.

55. C: Contingent job offers are the first possible step in the hiring process and should precede any pre-employment assessments that do not test a job candidate's abilities or fit for the position they are interviewing for. Pre-employment testing such as a drug test comes after a contingent job offer but before the formal employment contract or written job offer. Notifying non-selected candidates is an important step that can vary in its appropriate timing; however, in nearly all situations it is advisable to at least learn of the preferred candidate's answer to a contingent job offer prior to notifying non-selected candidates.

56. D: The common good approach to solving an ethical challenge asks the question: "Which solution will best help advance the common good?" This approach considers what is best for society and the community as a whole and looks at the future of society. In contrast, a utilitarian approach considers the most good for the greatest amount of people while inflicting the least harm. While the group is considered, this approach considers both the individual and the collective whole. A fairness approach (also referred to as a justice approach) considers the solution that will treat all involved parties the same way. A virtue approach considers what the morally "right" decision might be from a character-building standpoint.

57. D: An ESG approach to business seeks to make decisions in a way that positively impacts all parties who may be affected by the business (stakeholders) and not just stock owners (shareholders). While some elements of ESG may at times require putting employee value ahead of leadership value or HR principles ahead of a monetary bottom line, the main tenet of an ESG approach to business is more holistic and aims to put the long-term good of the whole ahead of the short-term good of just those who stand to make money.

58. B: The ERG Theory of 1969, which looks at the levels Existence, Relatedness, and Growth among employees, is attributed to Clayton Alderfer. Fredrick Herzberg is credited with the Motivation/Hygiene Theory of 1959; Victor Vroom is credited with the Expectancy Theory of 1964; Abraham Maslow is credited with the Hierarchy of Needs Theory of 1954.

59. D: The acronym BFOQ stands for *bona fide occupational qualification* and describes an exception to any of the anti-discrimination laws for employment. (For instance, an acting company may advertise to hire only female applicants when recruiting for a female character in an upcoming show.) EEOC refers to the Equal Employment Opportunity Commission. AAP refers to an affirmative action plan. KPM refers to Key Performance Measures.

60. D: Corporations fund business operations through the sale of stock. The purchasers of the stock are known as shareholders, and they are the ultimate owners of the corporation. They appoint a board of directors, which oversees the day-to-day managers of the corporation. When a corporation is successful, shareholders are paid dividends. When a corporation is unsuccessful, the value of stock shares may plummet.

61. A: The instructional design acronym known as the ADDIE model begins not with Administration but with Analysis. The other options – Design, Development, Implementation, and Evaluation – are all elements of the ADDIE acronym.

62. A: The piece of legislation to which the quote refers is the Occupational Safety and Health Act of 1970 (OSHA). The Americans with Disabilities Act (ADA) is focused specifically on providing rights for employees with disabilities in the workplace. The Drug-Free Workplace Act is focused on the substance abuse policy for federal contractors. The Sarbanes-Oxley Act is focused on the legal obligation that organizations have to record and report financial information.

63. B: A drug screening test can be required of any candidate for a job, and the medical examination conditions of ADA do not prevent a candidate from being tested for illegal drug use, regardless of disability. Polygraph tests, driving tests, and aptitude tests are not part of potential medical examinations, and all of these tests must be administered with certain stipulations from ADA.

64. B: One provision of the Fair Labor Standards Act of 1938 is that overtime pay must be 1.5 times the normal hourly wage. Employers may give compensatory time off in lieu of overtime pay. An employee should receive 1.5 times as much compensatory time off as he has worked in overtime. The FLSA established that children may only work limited hours, that the maximum work week is 40 hours, and that some previous compensation laws remain valid.

65. A: In a team-based model of career development, employee movement is generally lateral. The members of a work team are on the same level, and so position change is not generally considered as promotion or demotion. Some organizations encourage this sort of lateral movement because it gives employees a broader set of skills and reduces burnout.

66. C: The exemption status for the first (or last) week of employment only applies if the employee works less than the full week. As the employee is working the full week during the first week of employment, no exemption status is appropriate. The other answer choices—unpaid leave under FMLA, suspensions for inappropriate workplace behavior, and offsetting military pay—are all eligible for exemptions.

67. A: Construct validity is the measurement of the relationship between the characteristics of each employee and his actual performance in the position. Criterion validity results when a certain criterion (or work trait) is predicted and then results. Concurrent validity is a type of criterion

validity (along with predictive validity). Content validity is simply a test that measures whether or not a candidate is qualified to complete an important part of the job.

68. D: This would not be considered a work-related illness because the food was prepared at home for personal consumption. If the tuna sandwich had been provided by Hubert's employer, his illness would be considered work-related. It does not matter that Hubert ate the sandwich or became sick at the workplace.

69. B: If OSHA fails to issue the final order, the employee then has the right to file a law suit in a U.S. district court. The employee may choose to contact his congressional representative, but more than likely, the representative will simply review the employee's legal rights and encourage filing suit. Requesting a restraining order is not necessarily an appropriate step in this case; filing the full law suit, however, is. Submitting an official request about an improvement to the whistleblower policy is unlikely to accomplish much; the employer's actions would call for a larger response from OSHA and the legal system.

70. C: The typical hours of the swing shift are 4 p.m. to 12 a.m. The day shift typically runs from 8 a.m. to 4 p.m., and the graveyard shift typically extends from 12 a.m. to 8 a.m. Some employees receive extra compensation for working the swing or graveyard shift.

71. C: The employer's decision is voluntary, and thus a voluntary-recognition election bar will result, preventing the labor union from conducting elections in the immediate future. A prior-petition bar results when the union withdraws an election request petition and then resubmits it. A certification-year bar results when the NLRB has recently recognized and certified a representative for bargaining on behalf of the union. A blocking-charge bar occurs when an unfair labor practice charge remains pending.

72. D: According to the expectations of ERM, a human resources professional should apply reasonable techniques to correcting a problem. In Harold's case, the best option for addressing the problem of the incomplete documentation would simply be to establish a quarterly review of the paperwork to ensure that it is completed. As for the other answer choices, they each contain extreme responses that do not fit with the requirements of ERM. Terminating the responsible employee does not guarantee that the problem will be fully addressed. Creating a new department simply adds more paper work that can further complicate the process of completing the documentation. There is nothing within the process of ERM that suggests a human resources professional can request a reprieve from a federal agency; the rules are in place already and need to be observed.

73. C: Market pricing and establishing a pay policy line are directly linked to market compensation practices and do not offer a wide variability of options in pay rates. Pay grades offer some additional flexibility and set a minimum and maximum pay rate for a position or for a set of related positions. Broadbanding combines sets of pay grades and a greater number of positions into a larger range of pay options. This technique allows managers greater agency and flexibility in how they choose to reward or value their employees.

74. D: The Youngblood Company's arrangement is known as a health purchasing alliance. This gives smaller businesses more purchasing power and leverage in negotiations with health insurance providers. In an administrative services only plan, the employer creates a claim fund and then hires an insurance company to manage it. In a third party administrator plan, a business besides the employer or the insurance company handles claims. In a partially self-funded plan,

employers only provide a certain amount of coverage. This type of plan ensures that a small business will not be ruined by a single large claim.

75. B: When employees leave work early or purposefully work at a slow pace, they are engaging in production deviance. In other words, they are intentionally performing at a less than optimal rate. Property deviance is the destruction or damaging of company equipment. Property deviance also includes misrepresentation of hours worked, since the time during which the employee claims to be working is technically the property of the company. Political deviance is dysfunctional interpersonal behavior, as for instance spreading rumors or undermining the authority of superiors. Personal aggression includes antisocial and even criminal behaviors like stealing, sexual harassment, and physical violence.

76. C: In a collective bargaining agreement, a union shop clause requires all new employees to join the union within a defined interval. In all industries except construction, this interval must be at least thirty days. In construction, it must be at least a week. A maintenance of membership clause requires employees who choose to join the union to remain enrolled until the union contract expires. However, this clause does not force employees to join the union in the first place. A closed shop clause requires any new employees to join the union. A contract administration clause contains all the administrative details.

77. A: Interviews conducted by the researcher would be considered primary research. Primary research is distinguished by having been conducted by the researcher. Secondary research, on the other hand, is created by someone else. In most cases, it is good to have a mixture of primary and secondary research.

78. B: A short-form application is appropriate for job transfers and job promotions within the same company, so this would be appropriate for Michal's situation. A job-specific application is useful for companies that hire a number of workers for the same type of (or similar) jobs. A long-form application is considered standard for allowing candidates to include their entire educational and work history. A weighted application is appropriate for companies that need to focus on certain candidate qualifications over others.

79. D: Title VII of the Civil Rights Act of 1964 covers the following types of document retention: apprentice selection records, employee resumes, and tax deductions. It does not, however, apply to a business's affirmative action plan, which falls under Executive Order 11246.

80. C: Before submitting to the employer a demand for recognition, the labor union must acquire signed authorization cards from employees. This essentially provides an official statement from employees about their intent to unionize and lets the NLRB know that unionizing activity has support from employees. Petitioning the NLRB for voluntary recognition occurs next. Establishing a bargaining position and meeting with the employer to discuss alternatives are activities of the union itself, but they are not part of the actual unionization process.

81. D: The EEO-1 report must be completed on or before September 30 of each year (as this reflects the federal fiscal calendar). The other dates – January 31, April 1, and June 15 – all reflect possible times for submitting the report, if viewed as falling "before" September 30, but they do not reflect the required date. Also, it is unlikely that any human resources professional would submit the report on these dates. It is far more likely that the report will be completed and submitted closer to the required date.

82. C: In a matrix organization, each employee reports to two managers: a product manager and a functional manager. That is, each employee reports to someone responsible for overseeing the

203

development of a particular product, and someone responsible for overseeing certain types of employees. Matrix organizations require a great deal of cooperation and communication.

83. C: The President may require a cooling-off period for 80 days, if the strike is deemed to have national consequences. In other words, if the strike has the potential to result in serious consequences to national activities, the President may get involved and require the parties to come together and discuss the issue. The options for 30 days and 50 days are too low, and the option for 100 days is too high. (It should be noted that the President does not have to require the full 80 days, but the full 80 days is provided as an option.)

84. A: When a department within a company is planning interviews to hire new employees, the human resources professional's role is primarily one of assisting. The human resources professional is not responsible for choosing the members of the prospective interview board (answer choice B), since this role will fall to the department and those who will be working with the new employee or employees. Additionally, the tasks of creating an official list of questions for the interview (answer choice C), and conducting the actual interviews for prospective employees (answer choice D), belong not to the human resources professional but to the manager or supervisor of the department in which the employees will work.

85. A: In a limited liability partnership, partners exist mainly as investors, without much influence on daily operations. This arrangement, which is also known simply as a limited partnership, is typical of professional businesses, like legal or accounting firms. A sole proprietorship is initiated and operated by a single person. This person is entitled to all of the profits, but is liable for all business activities. In a general partnership, the business operates according to a preset agreement, and liability is shared by a group of partners. The joint venture is a form of general partnership created for a particular purpose or a restricted amount of time.

86. D: The Privacy Act of 1974 reflects data collection activities within federal agencies. It does not apply to private employers. The Fair Credit Reporting Act of 1970, the Immigration and Nationality Act of 1952, and the Civil Rights Act of 1991 all currently have elements that apply to private employers.

87. B: The process of succession planning requires that a human resources professional consider employees within their current positions. As a result, answer choice B falls outside the focus on employees within the positions and instead focuses on the position itself. This is not a part of succession planning. Answer choices A, C, and D all belong to the process of categorizing employees who are currently in positions within an organization.

88. A: Depending on the conversation, each of the answer options may be an important component of a successful conversation; however, active listening and its various building blocks (reflections, open-ended questions, affirmations, etc.) is the most impactful tool due to its ability to gain the trust of the other conversation participants as well as reduce any noise that may interfere with clear communication. A well-researched response is only as strong as the other party's willingness to listen. An assertive opening statement can be important in certain situations, but if the other party has their own priorities they wish to share, that can reduce the impact of a strong opening statement. Confident body language can be an important piece of conveying authority but can be misconstrued as aggressive if the conversation itself does not progress in a mutual give-and-take between participants.

89. A: While polygraph testing might have the goal of "justice" in mind, it actually falls under the Department of Labor. The Federal Trade Commission governs fair credit reviews, while the USCIS (or the United States Citizenship and Immigration Services) governs immigration laws. For employers, the Department of Justice is involved in privacy laws that apply to employees.

90. B: In order to build trust and respect within the workplace, it is important for human resources professionals and organizational leaders to set the example for open communication. Establishing and maintaining open door policies can give employees somewhere to go if they need to talk through interpersonal challenges, seek advice pertinent to their working team, or file a complaint or report inappropriate behavior. Restricting topics of conversation is unrealistic and unlikely to be an effective approach. Monitoring social media is a passive approach that may also breach employee privacy. While some parts of employee speech are protected, the First Amendment does not apply to employees in the private sector; additionally, speech that causes harm can fall into the buckets of harassment or discrimination and is not protected.

91. A: If employment is terminated due to "gross misconduct," the former employee is not entitled to any COBRA coverage. The other answer choices are too high; the employer has no obligation to support COBRA coverage for the terminated employee.

92. C: Derek should arrange the seats in the classroom style. In this style, participants are placed behind desks facing towards the front of the room. This seating arrangement is most appropriate for presentations delivered by a single person, especially when the participants will need to be making notes. In conference-style seating, participants are placed around a large square table. In the U-shaped seating style, participants are placed around three sides of a large table, and the presenter stands on the fourth side. In the Chevron style of seating, participants are placed in rows that face the front of the room at an angle, so that they are facing both the presenter and, to a lesser extent, one another.

93. B: Handing out documents supplementary to lecture materials would help reduce information overload during orientation. Though it may seem that giving new employees more material to look over would contribute to information overload, research has suggested that employees are better able to understand complex subjects when they receive instruction in multiple modes. A focus on the positive aspects of the organization would not necessarily decrease information overload. Conducting a program in one installment would be more likely to overwhelm new employees. Finally, failing to allow employees to raise questions and concerns after a presentation will contribute to information overload.

94. C: The distinguishing characteristic of a seamless organization is a lack of hierarchy. In a seamless organization, employees are not placed in departments and restricted in their communication. The traditional boundaries within an organization, whether departmental or geographic, do not exist.

95. A: An executive order must be published in the Federal Register for 30 days before it becomes law. Executive orders are proclamations by the President of the United States. They may be challenged in the judicial system.

96. C: Private employers with 100 employees or more – except for those within excluded categories – must complete the EEO-1 report. The other answer choices are either too low (50 and 75) or too high (200). In the case of answer choice D, this number of employees falls well within the required reporting, but it does not reflect the *minimum* stated by law.

97. A: The Portal to Portal Act, created in 1947, determined that employers cannot be required to compensate employees who commute long distances to work. The Equal Pay Act of 1963 forbids any type of discrimination based on the employee's gender. The Davis Beacon Act of 1931, and the

National Labor Relations Act of 1935 were both created before the legislation of the Fair Labor Standards Act of 1938, so they are irrelevant.

98. C: OSHA does not require businesses to create a sanitation plan, though the act does require businesses to meet certain standards in this regard. OSHA does require emergency action, safety and health management, and fire prevention plans. These plans must include a summation of company policy, the process for communicating this policy, record-keeping protocols, and identification of relevant officials.

99. C: Turnover analysis results from dividing the average number of employees over a given time frame by the number of employees who left the business over that same time frame. Accession rate describes the number of new hires when compared to the full number of employees in a business. The replacement cost shows businesses the cost of hiring new employees; these costs might include marketing costs, time spent costs, overtime costs, training costs, and more. The quality of hire is determined when a business establishes an example of a quality hire and then compares other employees or new hires against it.

100. A: Though picketing is legal under certain circumstances, one instance when picketing is illegal occurs when an election for union representation has occurred within a 12-month period. Answer choices B, C, and D are all incorrect because they represent occasions when picketing would be considered legal.

101. C: Businesses can decide to test certain job groups only. Some businesses restrict their drug testing to employees who will have great responsibility or who will be operating heavy machinery. Scheduled drug testing programs are less effective, because drug-using employees are given a chance to devise ways around the test. Testing for illicit drugs is not considered to be a medical exam; however, testing for alcohol is considered a medical exam and is regulated by the ADA as such. Pre-employment drug testing should not precede an offer of employment but, rather, be a contingency of the offer of employment.

102. A: According to NIOSH, this is the definition of stress that affects employees in the workplace. Answer choices B, C, and D are incorrect because they could be considered as possible effects of stress but do not fulfill the requirements of the definition on their own

103. B: Human resources professionals play a critical role in communicating and leading the way for change in an organization. Transparency in communications helps build trust and reduce fear even if the information is not all good news; the unknown can be a powerful driver of employee fear, distrust, and discontent. Compartmentalization and information restriction may be required in some situations with sensitive or proprietary information, but they should not be the main strategies unless there is an absolute business necessity; without buy-in from the workforce to support the change, the process can be more challenging or may fail outright. Reassuring the workforce can help soothe nerves surrounding change in the short term but can be viewed as disingenuous or deceitful if the change process leads to unfavorable or uncomfortable outcomes for some employees.

104. C: One consequence of the Sarbanes-Oxley Act is that CEOs may be punished for fraudulent financial reports. This act was passed in 2002 after several large corporations, most notably Enron, collapsed under the weight of unethical accounting and executive mismanagement. The intention of the Sarbanes-Oxley Act was to make top officials culpable for dishonest and reckless accounting. The act explicitly forbade employees from trading stocks during pension fund blackout periods, and

asserted that companies must have their stock appraised by a certified external organization. The act also declared that audit partner assignments must alternate every five years.

105. C: The HAY system classifies jobs according to knowledge, accountability, and problem solving. This system, which was developed in 1943, is a form of point factor grading. A job's accountability is the degree to which other members of the organization rely on that employee.

106. A: Polygraph tests are allowed among federal defense contractors but may only be administered to those who will be working in the defense-related jobs. Most large contractors will not limit their contract work to the government, so it is entirely possible that the company will have employees doing work that is unrelated to the defense jobs. What is more, the employees who do work in connection with the defense agency but don't do sensitive work will not require polygraph testing. Answer choice B is incorrect because federal law does allow for polygraph testing in certain situations. Answer choice C is incorrect because it does not really address the question and because the information is not accurate--polygraph tests must be administered by certified professionals. Answer choice D is also incorrect because the nature of the contractor's work for the defense agency will likely justify polygraph testing for many of the employees.

107. B: A high school janitor with the keys to the school generator would be most likely to receive on-call pay, compensation given to employees who must be available in case of emergency. Many doctors are on call, but they rarely receive special pay for this time, and dermatologists field few emergency requests. A receptionist would not need to be on call very often. A police officer is always on call, and does not receive special pay.

108. A: It takes only one complaint about a potential FLSA violation for a government audit to occur. As a result, businesses are expected to take FLSA rules seriously, and the human resources professional must be very familiar with the rules to avoid even an unintentional violation. The other answer choices (2, 3, and 5) are all too high. By the time that many complaints arise, the audit will already be in progress or have been completed.

109. A: A bank is a financial institution and must complete an annual EEO (equal employment opportunity) survey. This form must be completed before September 30, and must use employment data from a pay period of the most recent July, August, or September. The point of this survey is to ensure that employers are not discriminating in their hiring or promotion practices. Institutions of higher education, state and local governments with fewer than 100 employees, and federal subcontractors with fewer than 50 employees are not required to file an EEO survey.

110. A: The Department of Justice is responsible for enforcing privacy laws. The Equal Employment Opportunity Commission (EEOC) enforces civil rights laws and defends workers against discrimination in the workplace. The Federal Trade Commission (FTC) enforces antitrust laws and protects consumers. The Department of Labor (DOL) enforces labor laws pertaining to workplace safety, wage laws, federally required benefits, and other worker related protections.

111. D: According to Maslow's hierarchy of needs, physiological needs must be met first. Physiological needs are food, shelter, warmth, and water. Until they have been attained, a person cannot focus on higher needs. According to Maslow, needs must be fulfilled in the following order: physiological, safety, social, esteem, and self-actualization. Self-actualization is the need to express and evolve the personality.

112. A: Workers' compensation laws state that employers are responsible for any work-related injuries or problems that employees sustain on the job. Answer choice B is incorrect because employers are not responsible for an individual's health problems unless they were caused at work.

Answer choice C is incorrect because the workers' compensation laws do not necessarily place the full burden of proof on employees to prove the nature of the injury or problem. Answer choice D is incorrect because the workers' compensation laws do not provide for federal aid.

113. B: The Labor-Management Relations Act (LMRA) of 1947 is also known as the Taft-Hartley Act (or just Taft-Hartley). The Norris-LaGuardia goes by no other name. The Wagner Act is the alternative name for the National Labor Relations Act (NLRA). And the Landrum-Griffith Act is also known as Labor-Management Reporting and Disclosure Act (LMRDA).

114. B: A business must complete the I-9 form for new employees within 3 days of employment. The business may certainly complete the form within 1 day, but this is not the stated maximum. Completing the forms after 3 days (i.e., 5 days or 7 days) violates the law.

115. C: Reporting pay is defined as pay legally required whether or not an employer has immediate work available for an employee. Geographic pay is simply the pay scale that applies to employees in different geographic locations (ensuring that they receive a similar ratio of compensation, regardless of location). On-call pay is defined as pay provided for employees who respond to a work situation at short notice. Call-back pay is defined as pay provided for employees who must come into work beyond the scheduled work hours.

How to Overcome Test Anxiety

Just the thought of taking a test is enough to make most people a little nervous. A test is an important event that can have a long-term impact on your future, so it's important to take it seriously and it's natural to feel anxious about performing well. But just because anxiety is normal, that doesn't mean that it's helpful in test taking, or that you should simply accept it as part of your life. Anxiety can have a variety of effects. These effects can be mild, like making you feel slightly nervous, or severe, like blocking your ability to focus or remember even a simple detail.

If you experience test anxiety—whether severe or mild—it's important to know how to beat it. To discover this, first you need to understand what causes test anxiety.

Causes of Test Anxiety

While we often think of anxiety as an uncontrollable emotional state, it can actually be caused by simple, practical things. One of the most common causes of test anxiety is that a person does not feel adequately prepared for their test. This feeling can be the result of many different issues such as poor study habits or lack of organization, but the most common culprit is time management. Starting to study too late, failing to organize your study time to cover all of the material, or being distracted while you study will mean that you're not well prepared for the test. This may lead to cramming the night before, which will cause you to be physically and mentally exhausted for the test. Poor time management also contributes to feelings of stress, fear, and hopelessness as you realize you are not well prepared but don't know what to do about it.

Other times, test anxiety is not related to your preparation for the test but comes from unresolved fear. This may be a past failure on a test, or poor performance on tests in general. It may come from comparing yourself to others who seem to be performing better or from the stress of living up to expectations. Anxiety may be driven by fears of the future—how failure on this test would affect your educational and career goals. These fears are often completely irrational, but they can still negatively impact your test performance.

> **Review Video: 3 Reasons You Have Test Anxiety**
> Visit mometrix.com/academy and enter code: 428468

Elements of Test Anxiety

As mentioned earlier, test anxiety is considered to be an emotional state, but it has physical and mental components as well. Sometimes you may not even realize that you are suffering from test anxiety until you notice the physical symptoms. These can include trembling hands, rapid heartbeat, sweating, nausea, and tense muscles. Extreme anxiety may lead to fainting or vomiting. Obviously, any of these symptoms can have a negative impact on testing. It is important to recognize them as soon as they begin to occur so that you can address the problem before it damages your performance.

> **Review Video: 3 Ways to Tell You Have Test Anxiety**
> Visit mometrix.com/academy and enter code: 927847

The mental components of test anxiety include trouble focusing and inability to remember learned information. During a test, your mind is on high alert, which can help you recall information and stay focused for an extended period of time. However, anxiety interferes with your mind's natural processes, causing you to blank out, even on the questions you know well. The strain of testing during anxiety makes it difficult to stay focused, especially on a test that may take several hours. Extreme anxiety can take a huge mental toll, making it difficult not only to recall test information but even to understand the test questions or pull your thoughts together.

> **Review Video: How Test Anxiety Affects Memory**
> Visit mometrix.com/academy and enter code: 609003

Effects of Test Anxiety

Test anxiety is like a disease—if left untreated, it will get progressively worse. Anxiety leads to poor performance, and this reinforces the feelings of fear and failure, which in turn lead to poor performances on subsequent tests. It can grow from a mild nervousness to a crippling condition. If allowed to progress, test anxiety can have a big impact on your schooling, and consequently on your future.

Test anxiety can spread to other parts of your life. Anxiety on tests can become anxiety in any stressful situation, and blanking on a test can turn into panicking in a job situation. But fortunately, you don't have to let anxiety rule your testing and determine your grades. There are a number of relatively simple steps you can take to move past anxiety and function normally on a test and in the rest of life.

> **Review Video: How Test Anxiety Impacts Your Grades**
> Visit mometrix.com/academy and enter code: 939819

Physical Steps for Beating Test Anxiety

While test anxiety is a serious problem, the good news is that it can be overcome. It doesn't have to control your ability to think and remember information. While it may take time, you can begin taking steps today to beat anxiety.

Just as your first hint that you may be struggling with anxiety comes from the physical symptoms, the first step to treating it is also physical. Rest is crucial for having a clear, strong mind. If you are tired, it is much easier to give in to anxiety. But if you establish good sleep habits, your body and mind will be ready to perform optimally, without the strain of exhaustion. Additionally, sleeping well helps you to retain information better, so you're more likely to recall the answers when you see the test questions.

Getting good sleep means more than going to bed on time. It's important to allow your brain time to relax. Take study breaks from time to time so it doesn't get overworked, and don't study right before bed. Take time to rest your mind before trying to rest your body, or you may find it difficult to fall asleep.

> **Review Video: <u>The Importance of Sleep for Your Brain</u>**
> Visit mometrix.com/academy and enter code: 319338

Along with sleep, other aspects of physical health are important in preparing for a test. Good nutrition is vital for good brain function. Sugary foods and drinks may give a burst of energy but this burst is followed by a crash, both physically and emotionally. Instead, fuel your body with protein and vitamin-rich foods.

Also, drink plenty of water. Dehydration can lead to headaches and exhaustion, especially if your brain is already under stress from the rigors of the test. Particularly if your test is a long one, drink water during the breaks. And if possible, take an energy-boosting snack to eat between sections.

> **Review Video: <u>How Diet Can Affect your Mood</u>**
> Visit mometrix.com/academy and enter code: 624317

Along with sleep and diet, a third important part of physical health is exercise. Maintaining a steady workout schedule is helpful, but even taking 5-minute study breaks to walk can help get your blood pumping faster and clear your head. Exercise also releases endorphins, which contribute to a positive feeling and can help combat test anxiety.

When you nurture your physical health, you are also contributing to your mental health. If your body is healthy, your mind is much more likely to be healthy as well. So take time to rest, nourish your body with healthy food and water, and get moving as much as possible. Taking these physical steps will make you stronger and more able to take the mental steps necessary to overcome test anxiety.

Mental Steps for Beating Test Anxiety

Working on the mental side of test anxiety can be more challenging, but as with the physical side, there are clear steps you can take to overcome it. As mentioned earlier, test anxiety often stems from lack of preparation, so the obvious solution is to prepare for the test. Effective studying may be the most important weapon you have for beating test anxiety, but you can and should employ several other mental tools to combat fear.

First, boost your confidence by reminding yourself of past success—tests or projects that you aced. If you're putting as much effort into preparing for this test as you did for those, there's no reason you should expect to fail here. Work hard to prepare; then trust your preparation.

Second, surround yourself with encouraging people. It can be helpful to find a study group, but be sure that the people you're around will encourage a positive attitude. If you spend time with others who are anxious or cynical, this will only contribute to your own anxiety. Look for others who are motivated to study hard from a desire to succeed, not from a fear of failure.

Third, reward yourself. A test is physically and mentally tiring, even without anxiety, and it can be helpful to have something to look forward to. Plan an activity following the test, regardless of the outcome, such as going to a movie or getting ice cream.

When you are taking the test, if you find yourself beginning to feel anxious, remind yourself that you know the material. Visualize successfully completing the test. Then take a few deep, relaxing breaths and return to it. Work through the questions carefully but with confidence, knowing that you are capable of succeeding.

Developing a healthy mental approach to test taking will also aid in other areas of life. Test anxiety affects more than just the actual test—it can be damaging to your mental health and even contribute to depression. It's important to beat test anxiety before it becomes a problem for more than testing.

> **Review Video: Test Anxiety and Depression**
> Visit mometrix.com/academy and enter code: 904704

Study Strategy

Being prepared for the test is necessary to combat anxiety, but what does being prepared look like? You may study for hours on end and still not feel prepared. What you need is a strategy for test prep. The next few pages outline our recommended steps to help you plan out and conquer the challenge of preparation.

STEP 1: SCOPE OUT THE TEST

Learn everything you can about the format (multiple choice, essay, etc.) and what will be on the test. Gather any study materials, course outlines, or sample exams that may be available. Not only will this help you to prepare, but knowing what to expect can help to alleviate test anxiety.

STEP 2: MAP OUT THE MATERIAL

Look through the textbook or study guide and make note of how many chapters or sections it has. Then divide these over the time you have. For example, if a book has 15 chapters and you have five days to study, you need to cover three chapters each day. Even better, if you have the time, leave an extra day at the end for overall review after you have gone through the material in depth.

If time is limited, you may need to prioritize the material. Look through it and make note of which sections you think you already have a good grasp on, and which need review. While you are studying, skim quickly through the familiar sections and take more time on the challenging parts. Write out your plan so you don't get lost as you go. Having a written plan also helps you feel more in control of the study, so anxiety is less likely to arise from feeling overwhelmed at the amount to cover.

STEP 3: GATHER YOUR TOOLS

Decide what study method works best for you. Do you prefer to highlight in the book as you study and then go back over the highlighted portions? Or do you type out notes of the important information? Or is it helpful to make flashcards that you can carry with you? Assemble the pens, index cards, highlighters, post-it notes, and any other materials you may need so you won't be distracted by getting up to find things while you study.

If you're having a hard time retaining the information or organizing your notes, experiment with different methods. For example, try color-coding by subject with colored pens, highlighters, or post-it notes. If you learn better by hearing, try recording yourself reading your notes so you can listen while in the car, working out, or simply sitting at your desk. Ask a friend to quiz you from your flashcards, or try teaching someone the material to solidify it in your mind.

STEP 4: CREATE YOUR ENVIRONMENT

It's important to avoid distractions while you study. This includes both the obvious distractions like visitors and the subtle distractions like an uncomfortable chair (or a too-comfortable couch that makes you want to fall asleep). Set up the best study environment possible: good lighting and a comfortable work area. If background music helps you focus, you may want to turn it on, but otherwise keep the room quiet. If you are using a computer to take notes, be sure you don't have any other windows open, especially applications like social media, games, or anything else that could distract you. Silence your phone and turn off notifications. Be sure to keep water close by so you stay hydrated while you study (but avoid unhealthy drinks and snacks).

Also, take into account the best time of day to study. Are you freshest first thing in the morning? Try to set aside some time then to work through the material. Is your mind clearer in the afternoon or evening? Schedule your study session then. Another method is to study at the same time of day that

213

you will take the test, so that your brain gets used to working on the material at that time and will be ready to focus at test time.

STEP 5: STUDY!

Once you have done all the study preparation, it's time to settle into the actual studying. Sit down, take a few moments to settle your mind so you can focus, and begin to follow your study plan. Don't give in to distractions or let yourself procrastinate. This is your time to prepare so you'll be ready to fearlessly approach the test. Make the most of the time and stay focused.

Of course, you don't want to burn out. If you study too long you may find that you're not retaining the information very well. Take regular study breaks. For example, taking five minutes out of every hour to walk briskly, breathing deeply and swinging your arms, can help your mind stay fresh.

As you get to the end of each chapter or section, it's a good idea to do a quick review. Remind yourself of what you learned and work on any difficult parts. When you feel that you've mastered the material, move on to the next part. At the end of your study session, briefly skim through your notes again.

But while review is helpful, cramming last minute is NOT. If at all possible, work ahead so that you won't need to fit all your study into the last day. Cramming overloads your brain with more information than it can process and retain, and your tired mind may struggle to recall even previously learned information when it is overwhelmed with last-minute study. Also, the urgent nature of cramming and the stress placed on your brain contribute to anxiety. You'll be more likely to go to the test feeling unprepared and having trouble thinking clearly.

So don't cram, and don't stay up late before the test, even just to review your notes at a leisurely pace. Your brain needs rest more than it needs to go over the information again. In fact, plan to finish your studies by noon or early afternoon the day before the test. Give your brain the rest of the day to relax or focus on other things, and get a good night's sleep. Then you will be fresh for the test and better able to recall what you've studied.

STEP 6: TAKE A PRACTICE TEST

Many courses offer sample tests, either online or in the study materials. This is an excellent resource to check whether you have mastered the material, as well as to prepare for the test format and environment.

Check the test format ahead of time: the number of questions, the type (multiple choice, free response, etc.), and the time limit. Then create a plan for working through them. For example, if you have 30 minutes to take a 60-question test, your limit is 30 seconds per question. Spend less time on the questions you know well so that you can take more time on the difficult ones.

If you have time to take several practice tests, take the first one open book, with no time limit. Work through the questions at your own pace and make sure you fully understand them. Gradually work up to taking a test under test conditions: sit at a desk with all study materials put away and set a timer. Pace yourself to make sure you finish the test with time to spare and go back to check your answers if you have time.

After each test, check your answers. On the questions you missed, be sure you understand why you missed them. Did you misread the question (tests can use tricky wording)? Did you forget the information? Or was it something you hadn't learned? Go back and study any shaky areas that the practice tests reveal.

Taking these tests not only helps with your grade, but also aids in combating test anxiety. If you're already used to the test conditions, you're less likely to worry about it, and working through tests until you're scoring well gives you a confidence boost. Go through the practice tests until you feel comfortable, and then you can go into the test knowing that you're ready for it.

Test Tips

On test day, you should be confident, knowing that you've prepared well and are ready to answer the questions. But aside from preparation, there are several test day strategies you can employ to maximize your performance.

First, as stated before, get a good night's sleep the night before the test (and for several nights before that, if possible). Go into the test with a fresh, alert mind rather than staying up late to study.

Try not to change too much about your normal routine on the day of the test. It's important to eat a nutritious breakfast, but if you normally don't eat breakfast at all, consider eating just a protein bar. If you're a coffee drinker, go ahead and have your normal coffee. Just make sure you time it so that the caffeine doesn't wear off right in the middle of your test. Avoid sugary beverages, and drink enough water to stay hydrated but not so much that you need a restroom break 10 minutes into the test. If your test isn't first thing in the morning, consider going for a walk or doing a light workout before the test to get your blood flowing.

Allow yourself enough time to get ready, and leave for the test with plenty of time to spare so you won't have the anxiety of scrambling to arrive in time. Another reason to be early is to select a good seat. It's helpful to sit away from doors and windows, which can be distracting. Find a good seat, get out your supplies, and settle your mind before the test begins.

When the test begins, start by going over the instructions carefully, even if you already know what to expect. Make sure you avoid any careless mistakes by following the directions.

Then begin working through the questions, pacing yourself as you've practiced. If you're not sure on an answer, don't spend too much time on it, and don't let it shake your confidence. Either skip it and come back later, or eliminate as many wrong answers as possible and guess among the remaining ones. Don't dwell on these questions as you continue—put them out of your mind and focus on what lies ahead.

Be sure to read all of the answer choices, even if you're sure the first one is the right answer. Sometimes you'll find a better one if you keep reading. But don't second-guess yourself if you do immediately know the answer. Your gut instinct is usually right. Don't let test anxiety rob you of the information you know.

If you have time at the end of the test (and if the test format allows), go back and review your answers. Be cautious about changing any, since your first instinct tends to be correct, but make sure you didn't misread any of the questions or accidentally mark the wrong answer choice. Look over any you skipped and make an educated guess.

At the end, leave the test feeling confident. You've done your best, so don't waste time worrying about your performance or wishing you could change anything. Instead, celebrate the successful

completion of this test. And finally, use this test to learn how to deal with anxiety even better next time.

> **Review Video: 5 Tips to Beat Test Anxiety**
> Visit mometrix.com/academy and enter code: 570656

Important Qualification

Not all anxiety is created equal. If your test anxiety is causing major issues in your life beyond the classroom or testing center, or if you are experiencing troubling physical symptoms related to your anxiety, it may be a sign of a serious physiological or psychological condition. If this sounds like your situation, we strongly encourage you to seek professional help.

Tell Us Your Story

We at Mometrix would like to extend our heartfelt thanks to you for letting us be a part of your journey. It is an honor to serve people from all walks of life, people like you, who are committed to building the best future they can for themselves.

We know that each person's situation is unique. But we also know that, whether you are a young student or a mother of four, you care about working to make your own life and the lives of those around you better.

That's why we want to hear your story.

We want to know why you're taking this test. We want to know about the trials you've gone through to get here. And we want to know about the successes you've experienced after taking and passing your test.

In addition to your story, which can be an inspiration both to us and to others, we value your feedback. We want to know both what you loved about our book and what you think we can improve on.

The team at Mometrix would be absolutely thrilled to hear from you! So please, send us an email at tellusyourstory@mometrix.com or visit us at mometrix.com/tellusyourstory.php and let's stay in touch.

Additional Bonus Material

Due to our efforts to try to keep this book to a manageable length, we've created a link that will give you access to all of your additional bonus material:

mometrix.com/bonus948/phr

Made in the USA
Coppell, TX
20 October 2022